WORLD FOOD CAFÉ VEGETARIAN BIBLE

WORLD FOOD CAFÉ VEGETARIAN BIBLE

OVER 200 RECIPES
FROM AROUND THE WORLD
CHRIS AND CAROLYN CALDICOTT

F

FRANCES LINCOLN LIMITED
PUBLISHERS

Frances Lincoln Ltd
74–77 White Lion Street
London N1 9PF
www.franceslincoln.com

A catalogue record for this book is
available from the British Library.

ISBN 978-0-7112-3464-2

Printed and bound in China
9 8 7 6 5 4 3 2 1

Contents

Introduction 6

North Africa & Arabia 10
Morocco - Tunisia - Egypt, Jordan &
The Levant - Turkey - Oman

West & East Africa 70
Mali - Ethiopia - Kenya - Tanzania -
Mozambique

The Indian Ocean 92
The Seychelles & Maldives - Sri Lanka

India 132

Pakistan & Nepal 204

Southeast Asia 222
Burma - China - Laos - Cambodia -
Thailand - Malaysia & Indonesia -
The Strait of Malacca

French Polynesia 284

Central & Southern America 294
Mexico - Guatemala & Belize -
Brazil - Bolivia - Peru - Ecuador -
Costa Rica

Caribbean 340
Jamaica - Anguilla - Nevis - Cuba

Puddings 360

Index 372

Pages 1–3
Images of Africa

This page
Top **View from Anguilla in the**
Caribbean; *middle* **fruit stall in**
Rajasthan, India; *bottom* **sherbet**
stall in Hyderabad India

INTRODUCTION

Ten years of travelling the world in search of images and stories as a freelance photojournalist and as the Expedition Photographer-in-Residence at London's Royal Geographical Society have given me a wealth of memorable experiences. Not the least of these have involved the diverse and delicious meals I have been privileged to eat in generous people's homes and remote expedition camps, at simple street stalls and fashionable restaurants, and in dozens of countries. I started to collect recipes whenever possible, in the hope of being able to reproduce the best at home.

In 1989 I met Carolyn, already an accomplished cook, who similarly found discovering and eating exotic foods one of the greatest pleasures of travel. We began travelling together, visiting Africa, the Middle East, the Indian subcontinent, Southeast Asia, and Central and South America, accumulating ideas for globally inspired recipes with the aim of one day opening a restaurant in which we could serve all our favourite dishes from around the world. Some of the recipes we gathered from people we met along the way who were kind enough to invite us into their homes to eat or stay with them, others are traditional dishes of specific regions. Some have been worked out by observing the skills of speedy chefs in busy pavement cafés on crowded city streets, still others patiently demonstrated by local people in jungles and deserts and on mountains — some of the world's remote places, where with so few distractions, food, especially the evening meal, is a very necessary pleasure.

As both Carolyn and I travelled as vegetarians we were used to the challenge of finding good things to eat in places where the traditional cuisine lends itself more naturally to meat or seafood. Although this is rarely a serious problem, there have been times when we felt we were missing out on some exciting dishes simply because they were never made meatless. In such cases we adapted the traditional recipe, replacing the meat or fish with suitable alternatives to produce vegetarian versions just as tasty, with all the flavours and tastes so evocative of distant lands.

In 1991 we opened the World Food Café in London. The opportunity came when our friend and co-founder Nicholas Sanders offered us a 56 square metre (600 sq ft) room on the first floor of a building he was restoring in Neal's Yard in Covent Garden. The building had previously been used as an animation studio by the Monty Python comedy team before being burnt to the ground in an accidental fire. Nicholas was in the process

The freshly washed front doorstep of a house in Orissa in eastern India

7

Introduction

of rebuilding it in its original exterior style, and filling it with new businesses. Our space had no plumbing, electricity or gas — not even a floor: just four walls and three wonderful huge windows opening out on to the tree-filled peace of Neal's Yard. We wanted the café to retain this bright, open character, to provide an appealing place where we could serve meals made up from a variety of dishes from the countries we had visited. The café was also a perfect venue to exhibit photographs taken on each trip, and to play compilations of music originating from as many countries as the food.

The idea of cooking in faraway places food that is just like the food people eat at home, and flying ingredients thousands of miles to achieve it, might seem to rob travel of one of its greatest pleasures, the excitement of discovering new cuisines; there is something strange about eating a meal of Italian pasta in the Maldives, or a Thai curry in the Caribbean. Yet most of us enjoy eating such dishes in our own cities without a second thought.

For centuries, all over the world local cuisines have been constantly changing. Only 500 years ago Europeans had never tasted tomatoes, potatoes, peppers, avocados or chocolate, no one in Asia had ever spiced their food with chilli, no African had grown a field of maize and not a single dish in the Americas had been garnished with coriander or spiced with pepper. So growing rocket in northern Kenya, organic lemon grass in Belize or vines in India is really just an inevitable consequence of ingredients and tastes migrating. Tourism may be the initial impetus that creates a demand for previously unavailable commodities, but in time, some of these will become part of the diet of local people.

ABOUT THE RECIPES
The recipes in this book can all be easily cooked at home with the right ingredients; where these might be difficult to find we have suggested alternatives. Some of the dishes were those we served every day in the World Food Café; others made only occasional appearances there. In the café the food was usually cooked without dairy products; cheeses, yoghurts and creams were offered as optional garnishes. Meat and fish were never used. In this book we have indicated some of the recipes that would traditionally use fish or seafood.

Spices both aromatic and hot are a common ingredient of food from the countries represented in this book. In certain extreme cases we have eaten dishes that were

Top **Food shop in India**

distinctive for an ability to induce almost hallucinogenic states of delirium, as cocktails of pounded chillies, garlic and ginger released their power and left mouths on fire, brows moist and heads reeling. Any pleasure derived from this level of spicing is a very personal one, not universally shared. We have tried to achieve moderation in the use of chillies, and quantities may be reduced or increased according to taste. A number of dishes contain lots of spices other than chillies: these combine in specific amounts to form complex and unique flavours and therefore should not be altered as freely as the chilli quantities. Some of the food in this book is a little more spiced than we would have normally pitched it for consumption in the café, reflecting our own passion for more authentic levels of spicing.

Rice is another ingredient that requires some personal choice. Our own preference at home is to use white Indian basmati rice, which has a distinctive aroma and taste. In the café we always used brown long-grain rice, usually Italian or American, which the customers seemed to prefer. Both brown and white rice work well with any of the dishes. Basmati rice does come in a brown version, and there are dozens of other types available both brown and white, long- and short-grain, and organic — it's simply a case of choosing your favourite.

Another aspect of eating in most of the countries we have visited is the serving of several dishes at a time. We have adopted this custom so that when we serve a plate of food from a particular country we include, alongside, a selection of salsas, salads, chutneys, pickles, sambols, sambals, dals, raitas, rice and bread, depending on the dish's origins. Recipes for many of these accompaniments are included in the following chapters so that meals can be constructed from different combinations of them.

The book is divided up geographically and does not pretend to be a comprehensive guide to the cuisine of the regions covered, but rather reflects our personal choice of dishes enjoyed in areas we have explored. It contains the best recipes we have found on our journeys and we hope you will enjoy cooking and eating these recipes as much as we do.

All the recipes in the book serve six people, unless otherwise stated.
V **Indicates vegan recipes.**

Bottom **Coco pods in West Africa**

North Africa &

Arabia

North Africa & Arabia

When Arab horsemen arrived in North Africa in the seventh century, they established Islam as a new religion, built magnificent cities, and introduced exciting new ingredients to be blended with local dishes and sold in the markets. From Dubai to Fez, these market areas or souks – which are to be found in the medina, the heart of every Arab city – are still thriving centres of trade and socializing. They offer a chance to taste local food and experience how similar ingredients can be used in very different ways. As a tourist it's easy to feel like a mere observer, unconnected to these scenes, which could be straight out of *The Arabian Nights*. It's also easy to get lost and, considering the dazzling choice of ingredients on sale, surprisingly hard to find a decent meal.

We found that the best way to taste the traditional cuisine of Fez at its best, and to have a more engaging experience of the souk without getting lost or missing any of the best bits, was to book a day's cookery course. This also presented an opportunity to find some new recipes to use at the World Food Café, many of which are included here.

When we turned up at the home of Abdelfettah Saffar, who introduced himself simply as Fettah, the women of his house were busy dictating him a shopping list of ingredients needed for the dishes we were going to learn how to cook. We were dispatched down alleyways of splintered sunshine into the heart of the medina to haggle our way through the list. With Fettah acting as guide, translator and financial adviser, we slowly filled our baskets with produce. We also bought a hand-made kitchen knife, an earthenware tajine, a pot of lavender honey, a giant jar of multi-coloured olives, several bags of spices, and a brass pestle and mortar to take home.

In Tunis you enter the medina from the elegant French colonial Ville Nouvelle quarter, through the Bab Bhar, a huge arched gateway. The souks beyond it cater specifically for tourists, and are dominated by stalls of stuffed camels and expensive spices in tiny packets. Even here there are plenty of atmospheric cafés serving typical Tunisian snacks such as *lablabi*, a hearty spiced chickpea soup, *mechouia*, a salad of roasted chopped vegetables, and *briq à l'oeuf*, triangles of deep-fried filo pastry with a fried egg inside. Further into the medina we found souks piled high with local produce and restaurants selling Tunisian specialities like couscous and *ojja*, a Tunisian version of egg and chips.

Even in ultra-modern Dubai there is still an old souk along the creek. Although it is almost entirely dedicated to selling gold, there are a few stalls on the fringe selling spices and frankincense. Most of the cafés here specialize in biryanis to cater for the armies of migrant workers from the Indian subcontinent. A few offer the local version of biryani, a pilau of rice with pulses, dried fruit, nuts and seeds served with the popular Middle Eastern spice mix duqqa, puréed beans and rose water-scented salads.

In Fez's ancient medina the merchants of the souk sell mounds of succulent olives, baskets of sweet dates, necklaces of dried figs, pyramids of multi-coloured spices, cartloads of oranges, glistening fish, and fresh vegetables and herbs. Bakers produce trays of warm bread from glowing ovens. Potters' kilns release clouds of black smoke from tall chimneys. Animal skins are draped over the walls of caravanserais and then immersed in a mosaic of pits filled with dyes, from indigo to saffron yellow. Behind secret doorways are opulent palaces and forbidden mosques. Laden donkeys force their way through the throng of locals, many dressed in long robes with hoods drawn over their faces.

Pages 10–11 **A kasbah of Skoura oasis in the Dadès valley, Morocco, the Atlas mountains in the background**

Right **Images of a North African souk**

MOROCCO

Moroccan cooking is a blend of traditions. From the Berbers came tajines, or slow-cooked stews; harira, a hearty soup; and couscous, the North African staple — grains of semolina with a fine coating of wheat flour, perfectly preserved until brought to life by steam and oil, and thus ideal for long desert journeys. Bedouin Arabs introduced dried pastas, dates and bread. More succulent additions of olives, olive oil, nuts, apricots and herbs came from the Andalusian Moors. All this, mixed with spices from the Orient, and a final French influence to give some finishing touches — such as fresh-baked baguette every morning — and Morocco couldn't go wrong. Even strict vegetarians find plenty of good things to eat, while if you don't mind a bit of lamb stock here and there it is very easy to eat in places such as the atmospheric night markets. When cooking at home the results can be just as delicious avoiding meat altogether.

We ate well in the markets and cafés while travelling, but the real privilege was spending time with the cooks in houses we stayed in. We were photographing beautiful houses in Marrakesh and Ouarzazate that are let out as holiday villas. Each house has a resident cook, and as we could only work in daylight we were free to spend the evenings watching and helping the cooks to prepare our evening meals, and to work out ways of keeping them meatless.

In Marrakesh, one of these houses was hidden deep in the medina, the old Arab quarter, of the city. A pair of weathered wooden doors in a dusty alley opened on to a vast courtyard filled with palms, fountains and a swimming pool and surrounded by pillared verandas shading elegant interiors. Sitting on the sumptuous cushions scattered around the flat roof, we were afforded superb views over the rooftops of the old city. Here we were served a delicious vegetable and chickpea tajine flavoured with the ubiquitous Moroccan spice mixture known as *ras el hanout*, Arabic for 'head of the shop'. As the name implies it is a mixture of the best spices available to any spice merchant or cook combined in various quantities to taste. Subsequently every chef has their own version. The one we had here at the Riad El Arsat was the best we tasted and included rose petals.

An olive stall in the
Marrakesh souk

MINT TEA

Mint tea is drunk in all the Moroccan pavement cafés, mainly frequented by men. It is unusual to see women in these places, unless they are of dubious morals. Tea is served in sturdy glasses, poured from a silver pot, and is usually very sweet. Traditionally it is made from gunpowder green tea; we also like it with Darjeeling, as it then needs little, if any, sugar.

MAKES 6 SMALL GLASSES

2 teaspoons gunpowder green tea
   or Darjeeling

6 sprigs of mint
sugar or honey to taste

Make tea in the conventional manner in a large pot, add the mint and allow to brew for about 5 minutes. Serve hot or chilled, with added sugar or honey to taste.

RAS EL HANOUT v

This recipe yields the right quantity for the vegetable tajine recipe that follows.

2.5cm/1in piece of cinnamon stick
1 teaspoon cumin seeds
1 teaspoon coriander seeds
½ teaspoon black peppercorns
½ teaspoon cloves
½ teaspoon cardamom seeds (from green cardamom pods)

large pinch of saffron
1 teaspoon ground ginger
½ teaspoon cayenne pepper
⅓ teaspoon freshly grated nutmeg
1 teaspoon dried thyme
1 teaspoon rose petals or 1 teaspoon rose water

In a small frying pan, dry-roast the cinnamon stick, cumin seeds, coriander seeds, peppercorns, cloves and cardamom seeds until they become aromatic. Grind to a powder and combine with the remaining ingredients.

VEGETABLE AND CHICKPEA TAJINE v

A deep frying pan or casserole with a fitted lid can be used instead of a tajine. The vegetables are cut large and cooked slowly to caramelize the sauce.

6 tablespoons olive oil
1 red onion, cut into thin semicircles
4 garlic cloves, finely chopped
ras el hanout (see above)
3 carrots, cut into quarters lengthwise
2 red peppers, cut into 2.5 x 2.5cm/ 1 x 1in strips
350g/12oz pumpkin, peeled, seeded and cut into large chunks

350g/12oz sweet potatoes, cut into large chunks
350g/12oz marrow, peeled, seeded and cut into 7cm/3in chunks
2 dessertspoons tomato purée
225g/8oz cooked chickpeas
about 28 dried hunza apricots
large pinch of saffron
large handful of coriander leaves, chopped
salt to taste

In a large tajine or similar, heat the olive oil and gently fry the onion until it caramelizes. Add the garlic, fry for 1 minute and stir in the *ras el hanout*. Add the carrots and peppers and fry for a couple of minutes, stirring well. Then add the pumpkin, sweet potato and marrow. Fry for 3 minutes, stirring regularly. Add the tomato purée, chickpeas and hunza apricots and coat all the ingredients with the spices. Add 275ml/10fl oz of water, the saffron and coriander and salt to taste. Bring to the boil, cover the pan and simmer gently until the vegetables are soft and the sauce reduces. This should take about 30 minutes.

Serve with harissa cabbage, and sultana and onion chutney (page 33) and steamed couscous.

Above **At Zagora in the Draa Valley, modern civilization peters out: the only way forward is along the old caravan routes that link Morocco with Mali** *Opposite* **Ancient casbahs are dotted along the Draa Valley like sentinels. They were built to control the trade caravans supplying Marrakesh, west of the Atlas Mountains, with produce from across the deserts to the east**

A bedouin with camels in the Dubai desert

In Morocco meals usually start with appetizers of cooked salads, served cold with unleavened bread. Here are a couple of suggestions.

GRILLED PEPPER AND TOMATO SALAD v

4 large red peppers
6 medium tomatoes, roughly chopped
5 tablespoons olive oil
3 garlic cloves, thinly sliced
2 red chillies, finely chopped
2 teaspoons paprika
1 teaspoon ground cumin
¼ teaspoon ground white pepper
juice of ½ a lemon
salt to taste
large handful of chopped
    flat-leaf parsley

Grill the peppers until blackened on all sides. Place in a bowl and cover with cling film for 10 minutes; this should make them easier to peel. Peel and dice them.

Blend the tomatoes in a food processor until smooth. Heat the olive oil in a frying pan. When hot, add the garlic and chillies, and fry until brown. Stir in the spices, and then add the blended tomato, cover the pan and gently simmer until the sauce has reduced and the oil has returned. Add the peppers, lemon juice, salt to taste and parsley, and simmer, uncovered, for a further 10 minutes. Serve chilled.

AUBERGINE SALAD v

1½lb/750g aubergines, cut into
    quarters lengthwise
5 tablespoons olive oil
4 garlic cloves, thinly sliced
2 heaped teaspoons cumin seeds
3 teaspoons paprika
juice of 1 lemon
large handful of chopped
    coriander leaves
salt to taste

Cook the aubergine quarters in boiling water until soft. Drain and allow them to cool a little before scooping the flesh away from the skin and roughly chopping.

Heat the oil in a frying pan. When hot, add the garlic and fry until brown. Stir in the spices and then add the aubergine. Sauté for a few minutes, add the lemon juice, coriander and salt to taste, and gently simmer for 5 minutes. Serve chilled.

19

POMEGRANATE, BEETROOT AND WALNUT SALAD WITH GOAT'S CHEESE

When you buy cooked beetroot, make sure that it doesn't contain vinegar.

3 Little Gem lettuces, broken into
separate leaves and washed

12oz/350g packet cooked beetroot,
cut into cubes and any juice retained

1 pomegranate, cut in half and the
seeds scooped out

½ teaspoon paprika

½ teaspoon ground cumin

¼ teaspoon ground cinnamon

1 dessertspoon orange flower water

juice of ½ a lemon

3 tablespoons olive oil

1 dessertspoon honey

any juice retained from the
cooked beetroot

salt to taste

2 handfuls of walnuts

6oz/175g fresh goat's cheese,
cut into cubes

Arrange the lettuce leaves in a salad bowl, and place the chopped beetroot on top, followed by the pomegranate seeds. Make the dressing by combining the paprika, cumin, cinnamon, orange flower water, lemon juice, olive oil, honey, beetroot juice and salt to taste. Pour over the salad and then sprinkle the walnuts and goat's cheese on top. Chill before serving.

Pomegranate, Beetroot
and Walnut Salad with
Goat's Cheese

FENNEL AND ORANGE SALAD WITH ORANGE FLOWER WATER DRESSING

3 Little Gem lettuces, broken into
    separate leaves and washed
2 medium fennel bulbs,
    very finely sliced
2 large oranges, finely sliced
2 carrots, grated
large handful of finely chopped
    flat-leaf parsley, to garnish

For the dressing
juice of ½ a small orange
2 tablespoons lemon juice
2 dessertspoons orange flower water
1 dessertspoon honey
2 tablespoons olive oil
salt to taste

Layer the lettuce, fennel, orange and grated carrot on a large plate. Combine the dressing ingredients. Pour the dressing over the salad and garnish with the chopped parsley. Chill in the fridge until really cold before serving.

SWEET POTATO SALAD v

4 tablespoons olive oil
1 red onion, finely chopped
good pinch of saffron
½ teaspoon ground ginger
1lb 4oz / 565g sweet potatoes, peeled
    and cut into smallish cubes
1 teaspoon ground cumin
1½ teaspoons paprika

4 tablespoons lemon juice
zest of 1 preserved lemon or zest
    of 1 lemon, cut into strips and
    then blanched
large handful of black olives
handful of chopped flat-leaf parsley
handful of chopped coriander leaves
salt to taste

Heat the olive oil in a pan. When hot, add the onion and sauté until the onion is soft. Add the saffron, ginger, sweet potatoes and enough water to half cover. Cover the pan and bring to the boil; then reduce heat and simmer until soft. Add the cumin, paprika, lemon juice, lemon zest, olives, parsley and coriander leaves, and salt to taste. Cook until the sauce has reduced. Allow to cool before serving.

Fennel and Orange Salad with Orange Flower Water Dressing

GLOBE ARTICHOKE AND CHICKPEA COUSCOUS WITH ONIONS, HONEY AND RAISINS

6 globe artichokes, stalks cut away
2 large red onions, cut into
    eighths lengthwise
1lb 2oz/500g cooked chickpeas
1 teaspoon ground white pepper
½ teaspoon crushed saffron stamens
1 cinnamon stick
2oz/60g butter
2 tablespoons olive oil
8 coriander stalks, tied in a bundle
2 pints/1.25 litres vegetable stock
salt to taste

For the onions and raisins
2oz/60g butter
4 large red onions, thinly sliced
1 heaped teaspoon ground cinnamon
1 teaspoon ground ginger
½ teaspoon ground white pepper
good pinch of saffron
5oz/150g raisins
2 tablespoons honey
4fl oz/125ml water
salt to taste

For the couscous
1lb 2oz/500g couscous
2 tablespoons butter

Globe artichokes are a really sociable food. Once they are cooked, peel away the leaves, dip them in the stock and eat the soft end. When all the leaves have been eaten, carefully remove the hairy bit to reveal the heart, the most delicious part. Have a big bowl on the table to collect all the finished leaves.

The night market in the Djemaa el Fna and the Koutoubia mosque in Marrakesh, Morocco

First cook the artichokes. Place them in a large pan, cover with water, bring to the boil and simmer until the leaves easily peel away. Drain and set to one side.

Place the red onions, cooked chickpeas, white pepper, saffron, cinnamon stick, butter, olive oil, coriander stalks, stock and salt to taste in a heavy-bottomed saucepan. Cover the pan and bring to the boil; then reduce the heat and gently simmer until the onions are soft. Remove the coriander and add the cooked artichokes – you may need to transfer to a bigger pan – and simmer for a further 5 minutes or so.

Meanwhile make the onions and raisins. Heat the butter in a large frying pan. When hot, add the sliced onions, reduce the heat and gently sauté until the onions are nice and soft but not too brown. Stir in the cinnamon, ginger, pepper, saffron and raisins, sauté for a minute, and then add the honey and water and simmer until most of the water has disappeared. Season to taste.

Finally make the couscous. Pour the couscous into a large decorative bowl and pour over enough boiling water to just cover it. When the water has been completely absorbed and the couscous is soft, fluff it up with a fork and then stir in the butter.

Make a well in the centre of the couscous with a spoon, pour the chickpeas and stock into the well, and place the artichokes around the edge. Cover the chickpeas with the onions and raisins.

HARIRA SOUP

Serves 4—6

5 tablespoons olive oil
2 red onions, diced
2 garlic cloves, crushed
handful of flat-leaf parsley, chopped
1 teaspoon ground ginger
1 teaspoon coarsely ground
   black pepper
½ teaspoon ground saffron
 or turmeric
½ teaspoon cayenne pepper
1 tablespoon paprika
1 teaspoon ground coriander
2 medium potatoes, diced
3 carrots, diced

4 celery stalks, diced
125g/4oz green lentils
2 tablespoons tomato purée
450g/1lb tomatoes, puréed in a
   food processor
600ml/1 pint stock
225g/8oz cooked or drained
   canned chickpeas
60g/2oz cooked or drained canned
   white beans
125g/4oz vermicelli, broken up
juice of 1 lemon
salt

Heat the oil in a large saucepan. When it is hot, fry the onions and garlic until they soften.

Add the parsley, ginger, black pepper, saffron or turmeric, cayenne, paprika and ground coriander, stirring to prevent sticking. Then add the potatoes, carrots and celery, green lentils and tomato purée. Stir well and add the puréed fresh tomatoes, stock and enough water to cover all the ingredients well. Bring to the boil, reduce the heat and simmer for 45 minutes, adding more water when necessary (pulses do soak up a lot of water during cooking). The general aim is for a thickish soup.

Now add the cooked chickpeas, white beans and vermicelli and cook for a further 5 minutes, or until the vermicelli are soft. Finally pour in the lemon juice and season to taste.

By day the main square in Marrakesh, the Djmaa el-Fna, is the haunt of colourful snake-charmers, water-sellers and trinket-sellers; as night falls out come the story-tellers, fire-eaters, acrobats and magicians, who provide entertainment among the rows of open-air food-stalls lit by blazing kerosene lanterns. Customers sit at simple wooden tables on long benches and choose portions of whatever takes their fancy from the mounds of tempting food on display.

There are lots of different recipes for harira soup. We ate this version as an early snack before dinner in the night market, where it is served from huge pans and eaten with wooden spoons. Some stalls sell nothing but harira soup, and become very busy during the Islamic fasting month of Ramadan, when a bowl of harira is a popular way to break the day's fast.

The atmospheric night market in Marrakesh

MARRAKESH TAJINE v

Serves 4–6

5 tablespoons olive oil

2 red onions, thinly sliced

1 level tablespoon coarsely ground
   black pepper

1 heaped teaspoon ground cumin

½ teaspoon ground saffron
   or turmeric

1 teaspoon ground cinnamon

1 aubergine, cut in half lengthwise,
   then sliced into 1cm/½in
   half-rounds

4 small potatoes, cut into quarters

1 large sweet potato, chopped into
   large chunks

1 red and 1 green pepper,
   deseeded and cut lengthwise
   into 2.5cm/1in strips

salt

6 artichoke hearts (fresh or canned)

125g/4oz fine green beans

4 medium tomatoes, peeled and
   roughly chopped

1 tablespoon tomato purée

handful of flat-leaf parsley, chopped,
   plus more to garnish

handful of coriander leaves,
   chopped, plus more to garnish

small handful of raisins

small handful of dried apricots

85g/3oz stoned olives

harissa (page 32), to serve

crunchy baguette or couscous,
   to serve

Heat the oil in a large saucepan and, when hot, fry the onions until they start to soften.

Add the spices, stirring to prevent sticking. Add the aubergine, potatoes, sweet potato and green and red peppers. Sprinkle with a little salt as this helps prevent the aubergine from absorbing all the oil.

When the aubergine starts to soften, add all the remaining vegetables and the tomato purée with just enough water barely to cover the vegetables. Add the parsley, coriander, raisins, apricots and olives. Bring to the boil and simmer gently until all the vegetables are really soft and the sauce is reduced until it is thick and rich, with the oil returning on the top.

Garnish with lots of parsley and coriander, and serve with harissa and crunchy baguette or couscous.

The Marrakesh markets are full of every imaginable herb, spice and dried fruit, and we found that tajines tend to be much richer there than elsewhere in Morocco. We watched a sixty-year-old chef cook this tajine in the heart of the medina. Vegetables are cooked slowly and are served very soft, almost crumbling into the sauce. They are cut in large pieces to prevent them from disintegrating completely.

Marrakesh Tajine

OUARZAZATE COUSCOUS

SERVES 4–6

5 tablespoons olive oil

2 red onions, sliced from top to
   bottom into 4 wedges

1 large handful of flat-leaf parsley,
   chopped, plus more to garnish

3 tomatoes, skinned and
   roughly chopped

½ teaspoon ground saffron
   or turmeric

1 teaspoon ground ginger

1 teaspoon ground cumin

1 teaspoon coarsely ground
   black pepper

6 small carrots

6 small turnips, halved if large

1 small white cabbage (about 450g/
   1lb), cut into six lengthwise

600ml/1 pint stock

1 preserved lemon (page 34)

450g/1lb pumpkin, peeled, deseeded
   and cut into large cubes

6 small courgettes, part peeled
   lengthwise to create a
   striped effect

salt

harissa (page 32), to serve (optional)

For the couscous

450g/1lb fine couscous

600ml/1 pint boiling water

large knob of butter

125g/4oz toasted flaked almonds

ground cinnamon

In a large heavy-based saucepan, heat the oil and fry the onion until it starts to soften. Then add the parsley, tomatoes and spices. Stir to avoid sticking. Add the carrots, turnips and cabbage, and fry to soften.

Add the stock and the preserved lemon. If necessary, add more water so the vegetables are nearly covered in liquid. Bring to the boil, cover and simmer for 15 minutes. Add the pumpkin and the courgettes. Simmer for another 10–15 minutes or so, until all the vegetables are very soft, adding more water if needed. The end result should be quite soupy.

While the vegetables are cooking you can prepare the couscous: place the couscous in a large bowl, add the boiling water and leave to stand for 10 minutes. Now fluff the couscous with a fork or with your fingers until the grains are separated. To keep it warm, either sprinkle with water, cover and leave in a preheated low oven; or, if you have a steamer, steam on top of the vegetables for 10 minutes prior to serving.

We spent a few days in an amazing house overlooking a huge lake on the edge of the desert between the High Atlas and the Anti-Atlas mountains. Only a few miles along the Dades valley was an impressive collection of grand kasbahs (citadels) set among lush palmeraies in the oasis of Skoura. The house was very remote, but the wonderful resident cook brought our evenings alive with nightly cookery lessons.

The food in the desert is much simpler than that found in the cities. We particularly liked a dish of vegetables cooked almost like a soup and served with lots of fluffy couscous to soak up the sauce. The vegetables were kept whole and simmered until really soft, while the couscous was steamed for two hours over a huge pot. However, we have devised a much quicker way of making it, given in this recipe.

**The view on to the lake
at Ouarzazate**

To serve, season the vegetables and pour them into a colourful bowl, or a
tajine if you are lucky enough to possess one. Garnish with chopped parsley. Stir
the butter into the hot couscous, then pile on a large flat plate or bowl. Shape into
a mound and sprinkle with the toasted flaked almonds and cinnamon. If you like
spicy food, this is delicious served with harissa (page 32) to give it a kick.

HARISSA v

Makes 150ml/5fl oz

about 20 dried red chillies

5 garlic cloves, roughly chopped

2 tablespoons coriander seeds

1½ tablespoons cumin seeds

1 teaspoon sea salt

6 tablespoons olive oil

Soak the chillies in boiling water for half an hour. Meanwhile dry-roast the cumin and coriander in a small frying pan until aromatic. Remove from the heat and grind to a powder. Place all the ingredients in a food processor and blend until a thickish paste forms. Scoop into a jar and pour a little olive oil over the surface to form a seal.

Store in a fridge in an airtight container and serve with salads or couscous or to spice up cooked Moroccan vegetable dishes. Harissa is a strongly spiced condiment, so use with caution.

RED CABBAGE WITH HARISSA AND CORIANDER

SERVES 4–6

450g/1lb red cabbage cut into
  2.5cm/1in squares
4 tablespoons olive oil
1 large red onion, chopped
4 garlic cloves, finely chopped
2 teaspoons ground paprika
2 heaped teaspoons harissa (see left)

1½ tablespoons tomato purée
2 teaspoons of honey
1 teaspoon ground
  black pepper
handful of coriander leaves,
  chopped
salt to taste

A stall in the spice souk
at Essaouira

In a medium saucepan, cook the cabbage in salted boiling water until
it starts to wilt but remains crunchy. Remove from the heat and
immediately drain. Splash with cold water. In a large frying pan, heat
the olive oil. Fry the onion until it caramelizes. Add the garlic and
fry for 1 minute. Add the paprika and stir well. Add the harissa,
adjusting according to taste, and fry for 1 minute, stirring well. Add
the tomato purée, honey and black pepper and stir well. Add the
cabbage, and stir until it is well coated. Finally add the coriander and
salt to taste.

SULTANA AND ONION CHUTNEY

90g/3oz sultanas
60g/2oz butter
1 tablespoon olive oil
3 large Spanish onions, cut into
  thin semicircles
2 garlic cloves, finely chopped

1 teaspoon ground turmeric
1 teaspoon ground cinnamon
1 teaspoon ground ginger
pinch of saffron
60g/2oz brown sugar

Place the sultanas in a bowl. Pour over 275ml/10fl oz of boiling
water and set to one side. In a large frying pan, gently melt the
butter. Add the olive oil, onion and garlic. Fry on a low heat until
the onion caramelizes, stirring regularly. Stir the spices into the
onions while frying for 1 minute. Add the sultanas and water. Add
the brown sugar and bring to the boil. Simmer gently until the water
has reduced and the mixture is the texture of chutney.

PRESERVED LEMONS v

MAKES ABOUT 1 LITRE/1¾ PINTS

450g/1lb lemons (4–6), plus juice
of about 4 more lemons

60g/2oz salt

Cut the lemons into quarters, and cover the cut surfaces with salt. Put the lemons in a shallow bowl and cover with a weighted plate to help release juices. Leave for about 30 minutes.

Put the lemons and any juices that have collected in the bowl into a sterilized jar, pour on more lemon juice to moisten the lemons and just cover them, then seal. The preserved lemons can be used after about 3 weeks.

Alternatively, a quicker way is simply to cut lemons into quarters and blanch them in boiling water for 1 minute, then refresh them in cold water. This method isn't quite as authentic, but allows you to have almost the real thing in minutes, and you can do just enough for Ouarzazate Couscous (page 30)!

TOMATO AND CINNAMON CHUTNEY v

This very special, rather unusual chutney was served to us with a vegetable tajine in the heart of the medina in Marrakesh. Our hostess told us that many of her guests found it too strange, but she loved it – and so did I, although I am generally not a big fan of tomatoes.

MAKES ABOUT 100ML/4FL OZ

5 tomatoes
1 tablespoon brown sugar

2 cinnamon sticks, ground

Blend all the ingredients together in a food processor, chill for about 1 hour and serve.

Preserved lemons are an ingredient in many Moroccan dishes, and harissa (page 32) is used as a condiment all over the Maghreb. Both are easy to make and keep well in airtight jars in the fridge.

A kasbah at Skoura oasis in the Dades valley
Inset **Preserved Lemons**

CHERMOULA v

SERVES 4–6

5 tablespoons olive oil

2 red onions, thinly sliced

3 garlic cloves, crushed

2 teaspoons ground cumin

1 teaspoon paprika

½ scant teaspoon cayenne pepper

6 smallish potatoes, cut into quarters

450g/1lb tomatoes, puréed in a
    food processor

5 small courgettes, quartered
    lengthwise

225g/8oz shelled fresh peas

225g/8oz shelled fresh broad beans

large handful of coriander leaves and
    stems, chopped

juice of 1 lemon

salt and pepper

fresh hot baguette, to serve

Heat the oil in a large heavy-based saucepan. When it is hot, fry the onion until translucent. Then add the garlic and spices. Stir to keep them from sticking.

Add the potatoes and turn to coat them in the spices, then fry for 5 minutes. Add 225ml/8fl oz water and the puréed tomatoes. Bring to the boil and cook briskly until the sauce has reduced to a thick rich consistency with the oil returning on the top, adding the courgettes halfway through.

Add the peas, the broad beans and the chopped coriander, cover with a lid and simmer until all vegetables are soft. You may need to add a little more water to loosen the sauce and prevent sticking.

Finally pour in the lemon juice and add salt and pepper to taste. Serve with lots of fresh hot baguette.

We ate this dish when our car broke down near the fishing port of Essaouira and we were waiting for the fan belt to be fixed. Everyone was incredibly helpful and we had four mechanics on the job.

Chermoula is traditionally a fish dish and always includes a mixture of cumin, paprika, cayenne and lots of fresh coriander. If you do eat fish, simply fry fillets of white fish until they are crunchy and add to the mixture at the end of cooking. If fresh peas and broad beans are not available, frozen are the best option.

CARROT SALAD v

Serves 4–6

350g/12oz carrots
salt and pepper
1 red onion
2 garlic cloves, crushed
2 tablespoons olive oil, plus more
   for sprinkling

½ teaspoon ground turmeric
½ teaspoon ground cumin
juice of 1 lemon
lots of flat-leaf parsley, chopped,
   to garnish

Peel the carrots and slice them thickly. Cook them in boiling salted water until soft.

Meanwhile, cut the red onion in half, then slice the halves thinly. Fry the sliced onions and the garlic in 2 tablespoons of the olive oil until soft. Stir in the turmeric and cumin.

Drain the carrots and refresh with cold water. Place in a serving bowl and add the cooked onion, garlic and spice mixture, with a good sprinkling of olive oil and the lemon juice. Season to taste and mix well.

Garnish with lots of flat-leaf parsley. Allow an hour for the flavours to penetrate the carrots before serving.

MOROCCAN MIXED SALAD PLATE v

In Morocco, a salad of cucumber, tomato, red onion and olives is served with almost everything, so here is a suggested mixed plate. When buying tomatoes, it is always worth choosing plump beef tomatoes, or tomatoes on the vine, for a fuller flavour.

On a large plate, arrange slices of peeled cucumber, chunks of tomato, thin slices of red onion, and black and green olives. Then smother them in olive oil, lemon juice, black pepper and chopped fresh mint.

DATE, FIG AND CINNAMON TAJINE

6 largish carrots, cut into
    quarters lengthwise
3 sweet red capsicums (the ones that
    look like big red chillies), cut into
    thirds lengthwise
1lb/450g sweet potatoes, peeled and
    cut into 2 x 1in/5 x 2.5cm chunks
1lb/450g butternut squash, peeled and
    cut into 2 x 1in/5 x 2.5cm chunks
12oz/350g Jerusalem artichokes, left
    whole unless large, in which case cut
    down the middle
1 medium red onion, thinly sliced
18 stoned dried dates

18 dried figs
2oz/60g butter, diced
1 teaspoon ground white pepper
1 teaspoon ground ginger
1 heaped teaspoon ground cinnamon
½ teaspoon ground turmeric
good pinch of saffron
1 dessertspoon honey
16fl oz/500ml warm water
salt to taste
2 cinnamon sticks, broken into quarters
3oz/90g almonds, to garnish
2 tablespoons sesame seeds, to garnish

Layer the vegetables, dates and figs in the bottom of a tajine or saucepan, in the order listed in the ingredients, and dot with the butter. Combine the pepper, ginger, cinnamon, turmeric and saffron with the honey and 8fl oz/250ml warm water, and pour over the vegetables. Add salt to taste and the broken cinnamon sticks and 8fl oz/250ml water. Cover the pan, bring to the boil, and then reduce heat to a minimum and gently cook until the vegetables are really soft.

Meanwhile sauté the almonds in a little butter until golden and dry roast the sesame seeds in a small frying pan until golden.

Serve garnished with the almonds and sesame seeds with crusty bread and any of the salads in this section.

Traditionally Moroccans cook tajine dishes in an earthenware pot with a tall conical lid designed to capture all the flavours of the spices and infuse them into the ingredients as they slowly cook. These tajines are easily found in every Moroccan market for a few dirhams. They are quite fragile but can be carried home with care. More fancy versions, often gaily painted, can be found in kitchen shops outside Morocco; however, a large thick-bottomed saucepan with a lid will make a good substitute. In nearby Tunisia a tajine is a completely different dish to the Moroccan version, more like an Italian frittata made with eggs and served cold with salad.

CAULIFLOWER, FENNEL AND PEA TAJINE v

1 medium cauliflower, cut into
   large florets
3 medium fennel bulbs, cut into
   quarters lengthwise
1lb/450g baby new potatoes,
   cut down the middle
9oz/250g shelled peas, fresh or frozen
9oz/250g shelled broad beans,
   fresh or frozen
18 green olives
2 garlic cloves, finely chopped
1 heaped teaspoon ground
   white pepper
2 teaspoons ground ginger

2 teaspoons paprika
2 teaspoons ground cumin
1 teaspoon ground turmeric
large pinch of saffron
4 tablespoons olive oil
16fl oz/500ml warm water
salt to taste
large handful of chopped
   flat-leaf parsley
large handful of chopped
   coriander leaves
zest of unwaxed lemon, peeled into
½in/1cm strips

Layer the vegetables in the bottom of a tajine or heavy-bottomed saucepan, in the order listed in the ingredients. Add the olives and chopped garlic. Combine the spices with the olive oil and then stir in 8fl oz/250ml of warm water. Pour over the vegetables. Add salt to taste, the chopped parsley and coriander, the lemon zest, and 8fl oz/250ml of water. Cover the pan, bring to the boil, reduce heat to a minimum and gently cook until the vegetables are soft.

Serve with your choice of salad and bread.

COUSCOUS SALAD WITH GRILLED RED PEPPERS, TOMATOES AND FETA CHEESE

6oz/175g couscous

2 red peppers, cut in half lengthways

4 tomatoes, cut in half

6 tablespoons olive oil

2 garlic cloves, finely chopped

1 medium aubergine, cubed

2 courgettes, cubed

1 bunch of spring onions, sliced

large handful of chopped
  coriander leaves

handful of chopped mint leaves

3 tablespoons lemon juice

salt and freshly ground black pepper
  to taste

6oz/175g feta cheese, crumbled

Place the couscous in a bowl and pour over just enough boiling water to cover it. When the water has been absorbed and the couscous is soft, fluff it with a fork.

Grill the red peppers and tomatoes until blackened; then remove from heat and allow to cool a little. Peel the red peppers, remove the seeds and cut into cubes. Cut the tomatoes into cubes. Meanwhile heat half the oil in a wok. When hot, add the garlic and sauté until golden. Add the aubergine and courgettes and fry until soft.

Combine all the ingredients in a large bowl except the feta, and then sprinkle the feta over the top. Serve the couscous warm or chilled from the fridge.

DUQQA v

Duqqa is a spice mix used throughout the Middle East as a condiment — it is found on the table along with salt and pepper. We usually make it in advance and store it in our spice cupboard.

1 heaped tablespoon coriander seeds

1 heaped tablespoon cumin seeds

1 heaped tablespoon sesame seeds

Dry roast the ingredients in a small frying pan until they are aromatic, remove from the heat and grind to a powder. Store in an airtight container.

If you learn only one word of Arabic in Fez, it should be *barek*, meaning look out. It's a word you will hear often and a warning you will ignore at your peril. The medina of the old city, Fes el-Bali, is a labyrinth of over 9,000 winding lanes and alleyways between bazaars, mosques, *medersas* (Islamic colleges), souks, old caravanserais (lodges), hammams (baths), tanneries, bakeries, palaces and riads. Fighting their way between the pedestrians who crowd these narrow passages are determined donkeys pulling carts laden with improbable loads. To locals, a shout of '*Barek*' from a donkey driver is the cue for a mass shift to the side. For the tourist, distracted by the sights of the medina or engrossed in framing the perfect photograph, such moments are dangerous. The donkeys wear rubber shoes made of old tyres to help them grip on the steep gradients, so you don't hear them coming. Being tuned in for calls of '*Barek*' is your only chance.

In Fez I asked a guide for help in finding a Moroccan kitchen knife to buy for my cookery lesson the following day. We set off down a quiet alleyway that led eventually to a dead end and an old wooden door. The guide knocked on the door. It was slowly opened by an old woman who let us in with a look that suggested that she had played her role in this trick before. We climbed some stairs, which came out on to a flat roof. On the far side another doorway led down into a carpet shop and out on to another street in a completely different part of the medina. In the knife grinders' souk, men in cavernous workshops powered huge wheels of stone with their feet as sparks flew from their metal blades.

WHITE BEAN AND MINT PURÉE WITH DUQQA v

10oz/300g white butter beans
2 garlic cloves, roughly chopped
4 tablespoons olive oil
juice of 1 lemon
large handful of chopped mint leaves

salt and freshly ground black pepper
  to taste
olive oil, to serve
duqqa (opposite), to serve

Blend all the ingredients, except the duqqa, with a little water, in a food processor until smooth. Pour into a bowl and chill in the fridge.

Before serving, drizzle with some extra olive oil and sprinkle with as little or as much duqqa as desired. Serve with Rocket and Orange Salad with Rose Water Dressing (below).

ROCKET AND ORANGE SALAD WITH ROSE WATER DRESSING v

salad bowl of rocket leaves
3 medium oranges, peeled and sliced
large handful of coriander leaves
juice of ½ an orange

1 tablespoon rose water
3 tablespoons olive oil
salt and freshly ground black pepper
  to taste

Add the sliced oranges to the rocket and sprinkle over the coriander. Combine the orange juice, rose water, olive oil and salt and pepper to taste, and pour over the salad. Chill until ready to serve.

CHICKPEA, DATE AND PINE NUT PILAU

Pilau is a mixture of pulses, dried fruit, nuts or seeds, spices and rice. It is traditionally made with white rice; however, we prefer to make it with brown.

5oz/150g dried green lentils, soaked
   in water overnight
4 teaspoons coriander seeds
1in/2.5cm piece of cinnamon
8 cloves
½ teaspoon ground cardamom
2 tablespoons olive oil
2oz/60g butter
1 large red onion, sliced
3 medium carrots, cut into small cubes
2oz/60g pine nuts

1oz/30g pumpkin seeds
2oz/60g raisins
3oz/90g dates, cut into small pieces
10 oz/300g cooked brown rice
12oz/350g cooked chickpeas
5fl oz/150ml vegetable stock
2 large handfuls of flat-leaf
   parsley, chopped
handful of mint leaves, chopped
salt and freshly ground black pepper
   to taste

Cook the soaked green lentils in boiling water until soft, drain and set to one side.

Meanwhile dry roast the coriander seeds, cinnamon, cloves and cardamom in a small frying pan until aromatic, remove from the pan and grind to a powder. Heat the olive oil and butter in a wok. When hot, add the sliced onion and carrots, and sauté until soft. Add the pine nuts, pumpkin seeds, raisins and dates, and fry until the pine nuts are golden. Stir in the spices and fry for 1 minute. Then add the cooked lentils, cooked brown rice, cooked chickpeas and vegetable stock. Bring to the boil, cover the wok and gently steam until all the stock has been absorbed. Finally stir in the chopped parsley and mint leaves, and season with salt and pepper to taste.

Serve with White Bean and Mint Purée with Duqqa (page 41) and Rocket and Orange Salad with Rose Water Dressing (page 41).

Chickpea, Date and
Pine Nut Pilau

Tunisians love spicy food and harissa is the main ingredient used to provide the heat. It is very different to Moroccan harissa, using caraway seeds and grilled red pepper to add flavour. We make it in advance and store it in the fridge so that we always have it to hand.

TUNISIAN HARISSA v

1 red pepper

1 tablespoon ground caraway seeds

3 garlic cloves, crushed

2oz/60g dried red chillies, soaked in
   hot water

1oz/30g ground cumin

2fl oz/60ml olive oil

salt to taste

First grill the red pepper on all sides until blackened. Place in a bowl and cover with cling film for 10 minutes to make it easier to peel. Peel, deseed and dice the pepper. Combine all the ingredients in a food processor until smooth.

    Store in the fridge in an airtight container.

OJJA

In this recipe eggs are poached in a harissa, tomato and red pepper sauce.

3 tablespoons olive oil

4 garlic cloves, finely chopped

1 heaped teaspoon paprika

1 heaped teaspoon ground coriander

1 teaspoon caraway seeds

6 tablespoons tomato purée

3 medium tomatoes, diced

3 red peppers, cut in half and then
   thinly sliced

2 onions, diced

24fl oz/750ml water

harissa (above) to taste

salt and freshly ground black pepper
   to taste

6 large free-range eggs

Heat the oil in a wok. When hot, add the garlic and fry until golden. Add the paprika, coriander and caraway seeds, fry for 1 minute and then stir in the tomato purée, peppers, tomatoes, onions and three cups of water. Add harissa and salt and black pepper to taste. Bring to the boil, cover the wok, and then reduce the heat and gently simmer until the peppers are soft. Carefully break the eggs on top of the peppers, evenly spaced apart. Cover the pan and simmer until the eggs are poached.

    Remove from the heat and take straight to the table. Serve with fresh baguette or sautéed potatoes to mop up the sauce.

The Tunis medina,
Tunisia

BRIQ À L'OEUF

1lb 2oz / 500g potatoes,
  peeled and cubed
3 tablespoons olive oil
4 garlic cloves, finely chopped
1 teaspoon paprika
¼ teaspoon chilli flakes
½ teaspoon ground black pepper

12 black olives, roughly chopped
2 handfuls chopped coriander leaves
salt to taste
6 filo pastry sheets
6 small free-range eggs
wedges of lemon, to serve

Place the potatoes in a saucepan of boiling water and simmer until soft, drain off most of the water, leaving a little to moisten the mashed potato, and mash until smooth.

Heat the oil in a frying pan. When hot, add the garlic, fry until golden and then add the paprika, chilli flakes and black pepper. Stir into the mashed potato with the chopped black olives, coriander leaves and salt to taste. Divide the potato between the filo pastry sheets, placing some in the middle of each sheet. Then make a well in the middle of the potato, carefully break the egg into the well and fold the pastry like a parcel by folding in the sides and then folding the ends under the parcel, so that the thickest pastry is on the opposite side to the egg, moistening the edges of the pastry to seal the parcel. In a frying pan, heat ½cm of sunflower oil. When hot, place the parcels in the oil, two at a time, and fry on both sides for 2 minutes until quite brown. Remove from the pan and drain on a sheet of kitchen paper.

Serve with the lemon wedges and harissa (page 45) on the side.

This is a delicious and unusual snack or appetizer. Filo pastry is filled with potato mashed with olives and coriander and a whole egg. The parcel is then fried and served with a wedge of lemon. The trick with this recipe is to make sure that the egg yolk remains runny without being undercooked.

Pages 46–47, clockwise from top right
Lifeguard on duty in Dubai; three doorways in the Tunis medina; a café in the Tunis souk; a back street of Sidi Bou Said, Tunisia

Right **Briq à l'Oeuf**

LABLABI v

This spicy chickpea soup is very popular with Tunisians and is eaten for breakfast, poured on to broken baguette. Don't be put off by the amount of garlic, as cooking it for a long time mellows it.

To explore the vast medina of Tunis we chose to stay in the tiny and absurdly picturesque nearby seaside village of Sidi Bou Said. Although the cobbled streets that wind through the whitewashed houses with their blue painted shutters and studded wooden doorways attract coachloads of visitors every day, in the evenings and early mornings we almost had the place to ourselves. Regular commuter trains link the village with Tunis, so every morning after a peaceful breakfast and walk around the village we left for Tunis, just as the crowds began arriving in the village. On the way home in the afternoon we would stop off at the magnificent Roman and Phoenician ruins of Carthage stretched out over a hillside above the sea with great views across the Gulf of Tunis.

8 tablespoons olive oil
10 garlic cloves, finely chopped
12oz/350g chickpeas, soaked overnight and then drained
1 large red onion, diced
3 carrots, diced
6 celery stalks, diced
1 heaped teaspoon ground cumin
1 teaspoon ground coriander
1 teaspoon paprika
salt and freshly ground black pepper to taste
juice of 1 lemon
baguette, broken into chunks
handful of chopped coriander leaves, to garnish
harissa to taste (page 45), to serve

Heat half the olive oil in a saucepan. When hot, add the garlic and sauté until golden. Add the chickpeas and enough water to cover them by 1in/2.5cm. Bring to the boil, removing any foam that rises to the surface, and then reduce the heat, cover the pan and simmer until the chickpeas are soft.

Meanwhile heat the remaining olive oil in a wok. When hot, add the chopped onion, carrots and celery, and sauté until soft; it helps if you cover the wok and let the vegetables sweat. Towards the end of cooking, add the cumin, coriander and paprika. Stir the vegetables into the cooked chickpeas, followed by salt and black pepper to taste. Pour half the soup into a food processor and blend until smooth. Return it to the unblended soup, adding more water if necessary, and simmer for a further 5 minutes. Add the lemon juice.

Place baguette chunks, to taste, into the bottom of a soup bowl and pour over the soup. Serve garnished with chopped coriander leaves and harissa to taste.

A village mosque in Tunisia

EGYPT, JORDAN & THE LEVANT

In this section any of the recipes given may be eaten together in any combination: the best thing to do is to mix and match the dishes as desired, including roast pitta bread with every meal. Bread plays an essential part in the diet of this region. Its Arabic name, *aysh*, means 'life', and it is part of every meal, from the most basic street snack to the grandest Bedouin feast. All the breads of the region are unleavened; the most well-known, pitta, is widely available in Europe and the US and is an ideal accompaniment to all these dishes; it is especially good for serving falafel in.

When we sailed down the Nile between Aswan and Luxor we had to take enough food for five days. With no means of refrigeration in the scorching desert heat our fresh supplies soon diminished, and the copious amount of fresh bread our boatman-cook had included became completely stale. However, simply by sprinkling the dry loaves with Nile water and tossing them over the coals of our fire he was able to provide us with bread that seemed as delicious as if it had just been baked — although there may well be something about cooking and eating under the stars on the bank of a great river, after a day's sailing through dramatic desert landscapes, that makes even simple food taste delicious.

In the souks of Cairo, Amman and Damascus we saw lavish displays of healthy vegetables piled high, but found the extent of vegetarian café food to be limited — although there were occasional surprises, such as the wonderful rocket salad encountered in Aqabah (see page 63). From Aqabah we visited Wadi Rum, where *Lawrence of Arabia* was filmed. While the desert landscape was every bit as dramatic as it had been on film, we were slightly disappointed to find coach parties arriving for 'Bedu tent suppers'. At Petra, however, we had no such disappointment. Riding on horseback through the narrow entrance to the gorge to come upon the majestic ruins of the ancient rose-red city was a dream achieved. We spent three days exploring Petra, the highlight of our trip to Jordan.

The last tribes of Bedouin living in the Badia Desert of eastern Jordan maintain a passion for the traditional desert style of eating mutton known as *mensaf*. This dish is a vegetarian's nightmare: a freshly slaughtered sheep is served on a bed of rice soaked in fat from the cooking; delicacies such as the tongue and eyes are offered to guests with great insistence. I spent several weeks visiting the Bedouin in their tents while photographing their way of life for the Royal Geographical Society, and when I was introduced as a vegetarian they went out of their way to provide me with alternatives.

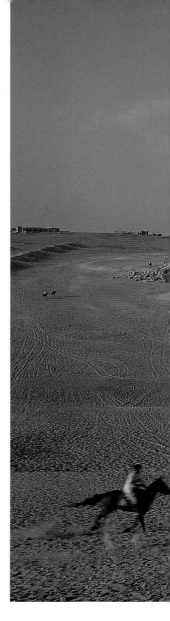

Early-morning riders at the pyramids at Giza

The Bedouin are warm, hospitable, generous and entertaining hosts. The harsh desert environment has inspired traditions of providing food, drink and shelter to any passing stranger. The extreme heat of the day makes any exertion undesirable, and the shade and ventilation achieved by the design of their tents create an ideal environment in which to sit around on cushions and camel saddles escaping the unforgivng sun and indulging in long, relaxing tea-drinking ceremonies. Relatively few Bedouin still live as nomads, as falling water levels and competition for land increasingly threaten their future, and I felt very privileged to have spent some time, however brief, living among some of the last of them.

Saffron
(Crocus sativus)

Native to Persia, saffron was among the earliest spices brought to the eastern Mediterranean by Arab traders, and it soon became much sought after. Greece is still a major producer. The Moors took it all the way to Morocco and Spain, where it is still grown and common in popular dishes such as tajines and paellas. The Mughals took it east to India; Kashmir remains one of the principal growers. From here its use spread via Tibet into China.

It is possible that saffron was one of the early spices introduced to northern Europe by Phoenician tin traders travelling to Cornwall many centuries before Christ, but attempts at commercial production were inspired by returning crusaders who brought back corms from Asia Minor between the fourteenth and sixteenth centuries. In England, the cultivatation of saffron became so well established around the Essex town of Walden that it changed its name to Saffron Walden. Saffron-growing spread through Italy and France too.

Because it is necessary to harvest by hand the stigmas of the crocus flowers that produce the spice, and a huge number of flowers is needed to supply even a kilo, saffron remains the most costly spice in the world. The most common use of saffron is to add colour and subtle flavour to rice dishes such as Indian biryani, Iranian pilaf and Milanese risotto.

Felucca **sailing boats on the river Nile**

The spice merchants in Aswan's glittering souk put a wonderfully creative effort into the visual splendour of their stalls, pandering to every fantasy a tourist might have of a spice market in an Arab bazaar. By day the illusion is compromised by the harsh desert sun and the heat, dust and flies that come with it. Nightfall relieves some of the heat. Darkness is kept at bay by a festival of lights as bright and gaudy as a fairground and the labyrinth of lanes and alleyways running along the east bank of the Nile is full of life. The picture is complete with turbaned men in dusty hooded cloaks (*jallabas*), masked women swathed in black and gold, donkey carts fighting their way through the crowds laden with oranges, tomatoes and bunches of coriander, the shouts of the merchants, the banter of bargainers, the wail of Arab music, clouds of incense and whafts of scented smoke from bubbling water pipes.

Saffron, the most valuable spice, is the one the Aswan merchants are most eager to sell. They know the tourists know it's expensive, but they also know most of them can't tell saffron from safflower. Saffron does not grow in the desert climate of Egypt, but thrives in the cooler mountain valleys of Persia, Kashmir, Spain and Morocco. Safflower is a thistle used as a vegetable dye that grows with abundance around Aswan and is of miniscule value compared to saffron. The spice sellers play a clever game. Well aware that tourists may be suspicious of their trade, their first attempt to sell saffron is to offer a scoop from a seductive mound of bright yellow Indian turmeric powder. Anyone taking issue with this offer is congratulated on their culinary experience. The turmeric mound is dismissed as inferior 'Sudanese saffron', and a theatrical display of pride accompanies the presentation of a few stigmas of safflower safely stapled up in a plastic bag. The impossibly low price demanded for this bag, the equivalent to about one English pound, immediately confirms the bogus nature of its contents. 'This is only Egyptian saffron, that is why it is cheap,' is the well-rehearsed reaction to this observation. 'You want best quality Persian saffron?' From a small tin hidden under the counter comes a much smaller plastic bag with a few dark orange twigs inside, but incredibly, this also costs only one pound. We buy it anyway and take it back to the cook on our boat and see if he can tell us what it is. He immediately recognizes it as ossfor: a near-worthless pickling herb.

EGYPTIAN LENTIL SOUP v

We had sailed to Aswan from Luxor on a boat called the Oberoi Philae. *The cooks on board came up with some above-average versions of the Egyptian staples and several dishes that were new to us. Of all the dishes on offer, however, our favourites were the Egyptian lentil soup and the bean purée.*

SERVES 4

For the soup
175g/6oz red split lentils
2 teaspoons cumin seeds
4 tablespoons olive oil
1 large onion, diced
2 garlic cloves, chopped
1 medium potato, peeled and cubed
2 leeks, washed and sliced
2 beetroots, peeled and cubed

575ml/1pt stock
juice of 1 lemon
salt and fresh ground black pepper

For the garnish
3 tablespoons olive oil
4 garlic cloves, chopped
1 teaspoon cumin seeds
handful of flat-leaf parsley

Rinse the lentils until the water runs clear. Dry-roast the cumin seeds for both the soup and the garnish in a small pan until they are aromatic, then grind them to a powder.

In a large saucepan, heat 4 tablespoons of olive oil. Add the onion and the garlic. Fry them until soft, then stir in 2 teaspoons of ground cumin.

Now add the potatoes, leeks and beetroots, stir well and cover the pan. Sweat the vegetables on a low heat until they start to soften. Add the red lentils, the stock and enough water to cover the vegetables well.

Bring to the boil, cover the pan and reduce the heat. Simmer until the lentils are soft and begin to break down, adding water as necessary (lentils soak up a lot of water during cooking). Scoop off any foam and discard it.

Blend the soup in a food processor until smooth, stir in the lemon juice and add salt and pepper to taste.

To make the garnish, heat 3 tablespoons of olive oil in a small pan, and fry the remaining 4 garlic cloves until light brown. Add the rest of the ground cumin and fry for a further few seconds. Pour a little on to the surface of each serving of soup and top with chopped parsley.

Cumin
(Cuminum cynimum)
Native to Upper Egypt and the eastern Mediterranean, cumin is a spice from antiquity, found in the tombs of the Pharaohs and used in the cooking of Classical Greece and Rome. There are biblical references to cumin being threshed with a rod in a style still seen in Egypt today. From early times cumin was traded west by the Phoenicians around the Mediterranean and east by the Arabs through Persia and on to India.

The ground powder of dry-roasted cumin seeds has a strong rather bitter taste, and is still an essential ingredient in the Egyptian condiment *duqqa*. In the Levant it is mixed with walnuts and pomegranate juice as a dipping sauce, in Persia it is a component of *advieh*, in Afghanistan of char masala and in India of garam masala. In India the seeds are also fried whole at the beginning of a recipe or added whole after dry-roasting (which brings out a nutty flavour), to dhal and to yoghurt sauces. In Morocco, as in India, ground cumin is often mixed with the sweeter powder of ground coriander, this is the case with both harissa and *ras el hanout*. By the sixteenth century cumin was being traded across the Atlantic to the Americas and it is a common ingredient in Mexican recipes such as mole sauces and chilli con carne.

EGYPTIAN BEAN PURÉE v

SERVES 4

For the purée

1 dessertspoon cumin seeds
4 tablespoons olive oil
1 red onion, cubed
4 garlic cloves, crushed
2 medium leeks, washed and sliced
150g/5oz dried fava beans or broad beans, soaked in water overnight
juice of a lemon

handful of flat-leaf parsley, chopped
handful of coriander leaves, chopped
salt and black pepper

For the garnish

2 tablespoons olive oil
5 spring onions, finely sliced
1 dessertspoon sesame seeds
handful of fresh dill

Dry-roast the cumin seeds until aromatic, grind to a powder and set to one side.

In a large saucepan, heat 4 tablespoons of oil and fry the onion, garlic and leeks until soft. Add the ground cumin and the drained fava beans, and stir well. Add enough water to just cover the beans, bring it to the boil, reduce the heat and simmer with a lid on until the beans become very soft.

Blend the beans with the lemon juice in a food processor until smooth. Stir in the chopped parsley, coriander, and salt and pepper to taste, then scoop the mixture into a bowl.

To make the garnish, heat 2 tablespoons of olive oil in a small pan, add the spring onions and sesame seeds and fry until golden. Pile on top of the bean purée. Sprinkle with dill and some additional olive oil. Serve with unleavened bread, such as pitta, and seasoned feta cheese

SEASONED FETA CHEESE

MAKES 200G/7OZ

200g/7oz block of feta cheese
1 teaspoon cumin and coriander seeds, mixed together, dry-roasted until aromatic and ground to a powder

1 teaspoon paprika
1 teaspoon freshly ground black pepper
olive oil
handful of flat-leaf parsley, chopped

Cut the cheese into three equal parts. Cover one of these in the cumin and coriander, one in the paprika and one in the black pepper. Sprinkle the cheese with olive oil and chopped parsley. Serve with olives, cubes of cucumber, tomatoes, fresh mint and red onion.

FUL MEDAMES v

SERVES 4–6

3 teaspoons cumin seeds

8 tablespoons olive oil

5 garlic cloves, crushed

350g/12oz dried fava or broad
   beans, soaked overnight

juice of 2 large lemons

large handful of flat-leaf parsley,
   chopped; more to garnish

salt and pepper

paprika, to garnish

2 lemons cut into wedges, to serve

For the Rocket and Grated Carrot Salad

2 handfuls of rocket

3 carrots, grated

lemon juice to taste

salt and pepper

For the Tomato and Cucumber Salad

4 large ripe tomatoes, diced

1 large cucumber, diced

1 red onion, cut into thin slices

4 sprigs of mint, chopped

lemon juice to taste

For the Beetroot Salad

3 cooked beetroots (with no added
   vinegar), diced

1 bunch of radishes, diced

2 red peppers, cut into cubes

handful of parsley, chopped

2 tablespoons olive oil

juice of 1 lemon

Dry-roast the cumin seeds in a small heavy pan until they are aromatic, then grind them to a powder.

In a large saucepan, heat 3 tablespoons of the olive oil. When hot, fry the garlic until soft. Add 2 teaspoons of the ground cumin and stir for a few seconds. Add the drained fava beans and stir until they are coated with oil.

Add enough water to cover the beans, bring to the boil, then simmer until the beans are nice and soft, for about an hour. You may need to add more water during this time to keep the beans moist and soupy.

Stir in the lemon juice, the remaining cumin and olive oil, the parsley, and salt and pepper to taste. As you stir, mash the beans so they start to break down.

Pile into a large bowl and sprinkle with paprika and chopped parsley to garnish. Place lemon wedges around the edge of the bowl. Make the three salads by simply combining the ingredients for each and serve with the ful medames.

Ful medames is served right across Egypt and Jordan, by everyone from street vendors and small cafés to the smartest hotels. It was our main dish on the last days of our boat journey down the Nile, and just the smell of the beans cooking brings back memories of our moonlit desert picnics.

We served a slightly more sophisticated version of ful medames in the café, accompanied by fresh salads of beetroot, radishes, red onion, tomato, cucumber, carrot, plenty of parsley and coriander leaves, and of course roasted pitta bread. Traditionally, the dish should be very garlicky and smothered in olive oil and spices. You can even serve the beans for breakfast, with fried eggs and slices of ripe tomato.

Clockwise from top left
**Tabbouleh (page 61),
Jordanian Rocket Salad
(page 63) and
Ful Medames**

HUMMUS v

SERVES 4–6

200g/7oz chickpeas, soaked
  overnight in plenty of water
2 garlic cloves
juice of 1½ lemons

3 tablespoons olive oil, plus
  more to dress
3 tablespoons tahina
ground cumin, to garnish

Drain the chickpeas and cook them in plenty of simmering water until soft.
Squash them between your fingers to see if they are done. Drain and allow
to cool.

Chickpeas are quite tough to blend, so do this in 2 batches if you have a
small processor. Put the chickpeas, garlic, lemon juice, oil and tahina in a
processor and blend until a thick paste forms. Now add a little water, bit by
bit, until the hummus becomes smooth and creamy. Season with salt to taste.
Turn out into a bowl and sprinkle with ground cumin, then drizzle with
olive oil.

TABBOULEH v

This is a beautiful speckled green salad from the mountains of Lebanon. We serve it with Falafel (page 62) and Hummus (opposite) or as part of a meze, a mixed salad plate.

SERVES 4–6

175g/6oz fine cracked
    bulghur wheat
6 medium tomatoes, finely diced
1 small cucumber, finely diced
4 tablespoons olive oil

juice of 2 lemons
salt and pepper
4 spring onions, thinly sliced,
    to garnish
lemon wedges, to serve

Soak the bulghur wheat in enough cold water to cover by 5mm/¼in and leave for 15 minutes. The bulghur will double in size and should be light and fluffy when broken up with a fork or the fingers. If you have added too much water you can simply pour off the excess.

Add all the remaining ingredients and mix well. Garnish with spring onions and serve with lemon wedges.

VARIATION

If you would like to serve tabbouleh with the less traditional dressing that we used at the World Food Café, try the recipe below.

1 level dessertspoon grainy mustard
½ teaspoon sweet paprika
1 teaspoon honey

juice of 1 lemon
1 tablespoon cider vinegar
4 tablespoons olive oil

Mix the mustard, paprika and honey until you have a smooth paste, then slowly add the lemon juice, vinegar and olive oil. Stir into the mixture of bulghur wheat, tomatoes and cucumber.

Serve garnished with spring onions and lemon wedges.

Far left The Rose Tomb at Petra, cut out of marbled sandstone rocks
Left The entrance to the siq (gorge) at Petra, revealing the ancient pillars of the Khazneh (Treasury), one of the city's finest ruins

FALAFEL v

We serve these deep-fried balls of spiced mashed chickpeas in pitta bread with Tabbouleh (page 61), Hummus (page 60), lettuce and a salad of grated carrots. As the falafel are a little fiddly to make, we advise making them in big batches and keeping them in the freezer, so they're always there and all you have to do is fry them. They also make great party food.

SERVES 4–6

225g/8oz chickpeas, soaked
   overnight and cooked until soft
2 pitta breads or 2 slices of
   dry bread
1 large onion, coarsely chopped
2 garlic cloves
2 dessertspoons ground cumin

1 teaspoon ground chilli
2 dessertspoons plain flour
1 teaspoon salt
handful of flat-leaf parsley, chopped
sesame seeds, for coating
oil for frying, preferably sunflower

Chickpeas are quite tough, so blend them in 2 batches if you think your food processor isn't powerful or big enough.

Reduce the bread to crumbs in the processor. Add the onion, garlic, cumin, chilli, flour, salt and parsley, and blend to a paste.

With the machine still running slowly, add the chickpeas, until a thick paste forms. The consistency of this paste can vary slightly, depending on the moisture in the onion: if the mixture is too wet, simply make more breadcrumbs and combine; if too dry, add a small amount of water while blending.

Roll the mixture between your hands into 2.5cm/1in balls and coat with sesame seeds. Fry the balls in hot oil until they are golden brown and crunchy.

If you are freezing the falafel, place cling-film between layers to make them easier to separate.

Falafel are served sizzling on pavements and in street cafés everywhere. In poorer rural areas they may share the pitta with little more than some dubious-looking limp salad (best declined) and a watery tahina (a creamed sesame paste with olive oil, garlic and lemon). In the bustling souks (markets) of Cairo, Amman and Damascus succulent concoctions of pickled vegetables, peppers, juicy tomatoes, crisp lettuce, yoghurt and thick creamy tahina are all crammed into the pitta along with the falafel balls to provide a whole meal on the hoof.

In restaurants falafel may be served on a side plate along with assorted dips such as baba ganoush (opposite) and various salads.

JORDANIAN ROCKET SALAD v

SERVES 4–6

3 large handfuls of rocket
handful of flat-leaf parsley, left on
the stalk
4 tomatoes, diced
2 red onions, cut in half then
thinly sliced

bunch of radishes, sliced
2 tablespoons olive oil
juice of ½ lemon
good pinch of ground cumin
salt and pepper

Mix the rocket and parsley. Make a bed of this in a salad bowl. On top of it,
pile the tomato, onion and radishes.

Make a dressing with the olive oil, lemon juice, cumin, and salt and
pepper to taste. Pour this over the salad and serve immediately.

BABA GANOUSH v

This aubergine dip is good served with warm pitta bread.

SERVES 4–6

1 large aubergine
2 garlic cloves
2 tablespoons tahina
1 tablespoon olive oil

salt and pepper
juice of 1 lemon
chopped flat-leaf parsley, to garnish
paprika, to garnish

Grill the aubergine until the skin starts to bubble, turning it regularly until
all sides are done and the aubergine feels soft. (This can also be done in a
hot oven.)

Halve the aubergine and scoop out the flesh into a food processor. Add the
garlic, tahina, olive oil, salt and pepper to taste and lemon juice, then blend
until smooth.

Pile on a flat plate, garnish with parsley and sprinkle with paprika.

TURKEY

Despite the extent and centuries-long duration of the Ottoman Empire, the Turks did not trade extensively with other nations nor really receive an influx of foreign populations or cuisines. However, Turkish cooking uses many ingredients common also to the cuisines of Greece to the west and the Arab countries to the south-east.

One of our favourite meals in Turkey is breakfast. Warm fresh bread with local honey and butter, salty black olives, white sheep's-milk cheese and lots of refreshing tea is the standard hotel breakfast from Istanbul to the seaside villages of the Aegean. I ate my most memorable breakfast one day when I was the only passenger out on the deck of a ferry on a winter crossing of the Sea of Marmara. It was a bitterly cold morning, but the sight of the mosques of Istanbul appearing in the distance through the sea mist was well worth braving the cold for — especially as breakfast was served with a winter speciality of hot sweetened milk flavoured with orchid-root and cinnamon.

Chillies and lemons hanging up for sale on the Mediterranean coast of Turkey

IMAM'S AUBERGINE

The main component of the Turkish meze (mixed plate) that we served in the World Food Café was this dish of aubergine and cabbage cooked in a herb and tomato sauce. We have come across similar dishes in Greek and Syrian cooking, usually known as 'the imam swooned', after a tale of an imam (Muslim prayer leader) who was so impressed with the taste that he fainted. We're not sure where the story or the recipe is originally from, so as we ate it first in Turkey we have included it here.

The rest of our meze is collected from all over the Middle East, including a mashed carrot salad, tabbouleh, hummus and olives.

SERVES 4–6

5 tablespoons olive oil
2 aubergines, diced
salt and pepper
275g/10oz white cabbage,
    thinly sliced
1 dessertspoon paprika
400g/14 oz creamed tomatoes (thick,
    smooth sieved tomatoes available

from good supermarkets) or
    passata, or 6 medium
    tomatoes puréed
large handful of flat-leaf parsley,
    chopped
6 sprigs of mint, finely chopped
juice of 1 lemon
1 tablespoon honey or brown sugar

Heat the oil in a large saucepan. When hot, add the aubergine and sprinkle with a little salt to prevent the aubergine absorbing all the oil and drying out. When the aubergine starts to soften, add the cabbage. Continue frying until both vegetables are soft. Add the paprika and stir until the vegetables are coated.

Add the tomatoes and a little water to make a sauce, bring to the boil and simmer until the oil returns on top and the sauce looks nice and rich. You may need to add a little more water to prevent sticking.

Finally, add the parsley, mint, lemon juice, honey or sugar, and salt and pepper to taste. Cook for a further 5 minutes to allow all flavours to combine.

Serve with Mashed Carrot Salad (page 67), black olives, yoghurt and cucumber, and pitta bread, or with Tabbouleh (page 61) and Hummus (page 60).

TOMATO, CUCUMBER AND GREEN PEPPER v

This works well in any Turkish meze. We ate it for breakfast, lunch and supper.

SERVES 4–6

4 ripe tomatoes, cubed
1 cucumber, cubed
2 green peppers, deseeded and cubed

olive oil
pepper

Simply combine all ingredients with olive oil and black pepper to taste.

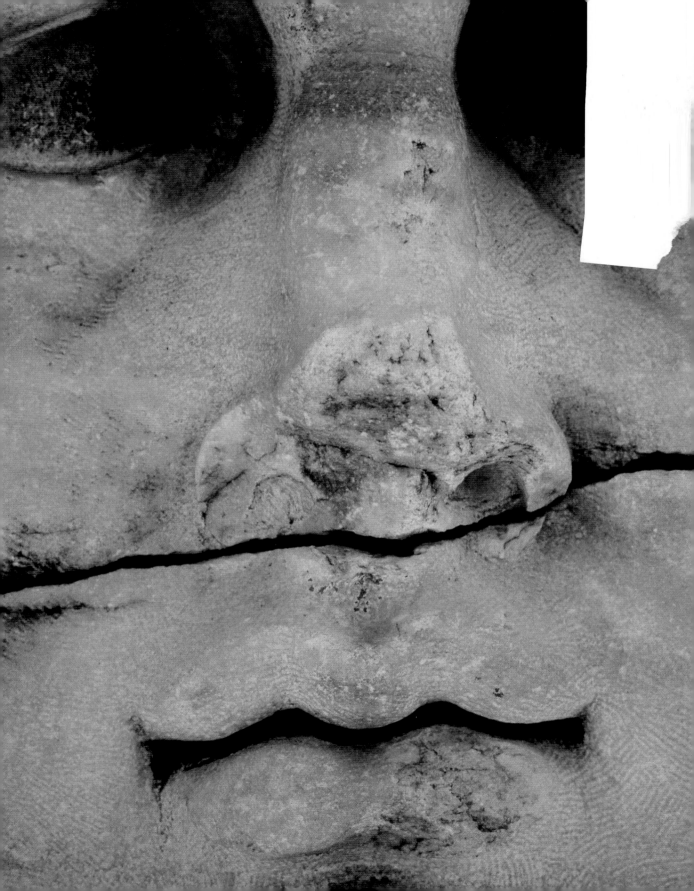

MASHED CARROT SALAD v

This recipe is also delicious with yoghurt stirred into it.

SERVES 4—6

500g/1lb 2oz carrots,
  peeled and sliced
salt
1 level dessertspoon cumin seeds

juice of 1 lemon
3 tablespoons olive oil
1 teaspoon ground black pepper
1 level dessertspoon sweet paprika

Cook the carrots in boiling salted water until soft. Drain and place in a large bowl, then mash with a potato masher until smooth.

Dry-roast the cumin seeds in a small pan, then grind to a powder. Add to the mashed carrot with the remaining ingredients and mix well.

YOGHURT WITH CUCUMBER

This makes a very popular side-dish with any meal.

SERVES 4—6

1 cucumber, peeled and finely diced
300ml/½ pint yoghurt, preferably
  sheep's-milk

4 sprigs of mint, chopped
salt and pepper
1 tablespoon olive oil

In a bowl, combine all ingredients except the olive oil. Just before serving, pour the oil over the top of the salad.

A detail of the cracked face of a statue in the ruins at Didyma, an ancient sanctuary and oracle of Apollo

OMAN

In Oman, where meat is the customary offering to guests, the most interesting regional vegetarian dishes we found were in the road-house truckstops on the desert highway that stretches for a thousand kilometres across the 'empty quarter', linking the capital, Muscat, with Salalah, capital of the southern Dhofar region. These highway rest-stops are typical of the extreme contrasts in Oman. They are as clean and modern as if they were in Muscat, yet located in the heart of one of the most rugged and empty parts of the globe. Just inland from the gleaming high-tech cityscapes of Muscat, the Jebel Akhdar is a mountainous region of dirt roads and ancient villages, inhabited by turbanned men and veiled women. Age-old traditions of hospitality are still observed and we often found ourselves guests in people's homes, consuming dates and cardamom coffee.

Salalah is in many ways the most modern city in Oman; investment has been encouraged by the government. It is also a historic centre of the frankincense trade, on the edge of Dhofar, a wild land of warring tribes, remote mosques and desolate coastline. One fairly new development has been the establishment of a dairy industry, and in pastures recalling rural England, imported Friesian cattle graze alongside camels nibbling frankincense trees — another of the wonderful juxtapositions of modern Oman.

ROSEWATER RICE

SERVES 4—6

30g/1oz butter
60g/2oz raw shelled whole
　pistachio nuts
125g/4oz raw almonds
125g/4oz seedless raisins
30g/1oz quartered dried apricots

450g/1lb rice
½ teaspoon ground
　cardamom seeds
4 teaspoons rosewater
grated zest of 1 orange,
　preferably organic

Melt the butter in a large pan and fry the nuts until they brown. Add the raisins and apricots and keep warm on a very low heat.

Cook the rice in a large pan of simmering salted water until it is just tender. Drain well and sprinkle with the cardamom.

Add the nuts and fruit, sprinkle with rosewater and orange zest, and serve.

It may have been partly our relief at finding civilization in the wilderness, or perhaps the temptation of an unlimited buffet, but one way or another gluttony was an easy sin at the highway rest-stops in Oman. Bowls of aubergines in puréed date and yoghurt sauce, and mounds of rosewater rice are two of the delicious vegetarian dishes we found.

The Jebel Akhdar
Mountains

AUBERGINE IN A PURÉED DATE SAUCE v

SERVES 4–6

4 tablespoons oil	¼ teaspoon ground allspice
3 medium red onions, thinly sliced	250ml/9fl oz stock
450g/1lb aubergine, cubed	150g/5oz dried dates
salt	juice of 1 lemon
1 teaspoon ground cinnamon	1 tablespoon rosewater
½ teaspoon ground ginger	

In a large pan, heat the oil. When hot, fry the onions until they are soft. Add the aubergine and sprinkle it with a little salt to prevent it from absorbing all the oil and drying out. Fry, stirring constantly, until the aubergine is browned. Add the spices and fry for 1 minute. Add the stock and simmer slowly for about 10 minutes.

In a food processor, purée the dates with the lemon juice and rosewater, adding enough water to make a creamy paste. Add this paste to the aubergine, stir in and serve.

West & East

Africa

WEST AFRICA

The countries of French-speaking West Africa have inherited many food customs from their colonial past. Croissants, baguettes and *café au lait* are ubiquitous in restaurants and cafés — even in Bamako, capital of Mali, one of West Africa's poorest and least developed states. However, the street food, cooked and served outdoors, belongs to quite another tradition: the ingredients and style are wholly African.

The highlight of our trip to Mali was the annual migration of Fulani cattle across the Niger at the island village of Diafarabe. Getting there took days of hard travel. We arrived at night to find a crowded village with no electricity; dawn revealed mud houses and a mosque among palm trees; fishermen casting nets into the Niger; and hundreds of cooking-fires filling the air with the smells of African breakfast. The herdsmen and cattle had been away in the Sahel for months, and their return was cause for celebration. Wives and families gathered on the river bank dressed in all their finery, as the Fulani chiefs, mounted on decorated horses and camels, galloped out of the desert in clouds of dust, then rode into the river, followed by thousands of long-horned cattle. The crossing continued long into the night, by which time Diafarabe was alive with music amplified with megaphones powered by truck batteries and dancing lit by hand torches.

WEST AFRICAN BEANS AND OKRA v

SERVES 4–6

4 tablespoons oil	300g/10oz green beans
1 onion, puréed	4 tomatoes, puréed in a
1 teaspoon cayenne pepper	food processor
1 tablespoon fresh chopped thyme	handful of chopped coriander leaves
18 medium-sized okra,	450g/1lb cooked black-eyed beans
cut in half lengthwise	salt and pepper

Heat the oil in a large pan and, when hot, fry the onion until soft, then add the cayenne and thyme, and cook briefly. Add the okra, green beans, tomatoes and coriander, and cook on a low heat for 15 minutes, stirring occasionally.

Add the cooked black-eyed beans, mashing them a little with a fork. Season to taste with salt and pepper and add a little water to loosen the mixture. Serve.

This is a typical West African dish using okra, one of the most common vegetables of the region. We ate it at the weekly market in Djenne, near the mighty 15th-century mud-built mosque. The market brought to life the dusty square in front of the mosque and the sleepy alleys; people poured in from the countryside, and food-stalls appeared all around the square.

Jollof is a style of eating rice that usually includes meat and makes a meal in itself. This recipe is designed to cook rice in a similar way, but without meat. It makes a good accompaniment to the bean and okra dish opposite, or to Sweet Potatoes in a Cayenne, Ginger and Groundnut Sauce (page 74).

Pages 70–71 **Fishermen hauling in nets on Elmina beach, Ghana**

Above **Pirogues – traditional canoes – on the Niger River**

WEST AFRICAN JOLLOF RICE

SERVES 4–6

45g/1½oz butter
2 large onions, thinly sliced
2 large green peppers,
    deseeded and diced
1 teaspoon cayenne pepper
1 teaspoon ground black pepper

½ teaspoon ground allspice
225g/8oz tomatoes, finely chopped
125g/4oz tomato purée
1 tablespoon fresh chopped thyme
450g/1lb rice, rinsed
salt

Heat the butter in a large saucepan and fry the onions, green peppers and spices over a high heat for 1 minute. Add the tomatoes and fry for another minute. Stir in the tomato purée and the thyme and fry for 1 more minute. Add the rice, mix well and add enough water to cover the rice by about 1cm/½ in. Cover and bring to the boil. Reduce the heat and simmer until all the water is absorbed, about 15 minutes. Season with salt to taste and serve.

SWEET POTATOES IN A CAYENNE, GINGER AND GROUNDNUT SAUCE v

SERVES 4—6

4 tablespoons sunflower oil

1 large onion, cubed

4 garlic cloves, crushed

5cm/2in piece of root ginger, peeled
    and finely chopped

750g/1¾lb sweet potatoes, cubed

450g/1lb white cabbage, cubed

1 dessertspoon paprika

1 teaspoon cayenne pepper

400g/14oz chopped plum (canned
    or fresh) tomatoes

300ml/½ pint pineapple juice

125g/4oz smooth peanut butter

salt and pepper

For the garnish

2 medium carrots, grated

2 medium raw beetroots, grated

2 bananas, sliced

juice of 1 lime

handful of coriander, chopped

Heat the sunflower oil in a large heavy pan. When hot, fry the onion until soft. Add the garlic and ginger, fry for a few minutes, then add the sweet potato and cabbage.

When the vegetables start to soften, add the paprika and cayenne pepper. Stir to coat the vegetables with the spices. Add the chopped tomatoes and pineapple juice. Cover the pan and simmer until the vegetables are soft.

Stir in the peanut butter until well combined. Season to taste.

Toss the carrot, beetroot and banana garnish in the lime juice and sprinkle over the dish, together with the coriander. Serve with rice.

This spicy sweet potato recipe is our all-time favourite West African dish, and one of our best memories of Mali. We tasted it on a riverboat journey along the Niger. Rather than eat the foul meals in the ship's restaurant, several Malians came equipped with stoves, pots and hampers of ingredients, and subsidized their fares by selling hearty stews.

We served our version every day in the World Food Café. Each time we tried to take it off the menu we were obliged by popular demand to bring it back. The ground peanuts — groundnuts — make a creamy sauce, enlivened with the fresh ginger, garlic and cayenne.

Sweet Potatoes in a Cayenne, Ginger and Groundnut Sauce

BAKED SWEET POTATO WITH WEST AFRICAN TSIRE (SPICED PEANUT BUTTER)

This utterly delicious take on baked potato using sweet potatoes and a typical West African style of spicy peanut butter called tsire makes a great simple supper.

6 medium orange-fleshed
    sweet potatoes
3oz/90g peanuts, with skins removed
⅓ teaspoon allspice
2in/5cm piece of cinnamon
8 cloves

1 teaspoon dried chilli flakes
1 teaspoon ground ginger
½ teaspoon freshly grated nutmeg
½ teaspoon crushed black peppercorns
½ teaspoon salt
4oz/115g unsalted butter

Preheat the oven to 400°F/200°C.

Bake the sweet potatoes for about 1 hour, until soft.

Meanwhile make the tsire. Dry roast the peanuts in a small frying pan until brown on all sides, remove from the pan and allow to cool. In the same pan, dry roast the allspice, cinnamon and cloves until aromatic, remove from the pan and grind to a powder. Combine with all the remaining ingredients except the butter and blend in a food processor until finely chopped. Gently melt the butter in a saucepan and stir in the spice mix. Cook for a couple of minutes and then remove from the heat.

Cut open the potatoes and spoon in the spiced butter. Serve immediately.

This weekly market at Djenné in Mali is typical of the country markets that are the main source of spices, vegetables, fruits and household items for most villagers in rural Africa

EAST AFRICA

East Africa is no paradise for vegetarians. Except in the Indian curry-houses of the cities, meat or seafood dishes are the most likely choice in any café or street stall anywhere in Kenya or Tanzania. However, spectacular skies, dramatic landscapes, wild animals and beautiful coastlines help to compensate for the lack of good vegetarian food. The most interesting dishes we found were on the Kenyan island of Lamu and the Tanzanian island of Zanzibar.

Apart from Zanzibar my main experience of Tanzania was photographing a Royal Geographical Society project in the heart of the savannah lands of Mkomazi Game Reserve. The reserve had never been developed or promoted as an international attraction, and the scientists were living in a group of huts on an escarpment overlooking

A Masai tribesman on the edge of the Rift Valley in Tanzania

the grasslands and the Paree Mountains beyond, in the midst of an undisturbed wilderness. On arrival I was allocated a Land Rover and a ranger with a gun, and was given the freedom of the reserve. This turned out to be a dream assignment, giving me unlimited opportunity to photograph the African bush and enjoy some thrilling encounters with truly wild animals.

My next job was to photograph an upmarket luxury safari in the Serengeti and Ngorongoro Crater parks, including dawn balloon rides, lavish catering and five-star accommodation. Having previously imagined that *this* would be the dream assignment, in practice I found the experience of being driven around the bush with a group much less exciting than that of being out on my own.

ZANZIBAR BEANS IN COCONUT SAUCE v

Zanzibar, politically part of Tanzania, owes its cooking traditions more to Arab and European colonialism and to Indian traders than to mainland East Africa. Coconut-palm groves and spice plantations provide ingredients for tasty sauces.

We rented a house with a cook on the quiet east coast. He was most enthusiastic about cooking us lobster, giant prawns and fish fillets in a rich coconut-cream sauce, but we did manage to get him to prepare the same sauce with beans and fried sweet potatoes, as given here, and it was just as good.

For a more authentic version of this dish, fresh fish or seafood can be used instead of the sweet potatoes.

SERVES 4–6

6 tablespoons oil
450g/1lb sweet potatoes,
    cut into 2cm/¾in cubes
1 large onion, finely chopped
6 garlic cloves, crushed
5cm/2in piece of root ginger,
    peeled and chopped
4 black peppercorns, coarsely ground
6 cloves, coarsely ground

4 cardamom pods, split
2 teaspoons ground turmeric
6 green chillies, cut into
    quarters lengthwise
handful of fresh coriander leaves
400ml/14fl oz canned coconut milk
450g/1lb cooked beans (pinto,
    black-eyed or cow pea)
salt

Heat half the oil in a heavy pan and, when hot, fry the sweet potato until almost cooked. Set aside.

In the remaining oil, fry the onion, garlic and ginger until soft. Add all the spices with the chillies and coriander, and cook, stirring, for 3 minutes.

Add the coconut milk, the sweet potato and the beans. Simmer gently until the sweet potato is quite tender. Season with salt to taste and serve.

BERBERÉ PASTE v

In Ethiopia, berberé means red chilli powder, but it is also the spicy paste that makes Ethiopian food so distinctive. It can be made in advance and kept in the fridge for up to 6 weeks.

SERVES 4–6

2 garlic cloves

1cm/½in cube of root ginger, peeled and coarsely chopped

3 spring onions or ½ medium onion, sliced

1 tablespoon vinegar

½ teaspoon black peppercorns

½ teaspoon cardamom seeds

½ teaspoon coriander seeds

½ teaspoon fenugreek seeds

4 cloves

1 teaspoon cumin seeds

7 dried red chillies

¼ teaspoon ground cinnamon

¼ teaspoon ground nutmeg

1 teaspoon salt

4 teaspoons ground paprika

¼ teaspoon ground allspice

In a food processor, blend the garlic, ginger, onion and vinegar until a paste forms.

Dry-roast the black peppercorns, cardamom seeds, coriander seeds, fenugreek seeds, cloves and cumin seeds in a hot frying pan until toasted. Add the chillies and grind the mixture finely in a spice grinder or using a pestle and mortar. Add to the paste.

Add the remaining ingredients and mix well. Store in a well-sealed container.

Ethiopia, in northern East Africa, can be a schizophrenic country for a vegetarian traveller. Ethiopians have a unique and interesting tradition of spicy stews, or wats (*w'ets*), based on lamb, goat or beef. However, many Ethiopians are Orthodox Christians required to 'fast' on Wednesdays and Fridays. 'Fasting' in this sense consists of eating wats without the meat — so a genuine retinue of tasty Ethiopian wats is made using vegetables, beans and lentils. During Lent in March and April there are several weeks of fasting, when vegetarians can feast daily without restriction.

The two recipes we give here are for berberé paste — the essential ingredient of a good wat — and for a wat made with mixed vegetables.

ETHIOPIAN VEGETABLE WAT

Any combination of vegetables can be used in this dish; the mixture used here is just a suggestion. In Ethiopia, the traditional accompaniment to this wat would be injera, a spongy, slightly fermented pancake-type of bread. In the café we served it with cheese-and-herb bread, cottage cheese and salad.

SERVES 4–6

45g/1½oz butter
1 large onion, thinly sliced
2 garlic cloves, crushed
1 tablespoon berberé paste
(see opposite)
1 teaspoon paprika
1 teaspoon ground turmeric
1 teaspoon ground cardamom seeds
1 clove, ground
7.5cm/3in piece of cinnamon stick, ground

3 medium carrots, cubed
3 medium potatoes, cubed
3 courgettes, chopped into chunks
200g/7oz green beans, chopped
200g/7oz spring greens, chopped
400g/14oz canned chopped tomatoes
250ml/9fl oz stock
salt and pepper
6 fresh basil leaves, torn up
handful of fresh coriander leaves, chopped

Melt the butter in a large heavy pan and, when hot, fry the onion, garlic and berberé paste for 3 minutes. Add the spices and cook, stirring, for 2 minutes more. Add all the fresh vegetables and stir into the spices. Continue to cook for 10 minutes, stirring occasionally.

Add the tomatoes with their liquid and the stock, bring to the boil and simmer until the vegetables are all cooked, adding more water if needed. Season to taste with salt and pepper.

Finally, add the torn basil leaves and coriander.

MKOMAZI CARDAMOM-MASHED SWEET POTATO WITH PEPPER RELISH

This mash, served here with a zingy relish, would also be good with an onion gravy.

SERVES 4–6

250g/9oz sweet potatoes	*For the relish*
250g/9oz sweetcorn kernels	3 garlic cloves
175g/6oz shelled fresh peas	3 fresh red chillies
250g/9oz spinach	4 tomatoes
45g/1½oz butter	1 onion, chopped
1 large onion, sliced	1 large red pepper,
1 teaspoon ground cardamom seeds	deseeded and chopped
salt and pepper	handful of fresh parsley
1 teaspoon honey	juice of 1 lemon
	salt and pepper

Well ahead, make the relish: in a food processor, blend together all the ingredients with 2 tablespoons water and seasoning to taste. Set aside, preferably in the fridge, and leave as long as you can – the longer the better.

Cook the sweet potatoes in boiling salted water until they are soft enough to mash. Drain.

Cook the corn and peas in boiling salted water until tender. Just before the end of cooking, add the spinach to wilt it briefly. Drain.

Melt the butter in a heavy pan, then fry the onion in it until it is well caramelized.

Combine the sweet potatoes and the onion, sprinkle with cardamom, salt and pepper and mash, adding more butter if desired. Add the other vegetables and mix in the honey.

Serve hot, with the relish and a green salad.

During my stay on the Mkomazi Game Reserve in Tanzania, the camp cook noticed my lack of enthusiasm for his meat stews and offered to cook me something special if I drove him to the village for some ingredients. Gathering the ingredients took about half an hour; sitting around in the bar meeting all his friends over several beers took the rest of the afternoon.

After weeks of meat stews, the others in the camp were so interested in my superb meal that the cook found himself making it for everyone the following evening.

Mkomazi Cardamom-mashed Sweet Potato and *(inset)* **Pepper Relish**

CASSAVA AND CELERY IN MUNG DAL GRAVY v

We were served this dish in a Nairobi home as a vegetarian alternative to the traditional meat sauces that accompany the maize-meal staple, ugali. We serve it with rice and salad instead of ugali. Cassava is not always easy to find (sometimes it is available frozen) and must be well cooked. Sweet potatoes make a perfectly acceptable alternative.

SERVES 4–6

250g/9oz mung dal
625g/1lb 6oz cassava or sweet potato,
    cut into 2cm/¾in cubes
4 tablespoons groundnut oil
2 large onions, finely chopped

1 teaspoon ground turmeric
1 teaspoon chilli powder
1 teaspoon paprika
1 head of celery, chopped small
salt

Cook the mung dal in boiling water until softish, drain and partially mash. Parboil the cassava in boiling salted water for about 10 minutes, drain and set aside.

Heat the oil in a large heavy pan. When hot, fry the onions until they are soft. Add the spices and fry for 1 minute more. Add the cassava and celery. Fry until the vegetables are tender, about 2–3 minutes.

Stir in the cooked dal, with salt to taste and enough water to give a sauce-like consistency.

Orphaned baby elephants in the Daphne Scheldrick Sanctuary of Nairobi Park

EAST AFRICAN PIRI PIRI v

8 large red chillies, roughly chopped
4 garlic cloves
2 teaspoons paprika
1 teaspoon ground black pepper

1 teaspoon salt
3fl oz/100ml lemon juice
4fl oz/125ml olive oil

Blend all the ingredients in a food processor until smooth. Store in the fridge in an airtight container.

The East African version of *piri piri*, the chilli-based sauce made all over Africa, is not as hot as the original Portuguese version made in Mozambique. This *piri piri* works well as a barbecue marinade or as a condiment. We make a jarful and store it in the fridge.

Left **Dhow crew, Mozambique**
Above **A natural rock pool in northern Kenya**

In Mozambique *piri piri* is served with absolutely everything. It is much more fiery than the *piri piri* found in other parts of Africa, so use it sparingly; and it is made with green chillies and fresh coriander, so it is green instead of red. As it is quite hot, this recipe yields less than regular *piri piri*.

MOZAMBIQUE PIRI PIRI V

1oz/30g thin green chillies
2 teaspoons crushed garlic
1 shallot, diced
3 tablespoons olive oil

3 tablespoons sunflower oil
3 dessertspoons lemon juice
handful of chopped coriander leaves
salt to taste

Blend all the ingredients in a food processor until smooth. Store in the fridge in an airtight container.

EAST AFRICAN WILDERNESS SWEET POTATO PATTIES

We enjoyed these sweet potato patties, served with mixed leaves and mung bean sprouts, as a snack after a game drive.

10oz/300g sweet potatoes, peeled
    and cut into cubes
10oz/300g white potatoes or yam,
    peeled and cut into cubes
2 teaspoons cumin seeds
2in/5cm piece of cinnamon
6 cloves
½ teaspoon ground turmeric
½ teaspoon cayenne pepper
½ teaspoon ground cardamom
2 tablespoons sunflower oil

1 medium onion, diced
1 small red pepper, diced
4oz/115g sweet corn kernels, fresh
    or frozen
1 tablespoon grated ginger
good knob of butter
1 small egg, beaten
handful of coriander, finely chopped
salt and freshly ground black pepper
    to taste

Place the potatoes in a saucepan of boiling water and simmer until soft.

Meanwhile dry roast the cumin seeds, cinnamon and cloves in a small frying pan until aromatic, remove from pan and grind to a powder. Combine with the remaining spices. Heat the oil in a wok. When hot, add the onion and pepper, and fry until soft. Add the sweet corn and ginger, sauté for a couple of minutes, and then stir in the spice mix; fry for 1 minute and then remove from the heat.

Drain the potatoes and mash, with the knob of butter, until smooth; then stir in the spice and vegetable mix, the beaten egg, chopped coriander and salt to taste. Shape the mixture into patties and fry in a non-stick pan with a little sunflower oil until brown on both sides.

Serve with East African Piri Piri (page 86), mixed leaves and mung bean sprouts.

You can use *piri piri* to add spice to any meal or mix it with extra oil and lemon to make a marinade. Any combination of vegetables or ingredients such as tofu, tempeh or halloumi cheese, marinated in the East African Piri Piri on page 86 and then cooked on a barbecue, will make a memorable meal.

**East African
Wilderness Sweet
Potato Patties with
East African Piri Piri**

KENYAN CURRY WITH OKRA AND PEAS, TOPPED WITH A FRIED EGG

There are obvious Indian influences in this recipe. Indians have been living in East Africa so long that it has become a local dish, using the popular African vegetable okra.

1 medium onion, roughly chopped

2 garlic cloves, roughly chopped

thumb-sized piece of ginger, peeled and roughly chopped

3 red chillies, roughly chopped

4 medium tomatoes, roughly chopped

2 teaspoons coriander seeds

1 teaspoon cumin seeds

2 teaspoons mustard seeds

1 teaspoon fennel seeds

½ teaspoon fenugreek seeds

1in/2.5cm piece of cinnamon

½ teaspoon ground turmeric

1 teaspoon paprika

4 tablespoons sunflower oil

1 medium onion, sliced

13oz/375g baby new potatoes, cut into chunks

5oz/150g okra, whole

5fl oz/150ml water

3 bay leaves

6oz/175g shelled peas, fresh or frozen

salt to taste

6 free-range eggs

chopped coriander leaves, to garnish

Blend the chopped onion, garlic, ginger, chillies and tomatoes in a food processor until smooth.

Make the spice mix by dry roasting the seeds and the cinnamon stick in a small frying pan until aromatic. Remove from the heat and grind to a powder. Combine with the turmeric and paprika.

Heat the oil in a wok and when hot add the sliced onion and fry until it starts to soften. Add the potatoes and okra, and fry until the potatoes start to brown, stirring regularly. Stir in the spice mix and fry for a couple of minutes. Add the blended onion, garlic, ginger, chillies, tomatoes, water and the bay leaves, and bring to the boil. Cover the wok and gently simmer until the potatoes are soft and the sauce has reduced. Add the peas and salt to taste and cook for a further 5 minutes.

Break the eggs into a non-stick frying pan and fry with a little oil, until cooked with a soft yolk.

Garnish the curry with the chopped coriander leaves and serve, topping each portion with a fried egg.

Samburu tribesman, northern Kenya

The Indian Ocean

The Indian Ocean

Many of the islands of the Indian Ocean are the perfect image of a tropical paradise, with white sand beaches lapped by azure seas and fringed with lush coconut palms. Predictably, coconut milk and fresh fish are common ingredients in the islands' recipes. We have created vegetarian versions of some of the traditional fish dishes, being careful to keep the flavours that make them so delicious, and we found plenty more good and varied vegetarian dishes among the islands.

The ultimate paradise islands are the Maldives, tiny sand-bar atolls scattered among coral reefs in shallow lagoons of crystal-clear water. As far as local cuisine is concerned, it can be rather limited. Beyond the capital, Male, the few islands populated by Maldivians are little more than simple fishing villages, where people make do with what they can grow and catch. By contrast the islands occupied by resort hotels can afford to import ingredients to feed their guests. As the logistics of this are still complicated, chefs have to be inventive and devise their recipes with ingredients that can be stored easily for long periods and combine them with locally available ingredients to create exciting versions of traditional dishes.

Sri Lanka, the nearest Indian Ocean island to the Maldives, is large enough to have its own very distinctive cuisine. Here we include many recipes we found along the west coast and up in the hill country of the interior, as well as some from Trincomalee on the east coast where there is more of a Tamil influence in the dishes.

As it is the largest natural harbour in Asia and an historic port, we expected Trincomalee to be a thriving urban hub of industry and commerce. It is more like a laid-back seaside town out of season. The main street, a parade of single-storey shops, opens out on to a large park with a cricket stadium in the middle and sandy bays either side. Spotted deer wander about on the grass without a care in the world; worshippers drift in and out of the Hindu temple on one side, while fishermen mend their nets on the other. The busiest place in town is the Siva temple perched on Swami Rock high above the old Portuguese fort guarding the entrance to the harbour.

Home-cooked food on the islands of the Seychelles reflects the mix of Asian, African and European people who have settled on them over the years. Typical Creole cuisine is made with the ingredients that grow easily in people's gardens. There is hardly a home without breadfruit and apple trees, a vegetable patch and a herb garden. Pineapples, bananas and wild herbs grow in the forest and coconut palms are everywhere.

Pages 92–93 **A rock on the shore of La Digue island in the Seychelles**

Right, clockwise from top right **A typical white sand beach in the Maldives; children in a Maldivian fishing village; a spa pavilion at Taj Exotica; a traditional** *dhoni* **fishing boat in Male harbour; the Indian Ocean**

THE SEYCHELLES & MALDIVES

La Digue is one of the 115 islands of the Seychelles. With a population of around 2,000 it is a friendly and relaxed place, with all the trappings of a tropical paradise. There are abundant forests full of fruits; palm-fringed beaches of white sand and warm, clear water full of fish; and long days of sunshine and blue sky. We also discovered some wonderful food.

We stayed in an old French colonial plantation house converted into a guest-house, in which the evening meals provided by the family that own and run it were exceptional. The cooks were more than happy to let us sit in on their preparations and find out how they created the meals we were eating. The recipes we give in this chapter are among our favourites.

La Digue was an uninhabited desert island until just over 200 years ago. It was first settled by French colonialists and their slaves, then gained by the British, along with most of the Indian Ocean islands, as spoils of the Napoleonic wars. With the abolition of slavery the British encouraged the migration of Indian and Oriental Asians to the islands. La Digue gradually developed as a community with the rich ethnic blend of African, Asian, Arab and European genes and cultural influences that define the Creole-speaking Seychellois and their food. The finest traditional cooking is probably found in the guest-houses, where meals are eaten communally as buffet feasts. Fresh fish and Creole sauces dominate, and there are also some delicious and inventive vegetable and salad accompaniments.

Much of the appeal of La Digue lies in the things it lacks — such as tropical diseases, crime, cars, poverty, pollution, large hotels, crowds, and dangerous wildlife. Being such an intimate island society, violent crime is virtually unheard of and even petty theft is extremely unlikely. Apart from the island's two taxis, vehicles are restricted to a few pickups used by the local farmers and traders, bicycles, and creaking ox-carts — which also operate as taxis.

The island is only 4 km (2.5 miles) long, and cycling is a pleasure on the shaded, carless roads which give access to most of the coast and the less mountainous parts of the interior. If you leave your bike, unlocked, at the end of a road and continue by foot, jungly tracks will take you to some of the most stunning beaches in the world.

One of the paradise
beaches of La Digue island

SWEET APPLE SALAD v

In the Seychelles Sweet Apple Salad is almost always served with Creole dishes. Golden apples – tart green apples rather like small Granny Smith's but with flesh that is drier and more yellow – are combined with bredes, a local variety of spinach which is in fact more like Chinese leaf. The resulting salad is a wonderful balance of sweet, savoury and spicy.

SERVES 4–6

4 tart apples, grated
½ medium head of Chinese leaf, thinly sliced
2 tablespoons sunflower oil
1 large red onion, cut in half and then thinly sliced

2 green chillies, thinly sliced
½ teaspoon ground turmeric
2.5cm/1in cube of root ginger, grated
juice of 2 limes
salt and pepper

Combine the grated apple and sliced Chinese leaf.

Heat the oil in a frying pan and fry the onion until it starts to soften. Add the chillies, turmeric and ginger and fry for a further 30 seconds.

Stir the contents of the pan into the salad, then sprinkle it with the lime juice and freshly ground black pepper. Add salt to taste and mix well.

Chill for half an hour before serving.

CARRI COCO CURRY

SERVES 4–6

125g/4oz butter
1 tablespoon sunflower oil
2 large onions, diced
5 garlic cloves, crushed
3.5cm/1½in cube of root ginger,
   peeled and grated
2 medium sweet potatoes
   (preferably orange-fleshed),
   cut into cubes
4 carrots, cubed
1 butternut squash, peeled and
   cubed (about 500g/1lb 2oz)
400g/14oz Chinese leaf, cut into
   2.5cm/1in strips
large handful of flat-leaf parsley,
   finely chopped

small handful of thyme,
   finely chopped
400ml/14fl oz coconut milk
salt and pepper

For the curry mixture
10 curry leaves
1 teaspoon ground cinnamon
½ teaspoon chilli powder
1 teaspoon ground allspice
¼ teaspoon cayenne pepper
1 teaspoon ground black pepper
1 teaspoon ground turmeric

For the garnish
2 plantains
2 tablespoons oil or 30g/1oz butter

Melt the butter in a large saucepan, without allowing it to burn. Add the oil. Fry the onion, garlic and ginger until soft. Add the curry mixture and stir.

Throw in the sweet potato, carrot and butternut squash. Stir until the vegetables are well coated with spice mix. Add just enough water barely to cover the vegetables. Bring to the boil, reduce the heat and simmer until the vegetables just start to soften.

Add the Chinese leaf, parsley, thyme and coconut milk. Cook gently for a further 10 minutes, making sure the coconut milk does not boil. Season with salt and pepper to taste.

While the curry is cooking, slice the plantain and fry the slices in hot oil until crunchy on the outside and soft inside. Sprinkle with salt.

Serve with rice, fried plantain slices and Sweet Apple Salad (page 97).

Coco curry is traditionally made with coconut milk and herbs, and served with fish. Sweet potato, cassava and bread fruit form a large part of the Creole daily diet, so those are what we cooked it with at the World Food Café. You can, however, make it with almost any vegetable. We have chosen sweet potato and butternut squash, which are more readily available.

Sweet Apple Salad *(front)* **and Carri Coco Curry** *(back)*

CORIANDER CHEELA

Cheela is a savoury gluten-free pancake made from gram flour (chickpea flour). Easy to make, it's a perfect quick meal. We have it for supper, stuffed with mung bean sprouts fried for 1 minute and sprinkled with lemon juice. It is also a brilliant alternative to rice and works well with Maldivian Mango and Chickpea Curry (page 103).

MAKES 12 PANCAKES

12oz / 350g gram flour

2 tablespoons cumin seeds,
    dry roasted until aromatic

1 tablespoon coriander seeds, dry
    roasted until aromatic and crushed

1 dessertspoon black peppercorns,
    crushed

2 teaspoons baking powder

1 teaspoon salt

1 pint / 500ml water

2 medium eggs, whisked

1 large red onion, finely chopped

large handful of chopped
    coriander leaves

Sieve the flour into a bowl, and stir in the spices, baking powder and salt. Gradually whisk in the water and eggs until a batter forms. Set to one side for half an hour.

Stir in the chopped red onion and coriander leaves. Heat a little oil in a non-stick pan. When hot, pour 3¼ fl oz / 100ml of batter into the pan, reduce the heat a little and cook until brown. Carefully turn and cook the other side. Serve immediately.

PAPAYA CHUTNEY v

2 tablespoons sunflower oil

2 teaspoons black mustard seeds

½ teaspoon ground turmeric

½ teaspoon ground black pepper

2 small papayas, peeled, deseeded
    and cubed

4 spring onions, finely sliced

2 large tomatoes, cubed

1in / 2.5cm piece of ginger, grated

2 tablespoons lime juice

salt to taste

Heat the oil in a frying pan. When hot, add the mustard seeds and when they crackle add the turmeric, black pepper and papaya. Fry for a couple of minutes and then turn out into a bowl. Add the spring onions, tomatoes, grated ginger, lime juice and salt to taste. This works really well with Paneer Tikka (page 118) and Spicy Rice Flat Bread (page 119).

No meal in the islands is complete without a selection of salads – such as sweet apples grated with ginger and then tossed with Chinese leaf and lemon juice – and *chatinis* (chutneys). Papaya is not only used in chutney but also blended with garlic and thyme into a soup, which is served with thin chips of fried breadfruit.

Evening fishing in a
bay on Mahé Island in
the Seychelles

DATE AND TAMARIND CHUTNEY

2 dessertspoons tamarind paste,
    dissolved in 12fl oz/350ml water
9oz/250g dates, stoned and
    finely chopped
2 garlic cloves, finely chopped
thumb-sized piece of ginger,
    peeled and grated

1 teaspoon chilli powder
2 tablespoons honey
juice of 2 limes
2in/5cm piece of cinnamon
1 teaspoon salt
2oz/60g sultanas
25 cashew nuts, roughly chopped

Combine all the ingredients except the cashews in a saucepan and bring to the
boil. Cover the pan and gently simmer until the dates have cooked down and are
of chutney consistency. Finally add the cashew nuts and cook for a further 5
minutes. Allow to cool. Pour into a jar and store in the fridge until required.

MALDIVIAN MANGO AND CHICKPEA CURRY

4 tablespoons butter

1 large red onion, finely chopped

3 garlic cloves, finely chopped

1in/2.5cm piece of ginger, peeled
and grated

10 curry leaves

1 dessertspoon black mustard seeds

1 teaspoon ground coriander

½ teaspoon ground cinnamon

½ teaspoon ground cardamom

½ teaspoon ground turmeric

½ teaspoon ground black pepper

1lb/450g butternut squash, peeled
and cubed

2 large tomatoes, chopped

1 cup water

14oz/400g cooked chickpeas

2 large mangoes, peeled and cubed

8fl oz/250ml coconut milk

4fl oz/125ml yoghurt

1 tablespoon lime juice

salt to taste

Melt the butter in a wok, add the onion, garlic, ginger and curry leaves, and sauté until the onion is soft. Add the mustard seeds, and when they crackle, add the remaining spices, stirring them into the butter. Add the cubed butternut squash and the tomatoes, and sauté until the squash starts to soften. Add the water and the chickpeas, bring to the boil, cover the pan and simmer for 5 minutes. Add the chopped mangoes and coconut milk, cover the pan and gently simmer for 10 minutes. Stir in the yoghurt, lime juice and salt to taste. Serve with Coriander Cheela (page 100) or rice.

FRESH COCONUT WITH LIME v

A good accompaniment to any curry.

½ a fresh coconut

1 garlic clove, finely chopped

2 green chillies, finely chopped

juice of 2 limes

salt to taste

Place the coconut in a plastic bag and give it a good bash with a rolling pin. Remove the flesh from the shell. Cut the coconut into strips with a vegetable peeler. Combine the remaining ingredients and pour over the coconut strips. Allow to marinate for 1 hour or so before serving.

Coriander Cheela
(page 100) with
Maldivian Mango and
Chickpea Curry

It was well worth being up at dawn for a swim in the warm, clear sea, and then a walk along the shore before breakfast. Fishing boats that spend all night at sea, their lamps twinkling on the horizon like the stars filling the sky, return in the morning to unload their booty. Rows of men haul immense nets ashore, and traders gather to barter for their share of the catch. Breakfast was always worth the wait; it was here that we discovered the pleasure of an omelette curry.

OMELETTE CURRY

For the omelette
5 large free-range eggs
2 medium red onions, diced
3 green chillies, finely chopped
10 curry leaves
large handful of chopped
    coriander leaves
juice of ½ a lime
1 dessertspoon soy sauce
    (optional)
sunflower oil, to fry

For the gravy
2 tablespoons sunflower oil
2 medium red onions, finely sliced
2 green chillies, finely chopped
15 curry leaves
2 teaspoons cumin seeds
1 teaspoon turmeric
14fl oz/400ml coconut milk
1 dessertspoon soy sauce (optional)
juice of 1 lime
1 heaped teaspoon roasted curry
    powder (page 119)
salt to taste

First make three omelettes. Whisk the eggs in a bowl and then stir in the remaining ingredients. Divide the mixture into three. Heat a little sunflower oil in a frying pan and when hot, pour in a third of the mixture. When one side is cooked, carefully turn and cook the other side. Cut the omelette into quarters and set to one side. Repeat until you have three omelettes.

To make the gravy, heat 2 tablespoons of sunflower oil in a wok. When hot, add the sliced onions and gently sauté until soft. Stir in the chillies and spices, fry for 1 minute, and add the coconut milk and soy sauce. Gently simmer for 10 minutes, taking care not to boil, as the coconut milk will split. Add the lime juice, salt to taste and omelette quarters, and simmer for a few minutes. Finally sprinkle the roasted curry powder over the top, cover the pan, turn off the heat and allow to sit for a few minutes.

Serve with rice and Date and Tamarind Chutney (page 101).

A *dhoni* fishing boat setting out to sea in the Maldives

DEVILLED POTATO CURRY v

This simple curry is delicious with Coconut Mellun Chutney (below) and Bringal Pickle (page 118).

4 tablespoons sunflower oil
1 large red onion, finely sliced
3 green chillies, finely chopped
½ teaspoon chilli powder
20 curry leaves
2 teaspoons dill seeds
2 teaspoons black mustard seeds

1½lb/750g potatoes, peeled and
    boiled until soft, and then cut
    into cubes
1 tablespoon soy sauce (optional)
6fl oz/190ml water
salt to taste

Heat the oil in a wok. When hot, add the onion and fry until soft. Add the chillies, chilli powder, curry leaves, dill seeds and mustard seeds, and fry for 1 minute. Add the cooked potatoes, fish or soy sauce and water, and gently simmer until the water has reduced and the potatoes start to brown, stirring to avoid sticking. Add salt to taste.

COCONUT MELLUN CHUTNEY v

1 tablespoon sunflower oil
1 medium onion, finely chopped
2 green chillies, finely chopped
¼ teaspoon ground turmeric
20 curry leaves

3oz/90g desiccated coconut
4fl oz/125ml water
juice of 1 lime
salt to taste

Heat the oil in a saucepan. When hot, add the onion and chillies, and sauté until the onion is soft. Stir in the turmeric and curry leaves, and fry for 1 minute. Add the coconut and water, and gently simmer until the water is absorbed. Add the lime juice and season to taste.

Pages 106–107, clockwise from top right **A Hindu temple on Trincomalee beach, Sri Lanka; fishermen at Trincomalee; La Digue island in the Seychelles; the Buddhas of Polonnaruwa, Sri Lanka; a fishing boat lamp; a Hindu temple in Trincomalee**

Above **Fish in the
Indian Ocean off an
island in the Maldives**

THYME AND LEMON RICE

A perfect accompaniment to Seychelloise food.

2 tablespoons butter
grated zest of 2 lemons
1 tablespoon chopped fresh thyme
½ teaspoon freshly ground
   black pepper

1lb/450g basmati rice, washed until
   the water runs clear
juice of 1 lemon
salt to taste

Melt the butter in a medium saucepan, add the lemon, thyme and black pepper,
and sauté for 1 minute. Add the washed rice and stir until the rice is coated with
the butter; then add the lemon juice and enough cold water to cover the rice by
½in/1cm. Cover the pan and bring to the boil, reduce the heat, and gently cook
until all the water is absorbed. Season to taste.

BANANA AND CHILLI FRITTER WITH PASSION FRUIT DIP

For the passion fruit dip
½ teaspoon mustard
juice of 1 lime
4 tablespoons olive oil
6 passion fruit, cut in half and the
    flesh scooped out
salt and freshly ground pepper to taste

For the fritters
4 tablespoons butter
2 eggs, lightly beaten
16fl oz/500ml natural yoghurt
2 teaspoons honey
8oz/225g plain flour

½ teaspoon salt
1 tablespoon baking powder
2 red chillies, finely chopped
3 large ripe bananas, mashed with
    a fork
sunflower oil

For the garnish
1 Chinese leaf, thinly sliced
sunflower oil
2in/5cm piece of ginger,
    peeled and grated
salt and freshly ground black pepper
    to taste

First make the passion fruit dip. Mix the mustard and lime juice in a bowl, and then gradually stir in the oil. Stir in the passion fruit and season to taste.

Melt the butter and allow to cool to room temperature. Mix the eggs, yoghurt and honey, and combine with the flour, salt and baking powder. Finally stir in the chillies and mashed banana. Heat a little sunflower oil in a non-stick frying pan. When hot, spoon the mixture into the pan in round fritter shapes and cook until bubbles form; then turn and cook the other sides.

Serve immediately, drizzled with the passion fruit dressing and garnished with thinly sliced Chinese leaf fried in a little sunflower oil. Add the grated ginger and season with salt and freshly ground black pepper to taste.

GREEN MANGO PICKLE

It seems that most mangoes we buy in supermarkets are underripe, which is useful for this recipe as it means that you can use them straight away without having to wait for them to ripen.

2 underripe mangoes
1 red chilli, finely chopped
1in/2.5cm piece of ginger,
  peeled and grated
2 garlic cloves, finely chopped
1 stick of lemon grass, finely sliced

1 teaspoon soy sauce (optional)
juice of 2 limes
handful of chopped coriander leaves
1 teaspoon honey
salt and pepper to taste

Left Bananas
Below Women on their way home from the shop on La Digue island in the Seychelles

Combine all the ingredients and then chill in the fridge for 30 minutes before serving.

MARINATED HALLOUMI WITH SEYCHELLOISE ROUGAILLE SAUCE

This dish is traditionally made with fish but halloumi is a good substitute. Blimbi are small cucumber-shaped vegetables that grow in most Seychelloise gardens; gherkins are similar, so we use them instead.

1lb 2oz / 500g halloumi, cut into
½ / 1cm strips

For the marinade
2 sticks of lemon grass, thinly sliced
1in / 2.5cm piece of ginger,
    peeled and grated
2 garlic cloves, finely chopped
1 green chilli, finely chopped
½ teaspoon ground turmeric
grated zest of 1 lime
juice of 1 lime
1 tablespoon sunflower oil

For the rougaille sauce
3 tablespoons sunflower oil

1 large red onion, diced
4 cloves garlic, finely chopped
2in / 5cm piece of ginger,
    peeled and grated
2 green chillies, finely chopped
1 dessertspoon black mustard seeds
½ teaspoon freshly ground
    black pepper
10oz / 300g cherry tomatoes, chopped
    in a blender
1 tablespoon soy sauce
6 gherkins, diced
4 spring onions, sliced
1 tablespoon chopped thyme leaves
handful of chopped parsley leaves
salt to taste

Marinated Halloumi
with Seychelloise
Rougaille Sauce

Combine the marinade ingredients and pour over the halloumi slices. Leave to marinade for 1 hour. Cook the marinated halloumi on a barbeque, under the grill or on a griddle until brown on each side. Retain any of the marinade that is left.

Heat the oil in a saucepan. When hot, add the onion, garlic, ginger and chillies, and sauté until the onion is soft. Add the mustard seeds and black pepper and fry for 1 minute. Add the chopped cherry tomatoes, soy sauce, gherkins, spring onions, thyme, parsley and retained marinade, and bring to the boil; then reduce the heat, cover and gently simmer until the sauce reduces and the oil returns. Add salt to taste.

Serve the sauce on the side of the grilled halloumi with Creole Pumpkin Chutney (opposite).

CREOLE PUMPKIN CHUTNEY

1½lb/750g peeled and cubed
   butternut squash
1in/2.5cm piece of ginger,
   peeled and grated
2 garlic cloves, finely chopped
1 red chilli, finely chopped
1 dessertspoon chopped thyme leaves

small handful of chopped coriander leaves
½ teaspoon freshly ground black pepper
2 tablespoons olive oil
juice of ½ a lemon
1 teaspoon honey
4 spring onions, finely sliced
salt to taste

Stew the butternut squash in a covered saucepan with the ginger, garlic, chilli and a
splash of water until soft. Mash the squash and then stir in the remaining ingredients.

SRI LANKA

Sri Lanka is a remarkably beautiful and deeply troubled island. Yet, considering the scale of the violence that is a daily reality for so many Sri Lankans, it is incredibly easy to be temporarily unaware of any trouble. We spent two weeks driving around the island's enchanting landscapes, meeting gentle, polite people, visiting serene Buddhist temple sites hosted by saffron-robed monks, or lazing on palm-fringed beaches. Nonetheless, there were sinister reminders of the island's tragedy lurking in the background, and our time was punctuated with police roadblocks, restricted travel and an atmosphere of tension.

Self-drive car hire is difficult in Sri Lanka, so we shared our trip with a driver. There is a certain relief in being freed from the stress of driving in a foreign country, but it can be a complicated equation having to share almost every hour of every day with a man you have never met before. Our driver, Cyril, took his job very seriously: he was a faultless chauffeur, always smartly turned out and punctual. In fact, he took everything very seriously, and seemed to be bored beyond words by yet another drive around the island with a couple of excitable tourists — that is, until we declared our intention of climbing to the summit of Adam's Peak. The ascent of Adam's Peak is a demanding pilgrimage of which, as a devout Buddhist, Cyril thoroughly approved. At the 2,223 metre (7,340 ft) summit of the pyramid-shaped mountain there is a large 'footprint' in the rock, left by the Buddha, or Adam, or St Thomas, or Shiva, or geology, depending on your preference.

We certainly earned Cyril's friendship. The climb lasted all night. When we set off in the relative cool of the evening, the almost party atmosphere among the ascending pilgrims and the lure of thousands of steps winding up the mountain lined by fairy-lights made a seductive combination. Several hours later in the chill of the pre-dawn air the romance was fading fast. Our energy was replenished by the spectacular sunrise — not to mention the excitement of seeing, just outside the summit temple, a bright red British Royal Mail-style pillarbox, with a daily collection at noon (which must demand an extremely fit postman). But then, disorientated as we were from lack of sleep, the descent, under an unrelenting tropical sun, down near-vertical steps, was punishing. We were as happy to see Cyril and his car waiting for us at the bottom as he had been to discover that his passengers were some sort of pilgrims.

A stilt fisherman at dusk in southern Sri Lanka

SRI LANKAN OKRA AND POTATO CURRY

In Sri Lanka curries are often described as white, to indicate mild spicing and use of coconut milk; red, to indicate use of powerful red chillies and tomato; or black, when roasted spices are used. This is a white vegetable curry, which would typically include the use of 'Maldive fish', pounded dried fish in powdered form. Here we use soy sauce.

SERVES 4

400g/14oz baby new potatoes, cut into cubes	2 teaspoons dill seeds
20 curry leaves	3 green chillies, finely chopped
½ teaspoon turmeric	300g/10oz okra, cut into 2.5cm/1in chunks
2 large red onions, cut into thin semi-circles	400ml/15fl oz coconut milk
3 teaspoons soy sauce	2 dessertspoons lime juice
3 tablespoons coconut oil	salt to taste

In a saucepan, boil the potatoes in 350ml/12fl oz of water until soft, along with half the curry leaves, the turmeric, half the sliced red onions and the soy sauce.

Meanwhile, in a wok, heat the oil and add the dill seeds. When they start to crackle add the rest of the curry leaves followed by the chilli and the remaining sliced onion. Fry until the onion starts to turn golden brown. Add the okra and fry gently until they start to soften.

Add the boiled potato mixture (including the liquid), the coconut milk, the lime juice and salt to taste, with 125ml/4fl oz of water. Gently simmer for 5 minutes, taking care not to boil as the coconut milk will separate.

Add salt to taste and serve with rice.

Curry Leaves
(Chalcas koenigii)
Curry leaves, or *kari patta*, grow feather-like along a stem. In southern India and Sri Lanka they are often dropped into hot oil, along with mustard seeds, and added at the last minute as a tempering to vegetable dishes, dhals and chutneys. Trade in them has been limited, however. They are a common constituent of curry powders in the recipes of Indian Ocean islands and the Caribbean. It was the name of this leaf that European languages adopted as a generic term to describe all spiced dishes.

Sri Lankan Okra and Potato Curry

PANEER TIKKA

1lb 2oz / 500g paneer, cut into
   1in / 2.5cm cubes
4 garlic cloves
2in / 5cm piece of ginger,
   peeled and grated
1 teaspoon salt
juice of 2 lemons
1 tablespoon coriander seeds
1 teaspoon cloves
1 teaspoon whole mace

1 teaspoon cumin seeds
½ cinnamon stick
1 teaspoon black peppercorns
3 bay leaves
1 teaspoon ground cardamon
2 teaspoons ground turmeric
½ pint / 300ml Greek-style yoghurt
3 tablespoons sunflower oil
salt to taste

Skewer the paneer cubes on to 12 small skewers. Blend the garlic, ginger, salt and lemon juice until a paste forms, coat the paneer cubes with the paste and set to one side.

   Dry roast the whole spices and bay leaves in a small frying pan until aromatic, remove from the pan and grind to a powder; then add the ground spices. Whisk the yoghurt and oil together in a bowl, and stir in the spice mix. Season to taste and coat the paneer skewers with the spiced yoghurt. Leave to marinate for 1 hour. Cook the skewers under the grill, in a griddle pan or on the barbeque until brown on all sides. Baste with a little of the marinade. Serve immediately. Papaya Chutney (page 100) and Spicy Rice Flat Bread (opposite) are the perfect accompaniments.

BRINJAL PICKLE

This is a very quick and easy-to-make pickle that can be served immediately.

1 small aubergine, thinly sliced
salt and ground turmeric to season
   the aubergine
sunflower oil
1 medium red onion, thinly sliced

2 green chillies, finely chopped
1 dessertspoon yellow mustard seeds,
   ground
juice of 2 limes
1 teaspoon honey

Season the aubergine slices with a little salt and turmeric; then heat the oil in a frying pan and fry until soft. Place in a bowl. Combine the remaining ingredients and pour over the aubergine. Allow to stand for 30 minutes before serving.

Twenty years ago I boarded an overcrowded, rusting ferry for the short sea voyage between India and Sri Lanka. Several hours after our scheduled departure, there was an announcement in Tamil which instantly caused a frenzied flight from the deck. Fearful that the ferry might be about to sink, I joined the fight for the exit. With relief I found that those in the exodus were merely heading for the ship's restaurant for a free meal that had been offered as compensation for the delay. My dining companions were unanimous in recommending Sri Lanka's east coast around the port of Trincomalee as the perfect beach to head for after visiting the island's hill stations and ancient cities.

   I never made it to Trincomalee. Soon afterwards, simmering disputes between the Sinhalese Buddhists and Tamil Hindus erupted into violent conflict. Until recently civil war between the Sri Lankan military and the Liberation Tigers of Tamil

SPICY RICE FLAT BREAD

You can eat this gluten-free bread spread with a little butter as a snack or with a meal instead of rice. It can be kept in the fridge for a day or so if you want to make it in advance.

14oz/400g rice flour
1 teaspoon salt
2 tablespoons sunflower oil
1 medium red onion, finely chopped
1–2 teaspoons red chilli flakes

1 dessertspoon ground turmeric
5 garlic cloves
2in/5cm piece of ginger, peeled and grated
butter, to serve

Place the rice flour in a saucepan and gently roast for a few minutes without browning. Add the salt and gradually stir in boiling water until a dough forms. Set to one side and allow to cool to room temperature.

Meanwhile heat the oil in a frying pan. When hot, add the red onion and fry until soft. Add the spices, fry for 1 minute and mix thoroughly with the dough. Allow to rest for 10 minutes.

Roll out a golfball-sized piece of dough, dusted with rice flour, until flat. Smear a little oil in a non-stick frying pan and cook the bread on both sides until brown. Repeat until you have used all the dough. Serve spread with a little butter.

SRI LANKAN ROASTED CURRY POWDER v

This spice mix is typical of Sri Lanka. It is not tempered but added at the end like a garam masala. We always make it in advance and store in an airtight container.

1 tablespoon white rice
1 tablespoon coriander seeds
1 dessertspoon cumin seeds
1 tablespoon desiccated coconut
2in/5cm piece of cinnamon

1 teaspoon cloves
20 curry leaves
1 teaspoon black peppercorns
1 teaspoon black mustard seeds

Dry roast the rice in a small frying pan until it starts to brown. Add all the spices and dry roast until they become aromatic and the coconut is golden brown. Remove from the heat and grind to a powder.

CASHEW NUT STUFFED CAPSICUM IN A COCONUT AND CURRY LEAF SAUCE v

Sweet capsicums look like large chillies but they are not spicy. They are available in both green and red varieties. We prefer red, but if you can only find green that's fine. They vary in size, so when choosing take into account how many you can eat.

10–12 sweet capsicums

1 large red onion, roughly chopped

1 tablespoon soy sauce (optional)

1 tablespoon lime juice

2 tablespoons desiccated coconut

4oz/115g cashew nuts

2 teaspoons roasted curry powder
    (page 119)

½ teaspoon chilli powder

1 tablespoon water

3 tablespoons sunflower oil

2 green chillies, finely chopped

½ teaspoon ground turmeric

20 curry leaves

14fl oz/400ml coconut milk

salt to taste

Wash the capsicums and then slit each one down one side and carefully remove the seeds, without breaking the capsicum.

Make the filling by blending together the chopped red onion, soy sauce, lime juice, desiccated coconut, cashew nuts, 1 teaspoon of the roasted curry powder, the chilli powder and the water until a paste forms. Stuff the capsicums with the filling and then heat the oil in a heavy frying pan and fry them on each side for a few minutes until brown. Remove from the pan and set to one side.

Add the chopped green chillies, turmeric and curry leaves to the pan, fry for a couple of minutes, and then reduce the heat and add the coconut milk, salt to taste and stuffed capsicums. Bring to the boil and gently simmer until the capsicums are soft and the sauce has reduced. Finally sprinkle the rest of the roasted curry powder over the top, cover the pan and allow to sit for 2 minutes before serving with rice.

Cashew Nut Stuffed Capsicum in a Coconut and Curry Leaf Sauce

CINNAMON AND COCONUT MILK CURRY v

3 tablespoons sunflower oil
1 large red onion, thinly sliced
2 garlic cloves, finely chopped
1½in/4cm piece of ginger,
    peeled and grated
2 green chillies, finely chopped
14oz/400g peeled and cubed
    butternut squash
1 cinnamon stick, broken into
    1in/2.5cm pieces
6oz/175g green beans,
    topped and tailed
4 celery sticks, cut into diagonal
    ½in/1cm slices
3 medium courgettes, cut into
    diagonal ½in/1cm slices
8fl oz/250ml water

⅔ small head of Chinese leaves, cut
    into 1in/2.5cm strip
2 sticks of lemon grass, finely sliced
handful of chopped parsley
1 tablespoon chopped thyme leaves
14fl oz/400ml coconut milk
salt to taste

For the curry powder
1 teaspoon ground cumin
1 teaspoon ground coriander
½ teaspoon ground cardamon
1 teaspoon ground turmeric
½ teaspoon ground fennel
1 teaspoon chilli powder
½ teaspoon ground cloves
½ teaspoon ground black pepper
15 curry leaves

Combine all the curry powder ingredients.

Heat the oil in a wok. When hot, add the onion, garlic, ginger and chillies, and sauté until the onion is soft. Add the butternut squash and cook until it starts to soften; then add the spice mix and the broken cinnamon stick, and cook for 1 minute. Add the green beans, celery, courgettes and water, and bring to the boil. Cover the wok, reduce the heat and gently simmer for 5 minutes. Add the Chinese leaves, lemon grass, parsley, thyme and coconut milk, cover the wok again and gently simmer for a further 10 minutes or so until the vegetables are soft and the sauce has reduced.

Season to taste and serve with Thyme and Lemon Rice (page 109).

Elephants bathing in the river at Pinnewala, Sri Lanka

COCONUT RICE

SERVES 4–6

500g/1lb 2oz basmati rice
30g/1oz butter
1 red onion, thinly sliced

4 green cardamom pods,
  lightly crushed
300ml/½ pint coconut milk
salt

Rinse the rice until the water runs clear.

Melt the butter in the pan in which you are going to cook the rice and fry the onion in it until softened. Add the cardamom and rice and stir until the rice is coated in the butter. Add the coconut milk and enough water to cover the rice by 1cm/½in, with salt to taste.

Cover with a tight-fitting lid and bring to the boil, then reduce the heat and simmer gently until all water is absorbed.

Adjust the season if necessary, fluffing the rice with fork as you do so. Leave to stand for a further 10 minutes, still covered, before serving

TOASTED COCONUT AND PINEAPPLE CHUTNEY v

Pineapple works particularly well with chilli, producing a delicious combination of sweet and sour.

SERVES 4–6

60g/2oz desiccated coconut
½ medium pineapple, peeled, cored
  and cubed

3 hot green chillies, thinly sliced
juice of 1 lime
salt to taste

Dry-roast the desiccated coconut in a hot pan, stirring constantly, until it just starts to brown. Turn it out of the pan and set aside.

Combine the pineapple, chillies, lime juice and salt to taste. Pour this over the coconut, mix well and serve immediately.

KANDY LEEK AND POTATO CURRY v

SERVES 4—6

1 heaped dessertspoon cumin seeds
1 heaped dessertspoon
    coriander seeds
1 teaspoon fennel seeds
4 tablespoons sunflower oil
1 red onion, thinly sliced
5 garlic cloves, crushed
5cm/2in piece of root ginger,
    finely chopped
4 medium white potatoes, cubed
    and parboiled

4 large leeks, cut into 2.5cm/
    1in slices
5cm/2in piece of cinnamon stick
½ teaspoon turmeric
1 teaspoon chilli powder
8 curry leaves
1 tablespoon vinegar
300ml/½ pint coconut milk
salt

fresh coriander leaves, to garnish

Kandy is the capital of the hill country and, in many ways, it is also the spiritual capital. The Temple of the Tooth houses Sri Lanka's most important Buddhist relic, the Sacred Tooth of the Buddha, which is believed to have been taken from the flames of his funeral pyre and smuggled into Ceylon in the fourth century, hidden in the hair of a princess.

During morning and evening ceremonies it is possible to 'view' the tooth. In fact you only see one of the many layers of casket in which it is housed and, needless to say, it is very heavily guarded. We ate this delicious leek and potato curry after the 'viewing'.

Dry-roast the cumin, coriander and fennel seeds in a small pan until they start to brown, then grind them to a powder using a spice grinder or pestle and mortar.

Heat the oil in a large heavy pan and, when hot, add the onion, garlic and ginger, and fry until soft. Add the potatoes and leeks and fry until the vegetables start to brown. Add the ground spice mix, cinnamon, turmeric, chilli powder, curry leaves and vinegar, stirring constantly to prevent sticking and ensuring that all the vegetables are coated in the spices.

Now add enough water barely to cover the vegetables and simmer gently until the vegetables soften. Add the coconut milk and simmer for a further 5 minutes.

Add salt to taste and sprinkle with the chopped coriander leaves. Serve with Coconut Sambol (page 127) and rice.

A young monk takes a photograph with my camera at the Buddhist cliff carvings at Polonnaruwa

COCONUT SAMBOL v

SERVES 4–6

85g/3oz desiccated coconut
6 shallots or 1 medium red onion, sliced
8 curry leaves

6 red chillies (fewer if you don't like it too spicy)
juice of 2 limes
salt

Soak the coconut in water until it swells and becomes fleshy. Place in a food processor with the remaining ingredients and salt to taste, then blend until well combined. If the mixture seems dry, simply add a little water.

You can store this sambal in an airtight container in the fridge for a few days. The coconut will continue to absorb any moisture, so re-moisten with a little lime juice and water before serving.

ONION SAMBOL v

SERVES 4–6

3 tablespoons sunflower oil
3 medium onions, finely chopped
4 garlic cloves, crushed
2 green chillies, thinly sliced
2.5cm/1in cube of root ginger, peeled and finely chopped
4 green cardamom pods, lightly crushed
1 teaspoon ground cinnamon

2 teaspoons garam masala
1 teaspoon salt
1 teaspoon brown sugar
1 tablespoon vinegar
150ml/¼ pint tamarind water (2 tablespoons tamarind purée dissolved in 150ml/¼ pint water)
1 tablespoon vegetarian Worcestershire sauce (optional)

Sambols are spicy dry chutneys. They are served as accompaniments to most meals or, as a light meal, simply with roti bread or hoppers (rice-flour pancakes).

Heat the oil in a heavy pan. When hot, fry the onions, garlic, chillies and ginger until soft. Add all the spices and stir them into the onions.

Now add all remaining ingredients and gently simmer until the water content reduces to give a chutney-like consistency. In a food processor, purée the contents of the pan, but be sure to retain some 'bite'. This sambal can be stored in an airtight container in the fridge for up to a month.

GREEN VEGETABLE MALLUNG v

Mallung, which means 'mixed up', is also the name of curries made with curry leaves, coconut and chilli. Mallung is most commonly made with green vegetables, of which there are many in Sri Lanka. Broccoli, for example, is abundant. This recipe can be made with any green vegetables, so feel free to substitute.

Traditionally mallung should contain fish paste, made from pounded dried fish. You might like to include vegetarian Worcestershire sauce instead. The flavour is quite similar to that of fish paste, but more subtle.

SERVES 4–6

4 tablespoons sunflower oil	175g/6oz spinach,
1 large red onion, thinly sliced	coarsely shredded
4 green chillies, thinly sliced	400ml/14fl oz coconut milk
12 curry leaves	1 tablespoon vegetarian
1 tablespoon black mustard seeds	Worcestershire sauce (optional)
350g/12oz broccoli florets	½ teaspoon ground saffron
350g/12oz peeled and	salt
cubed marrow	juice of 1 lime
60g/2oz desiccated coconut	chopped coriander leaves, to garnish

Heat the oil in a large pan and, when hot, add the onion and fry it for a few minutes, then add the chillies, curry leaves and mustard seeds. Fry until the mustard seeds 'pop'.

Add the broccoli, marrow and desiccated coconut, and stir until the vegetables are coated in the spices and the coconut is toasted. Pour over enough water partially to cover the vegetables and simmer until they are just starting to soften.

Stir in the spinach, the coconut milk, the vegetarian Worcestershire sauce if you are using it, and the saffron. Gently simmer until all the vegetables are soft. Add salt to taste and the lime juice.

Garnish with coriander leaves and serve with Onion Sambol (page 127) and rice.

After we had earned the approval of our driver, Cyril, by our ascent of Adam's Peak, he made it his mission to search out the best food he could find, and eagerly explained how things were cooked. Lunch that day was a mallung, or mixture, of green vegetables in a coconut-cream sauce with black mustard seeds, green chillies, yellow saffron and fresh curry leaves.

We ate the mallung while enjoying a grand view down towards the coastal plains. It tasted so delicious that we wondered if the setting, together with the healthy appetite from all our exercise, might be deceiving our senses, but every time we have cooked this dish since, its excellence has been confirmed.

Green Vegetable Mallung

BEETROOT AND BRINJAL BLACK CURRY v

This recipe works well with Toasted Coconut and Pineapple Chutney (page 124) and the combination of yellow and red looks wonderful.

SERVES 4–6

2 red onions, roughly chopped

3 garlic cloves

3–4 hot red chillies (either dried and soaked or fresh)

1 lemon grass stalk

1 dessertspoon cumin seeds

1 dessertspoon coriander seeds

1 scant teaspoon fennel seeds

4 tablespoons sunflower oil

450g/1lb raw beetroot (trimmed weight), peeled and cubed

5 baby aubergines (brinjal), cut into quarters

200ml/7fl oz stock

300ml/½ pint coconut milk

salt and pepper

125g/4oz cashew nuts

In a food processor, process the onions, garlic, chillies and lemon grass to a pulp. Dry-roast the cumin, coriander and fennel seeds in a small pan until they are dark brown (but not burnt or they will taste bitter). Grind to a powder using a spice grinder or pestle and mortar.

Heat the oil in a large heavy pan. When hot, add the onion paste and cook briskly for a few minutes, then throw in the ground spices, stirring continuously. When the spices are combined with the onion paste, add the beetroot and aubergine. Fry for a further minute or two on high heat, stirring constantly.

Pour in the stock and bring to the boil, then reduce the heat, cover and simmer until the vegetables are nice and soft. Add the coconut milk and cook for a further 5 minutes. Meanwhile, dry-roast the cashew nuts until golden.

Season the curry to taste with salt and pepper. Garnish the curry with the toasted cashew nuts and serve with Toasted Coconut and Pineapple Chutney and Coconut Rice (page 124).

We found this splendid recipe for Beetroot and Brinjal Black Curry at the delightfully 'olde worlde' New Oriental Hotel in Galle, on the west coast of Sri Lanka. Built in 1865 as an officers' barracks, the hotel is famous not only for its atmospheric Victorian interiors, but also for its food.

Hill country near Adam's Peak

India

India

Finding recipes for great vegetarian dishes in India is never a problem. Regional variations of ingredients and cooking styles mean that there is no such thing as typical Indian cuisine.

Hyderabad, the old Islamic capital of south India, is often ignored by tourists but it is well worth a visit. The bazaars of the old town around the impressive Charminar mosque are packed full of pearls, bangles, fabrics and huge pots for cooking biryanis. There are exquisite Islamic tombs of Mughal rulers, elegant merchants' houses and, outside the city, the ruins of Golconda, one of India's finest forts. The city's cuisine is dominated by complex biryanis that reflect the sophisticated, delicate tastes of its Mughal past. Beyond the city, much of rural Andhra Pradesh is engaged in tobacco production. For generations the villagers who work in the fields have had a habit of chewing tobacco, and as a consequence many have damaged their taste buds. To compensate, local cuisine is heavily spiced. On our drives through the countryside we ate the hottest food we have ever had in India.

In Rajasthan the combination of dramatic desert landscapes, the bright colours of Rajput turbans and saris, and the wealth of historic buildings is a seductive mixture. We travelled by car from Udaipur in the south to Jaipur in the north, staying in a collection of 'heritage hotels'. Some of these were rural palaces that are still the homes of families descended from the royal rulers who built them. Others were once the homes of wealthy merchants in cities and one was a tented camp in the middle of a working farm. We ate some sensational food, including some unique dishes that were the old family recipes of our hosts.

In Amritsar, every day a vegetarian feast is served free to pilgrims visiting the Golden Temple of the Sikhs. Up to 30,000 people a day are fed by an army of volunteers engaged in a mass catering operation on an awesome scale. Such generosity is typical of the welcome Sikhs offer visitors to their holiest shrine. The temple complex is a good reason to visit Amritsar, especially at sunset, when the golden domes of the Hari Mandir Sahib are reflected in the tranquil Pool of Nectar that surrounds it. From here we travelled by road up into the hill stations and villages of the Himalayas. In roadside dharbas we ate plenty of wholesome dhal and some interesting vegetable dishes such as spicy mashed pumpkin.

In Calcutta we went in search of restaurants serving traditional Bengali dishes. These are surprisingly rare. The local Bengalis spend hours socializing in tea houses but eat at home, and most of Calcutta's restaurants cater for migrants into the city who don't have extended families there to provide home-cooked feasts for them.

Pages 132–133 **Melas, or fairs, have for centuries attracted tens of thousands of pilgrims. These Rajput pilgrims have gathered at the desert oasis of Pushkar in Rajasthan for an auspicious bathe under a full moon**

Right, clockwise from top right **A girl from a nomadic clan in the Shekhawati region of Rajasthan; a village man, Rajasthan; a girl at the tomb of the Qutb Shahi kings of Hyderabad; a Rajput man in Shekhawati; a flower seller in a Calcutta bazaar; a picture in the window of a photographer's shop in Calcutta**

KICHURI

6 cups water

8oz/225g basmati rice

8oz/225g mung dhal, dry roasted in
a frying pan until golden brown

2in/5cm piece of ginger, peeled
and grated

2 teaspoons ground coriander

1 teaspoon ground turmeric

½ teaspoon chilli powder

2 teaspoons ground cumin

2 teaspoons jaggery or brown sugar

9oz/250g cauliflower, cut into florets

7oz/200g potatoes, cubed

6oz/175g mooli (white radishes),
peeled and cubed

5oz/150g shelled peas, fresh or frozen

4oz/115g shallots, peeled and left whole

6 green chillies, slit down the side

salt to taste

4in/10cm piece of cinnamon,
broken into smaller pieces

6 cloves

6 green cardamom pods

3oz/90g ghee or butter

6 dry red chillies

4 bay leaves

1 large red onion, thinly sliced

2oz/60g raisins

extra ghee or butter

chopped coriander leaves, to garnish

8floz/250ml yoghurt, whisked with
¼ teaspoon ground black pepper
and ¼ teaspoon ground
cardamom, to serve

hard-boiled egg, quartered, to
garnish (optional)

Bring the water to boil in a large pan, add the rice and dry roasted mung dhal,
cover the pan and gently simmer until the rice is half cooked.

Mix the ginger, coriander, turmeric, chilli powder and cumin with a little
water to make a paste and add to the rice and dhal along with the jaggery or brown
sugar. Add the vegetables and green chillies and salt to taste, and continue to
cook, covered with a lid, until the vegetables are soft.

Meanwhile dry roast the cinnamon, cloves and cardamom in a small frying pan
until aromatic and then grind to a powder. Heat the ghee or butter in a frying
pan. When hot, add the red chillies and bay leaves and fry for 1 minute. Add the
sliced red onion and raisins and fry until golden brown. Add the ground spice
mix, fry for 1 minute and then stir into the cooked kichuri.

Serve with extra melted ghee or butter poured over the top – as much or as little
as you like – and garnish with chopped coriander. Serve with yoghurt whisked
with black pepper and cardamom, and garnished with hard-boiled egg if desired.

Kichuri is traditionally
eaten during the
monsoon, when villages
get cut off and have to
rely on rice and dhal,
which are always kept in
the store cupboard.
Kichuri means a mixture,
so you can add any
vegetables you like. It is
also served with boiled
eggs; we love it with Egg
Curry (page 163).

**Jaggery or gur, made
of date palm sap, is
often used as a
sweetening agent in
Indian cookery**

MUSTARD SPICED CAULIFLOWER v

3 tablespoons black mustard seeds
3 tablespoons yellow mustard seeds
6 tablespoons mustard oil or
   sunflower oil
2 teaspoons nigella seeds

2lb/900g cauliflower, cut into
   small florets
1 teaspoon ground turmeric
12fl oz/375ml water
6 green chillies, slit down one side
salt to taste

Grind the mustard seeds to a powder and set to one side.

Heat the oil in a wok. When hot, add the nigella seeds. When they crackle, add the cauliflower and fry until golden brown. Add the turmeric and ground mustard seeds along with the water, chillies and salt to taste. Bring to the boil then reduce heat, cover pan and gently simmer until all the water has evaporated.

Serve with rice, Pumpkin with Chickpeas and Panch Phoran (page 164) and Tomato Chutney (page 164).

UTTAPAM

5oz/150g rice flour
3oz/90g urad dhal flour
1oz/30g fenugreek seeds, ground to
   a powder
1 heaped teaspoon baking powder
1 teaspoon sugar
1 teaspoon salt

3 medium tomatoes, finely chopped
1 red onion, finely chopped
2 large handfuls of finely chopped
   coriander leaves
3 green chillies, finely chopped
sunflower oil for frying
butter, to spread on top

Combine the flours, ground fenugreek seeds, baking powder, sugar and salt. Gradually add enough water to make a thick batter, making sure that there are no lumps. Add the chopped tomato, red onion, coriander and green chillies. Heat a little oil in a non-stick frying pan. When hot, pour in a ladleful of batter, using the back of the ladle to spread the batter into a pancake approximately 8in/20cm in diameter. When bubbles form and the batter has set, turn the uttapam and cook the other side.

Serve spread with butter and with Coconut Chutney (page 143) on the side.

The Indian version of pizza, uttapam is a wheat-free pancake, eaten for breakfast or mid-morning with chutney. You can improvise with toppings and fillings, but traditionally it is served with diced tomatoes, onion, chilli and coriander. The batter is usually left to ferment at room temperature for a minimum of 3 hours, but the cheat's method is to add baking powder.

METHI ALOO

Potatoes cooked with fenugreek leaves and yoghurt make a great combination. Fenugreek leaves are sold very cheaply, in big bunches, in Indian stores. You can also buy fenugreek dried, although it's not as good as fresh.

1lb 10oz/750g potatoes,
   peeled and cubed
1 medium onion, roughly chopped
5 garlic cloves
thumb-sized piece of ginger, peeled
   and roughly chopped
4 green chillies, chopped
2oz/60g ghee or butter
8 green cardamom seeds, crushed
6 cloves
2in/5cm piece of cinnamon

2 bay leaves
½ teaspoon fenugreek seeds
1 medium onion, thinly sliced
1 teaspoon ground coriander
½ teaspoon ground cumin
½ teaspoon ground turmeric
4oz/115g natural yoghurt
6oz/175g fresh fenugreek, roughly
   chopped, or 1oz/30g dried fenugreek
8fl oz/250ml water
salt to taste

Place the potatoes in a saucepan of boiling water and parboil until nearly soft, drain and set to one side.

Blend the roughly chopped onion, garlic, ginger and chillies in a food processor until smooth. Melt the ghee or butter in a wok, and then add the cardamom, cloves, cinnamon, bay leaves and fenugreek. Heat until they start to crackle. Add the sliced onion and sauté until the onion starts to brown. Stir in the ground coriander, cumin and turmeric, followed by the potatoes and the onion paste mix, and fry, stirring constantly for 3 minutes. Add the yoghurt, fenugreek and water, bring to the boil, cover the pan, reduce the heat and gently simmer until the potatoes are soft and the sauce is reduced. Add salt to taste.

Serve with Whole Green Chillies in Tamarind and Brazil Nut Sauce (opposite).

A tea picker in Darjeeling

WHOLE GREEN CHILLIES IN TAMARIND AND BRAZIL NUT SAUCE ᵥ

The amount of chillies in this recipe may look scary, but the large, almost pepper-like green chillies used, available in Indian and Middle Eastern stores, are not spicy.

12oz/350g large green chillies
2 tablespoons desiccated coconut
8 brazil nuts, roughly chopped
2 dessertspoons sesame seeds
4 tablespoons sunflower oil
1 large red onion, finely sliced
1 heaped teaspoon cumin seeds
1 heaped teaspoon ground coriander
½ teaspoon ground chilli

½ teaspoon ground turmeric
3 garlic cloves, crushed
3in/7.5cm piece of ginger, peeled
  and grated
10 curry leaves
14fl oz/425ml tamarind water
  (2 teaspoons tamarind paste
  dissolved in 1¾ cups water)
salt to taste

Boil the whole chillies in salted water until their colour changes and then drain and set to one side.

Dry roast the desiccated coconut, brazil nuts and sesame seeds in a small frying pan until toasted. Remove from the heat and grind to a powder.

Heat the sunflower oil in a wok. When hot, add the sliced onion and fry until golden brown. Stir in the cumin seeds, followed by the coriander, chilli and turmeric. Add the garlic and ginger and the nut and seed paste, and sauté for a few minutes. Add the chillies and the curry leaves, stir into the spices, and then pour in the tamarind water and salt to taste. Cover the pan and simmer for a further 5 minutes.

Serve with either Methi Aloo (opposite) or Hyderabadi Kacchi Biryani (page 140).

HYDERABADI KACCHI BIRYANI

1lb/450g basmati rice

salt to taste

6 tablespoons ghee or butter

2oz/60g raisins

3oz/90g whole almonds

3 medium onions, thinly sliced

3 garlic cloves, crushed

2in/5cm piece of ginger, peeled
and grated

2 teaspoons chilli powder

1 teaspoon ground turmeric

1lb 5oz/600g peeled and cubed pumpkin

4oz/115g unsulphured dried apricots,
cut into quarters

¾ cup water

14fl oz/425ml natural yoghurt, beaten

large handful of mint leaves, chopped

large handful of coriander leaves,
chopped

2 tablespoons lemon juice

2 pinches of saffron, dissolved in
3 tablespoons warm milk

For the pumpkin masala spice mix

3in/7.5cm piece of cinnamon

6 green cardamom pods

6 cloves

2 bay leaves

1 teaspoon caraway seeds

For the rice masala spice mix

2in/5cm piece of cinnamon

6 green cardamom pods, crushed

6 cloves

Dry roast the pumpkin masala spice mix in a small frying pan. When it becomes aromatic, remove from the pan and grind to a powder.

Wash the basmati rice before putting it in a saucepan with enough water to cover the rice by 1in/2.5cm. Add the rice masala spice mix and salt to taste. Cover the pan, bring to the boil and then reduce heat and simmer until the rice is three-quarters cooked. Remove the pan from the heat, drain the rice and set to one side.

Heat one-third of the ghee or butter in a frying pan. When hot, add the raisins and the almonds, sauté until toasted and then remove with a slotted spoon and combine with the rice. Add the sliced onions to the frying pan, cook until crisp and brown, and set to one side.

Heat the remaining ghee or butter in a heavy-bottomed casserole dish with a tight-fitting lid. Remove half and set to one side. Add the garlic and ginger and fry for a couple of minutes, and then stir in the chilli and turmeric, followed by the pumpkin, chopped apricots and salt to taste. Add the water and a quarter of the yoghurt, and gently simmer for 5 minutes.

Sikh volunteers
cooking free food for
pilgrims at the Golden
Temple, Amritsar

Now assemble the biryani. Layer half the fried onions and half the chopped mint and coriander leaves over the pumpkin, followed by half the rice. Pour over the remaining yoghurt, mint and coriander. Cover with the remaining rice, onions, lemon juice, melted ghee or butter and saffron milk. Cover the casserole with the lid and cook on a high heat for 3 minutes; then reduce the heat to a minimum and gently cook for a further 15 minutes.

Serve with Whole Green Chillies in Tamarind and Brazil Nut Sauce (page 139).

CHANNA DHAL

This is a dhal made from split chickpeas and tempered with fried fresh coconut and raisins.

8oz/225g channa dhal

3 pints/1½ litres water

1 teaspoon ground turmeric

½ teaspoon chilli powder

1 teaspoon ground coriander

2 teaspoons ground cumin

1 teaspoon garam masala

6 green chillies, slit down the side

2 teaspoons jaggery or brown sugar

salt to taste

2 tablespoons ghee or buttter

¼ small coconut, finely diced

2 tablespoons raisins, soaked in water

   for ½ hour and then drained

4 bay leaves

1 teaspoon garam masala

Place the channa dhal in a saucepan with the water and bring to the boil. Remove any foam that rises to the surface. Add the turmeric and chilli powder, cover the pan and gently simmer until the dhal is soft. Mash the dhal with a potato masher to break it up a little. Combine the coriander, cumin and garam masala with a little water until a paste forms, and add to the dhal along with the green chillies, jaggery or brown sugar and salt to taste. Continue cooking for a further 5 minutes.

   Heat the ghee or butter in a small frying pan. When hot, add the coconut and raisins, and fry until golden. Add the bay leaves and garam masala, fry for 1 minute and pour on to the dhal.

COCONUT CHUTNEY V

2½oz/75g desiccated coconut

3 tablespoons chopped ginger

3 red chillies, roughly chopped

4 tablespoons lemon juice

2 teaspoons black mustard seeds

1 teaspoon black peppercorns, crushed

1 teaspoon sugar

salt to taste

Blend the coconut, ginger, chillies and lemon juice in a food processor until smooth. Dry roast the mustard seeds and crushed peppercorns in a small frying pan until they pop and then add to the chutney, along with the sugar, salt to taste and enough water to make the chutney moist.

Channa Dhal

KORMA SHAH JAHAN

This recipe was apparently created in the royal kitchen of Shah Jahan, the Mughal emperor who built the Taj Mahal. We make it with paneer, a firm cottage cheese made for cooking and available in blocks from Indian shops and some supermarkets.

4 red chillies, roughly chopped
1in/2.5cm piece of ginger, peeled
   and roughly chopped
5 skinless almonds
15 pistachios, shelled
3 teaspoons white poppy seeds
3 dried figs, roughly chopped
4 teaspoons desiccated coconut
4 tablespoons ghee or butter
14oz/400g paneer, cut into cubes
1 medium onion, finely sliced
⅔ teaspoon ground nutmeg
⅔ teaspoon ground cardamom

pinch of saffron
4fl oz/125ml double cream
4fl oz/125ml water
salt to taste

For the garam masala
½ teaspoon cumin seeds
4 cloves
2 bay leaves
4 green cardamom pods
1in/2.5cm piece of cinnamon
6 black peppercorns
½ teaspoon mace

Dry roast the garam masala ingredients in a small frying pan until aromatic, remove from the pan and grind to a powder.

Make the korma paste by blending the chillies, ginger, almonds, pistachios, poppy seeds, figs and desiccated coconut in a food processor until a paste forms.

Heat the ghee or butter in a wok, add the paneer and fry until browned on all sides. Remove from the pan with a slotted spoon and set to one side. Add the sliced onion to the wok and fry until golden brown. Stir in the korma paste, fry for a few minutes, and then add the nutmeg, cardamom and saffron. Add the cream, garam masala, paneer, water and salt to taste. Cover the wok and gently simmer for 4 minutes.

Paneer is an unfermented cheese made from milk curd. Uncooked it is quite tasteless, so it is always used in cooked dishes, usually fried in cubes or strips and then added to the dish.

Sikh pilgrims at the Pool of Nectar in the Golden Temple, Amritsar

SPICY MASHED PUMPKIN

1lb 10oz/750g peeled and
   cubed pumpkin
4 dried red chillies
1½ heaped tablespoons
   coriander seeds
4 teaspoons cumin seeds

3oz/90g sesame seeds
1 teaspoon amchoor (dried
   powdered mango)
salt to taste
6 tablespoons ghee or butter
good pinch of asafoetida (hing)

Boil the cubed pumpkin until soft, drain and mash until smooth. Meanwhile dry roast the dried red chillies, coriander seeds, cumin seeds and sesame seeds in a small frying pan until aromatic, remove from the heat and grind to a powder. Add to the mashed pumpkin, along with the amchoor and salt to taste. Melt the ghee or butter in a small frying pan. When hot, add the asafoetida and then gradually stir into the mashed pumpkin. Serve with Korma Shah Jahan (opposite).

ROYAL BABY AUBERGINES

½oz/15g peanuts

1oz/30g desiccated coconut

2 teaspoons sesame seeds

4 dried red chillies

2 teaspoons coriander seeds

2 teaspoons cumin seeds

1 tablespoon honey

1 tablespoon chopped coriander leaves

1in/2.5cm piece of ginger,
    peeled and chopped

2 teaspoons ground turmeric

3 garlic cloves

1 teaspoon garam masala

salt to taste

1lb 2oz/500g baby aubergines

5 tablespoons sunflower oil

1 small onion, finely chopped

8fl oz/250ml tamarind water
    (1 heaped teaspoon tamarind
    paste dissolved in 1 cup water)

Dry roast the peanuts in a small frying pan until golden, and then add the coconut, sesame seeds, red chillies, coriander seeds and cumin seeds and continue roasting for a few more minutes. Remove from the heat and grind to a powder. Place the powder, along with the honey, coriander leaves, ginger, garlic, turmeric and garam masala, salt to taste and a little water, in a food processor and blend until a paste forms.

Slit the baby aubergines in half, keeping the stem intact, and fill the aubergines with the paste. Smear any remaining paste on the outside of the aubergines. Heat the oil in a wok. When hot, add the aubergines, four at a time, and fry until brown on all sides. Set to one side. In the same oil, fry the chopped onion until golden, add the aubergines and tamarind water, bring to the boil, cover the pan, reduce the heat and gently simmer until the tamarind has reduced to almost nothing and the aubergines are soft.

Serve with Prune and Date Chutney (page 169).

We had one of our most memorable nights in India staying in the tented camp of Chhatra Sagar at Nimaj, on the road between Jodhpur and Jaipur. The family who farm their ancestral land in this remote part of the state constructed a dam to provide irrigation for their fields and they accommodate guests in luxurious tents pitched along the dam wall, overlooking the lake. Staying here gave us the unique experience of sleeping under canvas deep in the Rajasthan countryside. The food served was the best we have ever eaten in India, all organically grown in the fields around the lake and cooked in an open-plan kitchen by the family.

PEAS AND SPINACH WITH GRAM FLOUR AND CURD

1 medium onion, roughly chopped
2 garlic cloves
3 green chillies, roughly chopped
2½fl oz/75ml yoghurt, beaten with
    1 cup water
½oz/15g gram flour (chickpea flour)
1fl oz/30ml lime juice
3 dried red chillies, powdered
1 teaspoon ground turmeric
1½ teaspoons cumin seeds

3 tablespoons sesame oil
2 garlic cloves, finely chopped
10oz/300g spinach leaves, washed,
    stems removed and cut into
    ½in/1cm strips
6oz/175g shelled peas,
    fresh or frozen
22fl oz/600ml water
salt to taste

Blend the onion, garlic and green chillies in a food processor until smooth.

Gradually stir the yoghurt and water mixture into the gram flour, making sure that there are no lumps. Add the lime juice, red chillies, turmeric, cumin seeds and blended onion mix.

Heat the sesame oil in a wok. When hot, add the chopped garlic cloves and fry until golden brown. Reduce the heat and allow to cool a little before stirring in the yoghurt and gram flour mixture, followed by the spinach, peas and water. Gently simmer until the sauce thickens, and then stir in salt to taste.

GHEE

A lot of Indian recipes use ghee, a form of clarified butter. It is incredibly easy to make and can be kept in the fridge for some time, so we thought we would include this recipe.

1 block butter, preferably unsalted

Melt the butter in a small pan. When the butter has melted, it will splutter. Reduce the heat and keep cooking until the spluttering stops and the milk solids that have risen to the surface sink. Pour into a container and allow to cool. Store in the fridge.

SOUTHERN INDIA

Southern India includes the Deccan plateau, the plains of the Malabar and Coromandel coasts and the mountainous Eastern and Western Ghats that separate them, and, in the far south, the flat lands of Tamil Nadu. While the food of the coasts inevitably involves a lot of seafood, vegetarian options are still plentiful; in Tamil Nadu, as in Gujarat, vegetarianism is the norm. Much use is made of coconut in creamy sauces and nutty chutneys; rice grows everywhere and is served in copious amounts at every meal. The Deccan does not have the wealth that the coastal states have accumulated through generations of sea-trading, so the food there is often more basic. The exception is Bangalore, the capital of Karnataka, which has blossomed into a dynamic and prosperous city on the back of its booming information technology industry. Its new wealth has attracted India's first Kentucky Fried Chicken outlet and many fast-food imitators, but thankfully there has been demand for fine new Indian restaurants too.

We left Bangalore by the night train for the north of Karnataka, where, after a first-rate thali and a good night's sleep, we woke up to find an India from another century. We drove past acres of sunflowers to the sleepy town of Badami, whose tree-lined avenues were almost devoid of motorized traffic; bullock-carts, horse-drawn tongas and bicycles were the only company for our car. In the cliffs above the town are some fifth-century caves full of exquisite stone-carving depicting scenes from Hindu and Buddhist mythology. As the Moguls fought their way south in the sixteenth century destroying such images, they missed these, which are almost intact today. Despite such treasures, relatively few foreigners pass through Badami and tourists are still a novelty. From Badami we drove south to the ruins of Vijayanagar at Hampi: these have not survived years of conflict as well as Badami has, but their sheer size and their setting among desolate, boulder-strewn hills make them just as impressive.

In Kerala vegetables come immersed in fragrant coconut cream laced with spices, while in Tamil Nadu we ate well on numerous fill-up thalis, served on a fresh banana leaf. As soon as any one of the many ingredients on the leaf is eaten a man appears and replaces it with more of the same: only when one folds over the leaf is there an escape from the unending meal. However, more than the plethora of vegetable and dal dishes, it is the chutneys and raitas that we remember most, and we have given the tastiest of them in this chapter.

An elephant in the morning mists in Tamil Nadu's Mudumalai Sanctuary

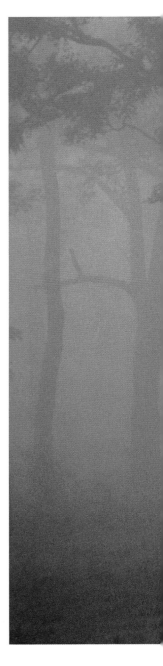

POTATO AND PEANUT PAWA v

Pawa is a type of flat rice available from Indian shops.

SERVES 4–6

4 tablespoons oil

1 teaspoon black mustard seeds

60g/2oz peanuts

3 medium potatoes, cut into small
   cubes and boiled until soft

1 teaspoon sesame seeds

½ teaspoon ground turmeric

½ teaspoon chilli powder

1 green chilli, finely chopped

1 tablespoon desiccated coconut

salt

sugar

125g/4oz pawa (dried flat rice),
   rinsed and drained

large handful of fresh
   coriander leaves

Heat the oil in a large frying pan, add the mustard seeds and cook until they pop, then add the peanuts. When they begin to brown, add the drained potatoes, sesame seeds and turmeric. Fry until the potatoes begin to brown. Add the chilli powder, green chilli and coconut, with salt and sugar to taste; mix gently.

Remove from heat and mix in the pawa flakes. Return to the heat and fry until the pawa flakes are heated through.

Add the coriander leaves and either eat warm or keep in a sealed container for your train journey.

In the town of Badami we found people friendly and hospitable — so much so that when we enthused about a lunch we ate in a café, we were not allowed to pay for it. The day we left Badami we persuaded the café owners to let us pay for a tiffin tin full to take away with us. The dish was very simple, using an ingredient we had seen often in markets but never known how to use. This was pawa — dried flattened flakes of rice.

Quite unappetizing in its raw state, once brought to life with oil, spices, potatoes and peanuts, pawa becomes a great snack food. It is very popular in southern India — families cook it up and take it with them in stainless steel tins to snack on during long train journeys.

CACHUMBERS v

A cachumber is a raw vegetable accompaniment that usually includes onion: we give the classic version with tomato.

SERVES 4–6

1 medium-to-large red onion,
   finely diced

3 tomatoes, cut into small cubes

juice of 1 lime

1 tablespoon coriander leaves, chopped

salt

Mix all the ingredients in a bowl with salt to taste.

The entrance to the cave temples at Badami in Karnataka

COCONUT CABBAGE v

Serves 4–6

4 tablespoons sunflower oil

5cm/2in piece of root ginger, peeled and cut into thin matchstick strips

2 green chillies, thinly sliced

8 curry leaves

1 level dessertspoon black mustard seeds

½ teaspoon ground turmeric

1 small white cabbage, finely shredded (about 675g/1½lb)

2 tablespoons desiccated coconut

1 teaspoon sugar

1 teaspoon salt

Make sure you have all the ingredients ready to throw in. Heat the sunflower oil in a wok and, when hot, add the ginger, chilli and curry leaves. Fry for a minute.

Add the mustard seeds and turmeric, and when the mustard seeds start to 'pop' add the cabbage. Stirring constantly, fry until the cabbage starts to wilt.

Add the coconut, stirring well until it begins to toast. Finally add the sugar and salt. Serve immediately.

CHANA IN A THICK SPICY GRAVY

The chickpea dish given here may be described as chana batura or chana masala. As chana batura, it is served with deep-fried batura bread and makes a popular fast-food dish in Bombay cafés. As chana masala, it can be a side-dish, along with vegetables and rice or chapatis, and appears all over India.

SERVES 4–6

handful of coriander leaves, chopped
handful of fresh mint, chopped
3 medium onions
12 garlic cloves
5cm/2in piece of root ginger
1 teaspoon whole cumin seeds
1 teaspoon whole coriander seeds
5cm/2in piece of cinnamon stick
7 dried red chillies
10 black peppercorns

2 bay leaves
1 teaspoon ground turmeric
4 tablespoons ghee
2 tablespoons tomato purée
250g/9oz dried chickpeas, soaked overnight and boiled until soft
2 medium potatoes, boiled and chopped small
300g/10oz spinach, chopped
salt

In a food processor, process the coriander, mint, onions, garlic and ginger to a paste.

Dry-roast the cumin and coriander seeds, cinnamon, chillies, peppercorns, bay leaves and turmeric in a dry frying pan over a medium heat, tossing continuously to avoid burning, then grind them all in a spice grinder into a dry masala.

Melt the ghee in a large heavy pan and fry the paste for 3 minutes. Add the dry masala and fry for another minute. Add the tomato purée and cook for 3 minutes more.

Add the drained chickpeas and chopped potatoes, followed by the spinach, and cook until the latter is wilted. Add water as needed to form a thick gravy. Season with salt to taste and serve.

A woman worships at the giant effigy of Ganesh, the elephant-headed Hindu god, at Hampi in northern Karnataka

COCHIN COCONUT MASALA V

<small>SERVES 4–6</small>

5 dried red chillies

2 tablespoons white poppy seeds

2 tablespoons coriander seeds

1 teaspoon cumin seeds

5 cloves

10 black peppercorns

60g/2oz desiccated coconut,
    dry-roasted in a hot pan until
    just brown

6 tablespoons sunflower oil

1 teaspoon black mustard seeds

1 teaspoon cumin seeds

pinch of hing (asafoetida)

5–10 green chillies, cut into
    thin strips

1 teaspoon ground turmeric

12 curry leaves

1 large onion, thinly sliced

1 large sweet potato, cut into chunky
    'chip' shapes

2 medium courgettes,
    cut into 'chips'

250g/9oz mooli, cut into 'chips'

125g/4oz okra, cut in
    half lengthwise

125g/4oz green beans, cut in half

400ml/14fl oz canned coconut milk

juice of 1 lime

salt

Dry-roast the red chillies, poppy seeds, coriander seeds, cumin seeds, cloves and peppercorns, then grind them all in a spice grinder. Mix with the roasted coconut and a little water to make a paste.

Heat the oil in a large heavy pan. When hot, fry the mustard seeds, cumin seeds, hing, green chillies, turmeric and curry leaves, then add the onion. Fry until the onion is soft. Add the sweet potato and fry for 3 minutes.

Add the spice paste and all the other vegetables, stirring everything for 5 minutes. Then add the coconut milk, reduce the heat and cook until the vegetables are tender, adding a little water if necessary to keep things loose.

Finally, add the lime juice and a little salt to taste.

After a minor accident in Cochin in Kerala, I spent a night in hospital. The next day my bed was needed for another patient so I had to transfer to a hotel, but I was told not to walk for three days. I was borne aloft on a stretcher through the streets until a suitable hotel was found.

I hadn't considered the complication of getting food without being able to walk — but I needn't have worried. Each day medical students arrived to change my dressing and supply me with fresh food from their canteen, assuring me that it was merely their duty to attend the wounded.

While I was laid up in bed, this dish was something I looked forward to every day. I loved the way the vegetables were cut, as well as the tastes — it felt as if someone was really looking after me.

Enormous Chinese-style fishing nets, used in Cochin, are seen here silhouetted against the evening sky

FRUIT LASSI

This refreshing and cooling yoghurt drink makes a perfect accompaniment to a spicy curry, and can be sweet or savoury. We often use mango, but you can use any soft fruit, such as banana.

SERVES 4–6

500g/1lb 2oz full-fat yoghurt
300ml/½ pint iced water
300ml/½ pint cold milk
½ teaspoon ground cardamom seeds

1 tablespoon rosewater
2 mangoes, peeled and cubed, or
   5 ripe bananas, peeled and sliced
flaked roasted almonds, to serve

Place all the ingredients in a blender or food processor and blend until smooth.
Serve with ice cubes and sprinkled with the flaked roasted almonds.

155

GREEN COCONUT CHUTNEY v

SERVES 4–6

handful of coriander leaves
handful of mint leaves
1 garlic clove
2.5cm/1in piece of root ginger,
    peeled and roughly chopped

2 green chillies
250g/9oz desiccated coconut
juice of 2 limes
1 teaspoon sugar
1 teaspoon salt

In a food processor, blend the coriander, mint, garlic, ginger, chilli, coconut and lime juice until they form a paste. Add just enough water to make a moist (but not wet) chutney. Mix in the sugar and salt.

If you are making this in advance, the coconut will absorb the water, so simply add more water to get the desired consistency before serving.

SWEET DATE AND TAMARIND CHUTNEY

SERVES 4–6

250g/9oz dates, chopped
1 level dessertspoon tamarind paste
1 dessertspoon cumin seeds,
    dry-roasted in a hot pan

1 teaspoon honey
salt

Place all the ingredients in a food processor with 250ml/9fl oz water and salt to taste, and blend until well combined.

In India no meal is complete without a chutney. There are hundreds of different recipes, for both fresh and cooked versions. Chutneys based on coconut are more common in the south, fruit chutneys in the north and west.

Raita is the term used for a variety of cooling yoghurt-based accompaniments. We've chosen two examples, one savoury, one sweet.

CUCUMBER AND MINT RAITA

SERVES 4–6

250ml/9fl oz yoghurt
½ cucumber, peeled and cut into small cubes
4 sprigs of mint, leaves removed and chopped

¼ teaspoon ground cumin
½ teaspoon sugar
salt and pepper
paprika

Whisk the yoghurt with a little water to thin it to a spoonable consistency. Add all of the remaining ingredients, except the paprika, with salt and pepper to taste. Mix well.

Chill the raita if you have the time. Sprinkle the paprika over the top before serving.

BANANA RAITA

SERVES 4–6

250ml/9fl oz yoghurt
1 teaspoon black mustard seeds
3 bananas, cut into 1cm/½in rounds

½ teaspoon sugar
1 green chilli, thinly sliced
salt

Whisk the yoghurt with a little water to thin it to a spoonable consistency. Dry-roast the black mustard seeds until they start to pop (cover the pan to prevent them jumping out). Add to the yoghurt with all the remaining ingredients and salt to taste. Mix well.

EASTERN INDIA

Bengal was tragically torn in half by the partition of India in 1947. Bengalis on the two sides of the artificial border share a language and traditions of cooking.

The area that was to be known as Bengal was incorporated into the early Mauryan and Gupta Buddhist empires before reverting to a long period of Hindu kingdoms that ended with the rule of Delhi sultans at the end of the twelfth century. The Islamic influence from the west began the conversions that 800 years later were to tear the state apart. Long before this, in 1341, Bengal had broken away from Delhi to form a separate sultanate. When the British East India Company chose to locate their centre of Asian operations at the Bengali port of Calcutta in the 1690s, it became one of the great trading cities of the world.

The friendly, gregarious and inquisitive nature of many Bengalis, combined with their passion for lively discussion, makes cafés and restaurants of the region places where even strangers are unlikely to feel lonely. *Panch phoron*, a spice mixture that Bengalis created out of local mustard seeds mixed with imported fenugreek, cumin, nigella and fennel, fried in ghee and added to vegetable masals and dhals, is popular on both sides of the border. We have eaten versions of the dish of *panch phoron* spiced vegetables (opposite) in Calcutta and Dacca.

BENGALI PANCH PHORON SPICE MIX v

Panch phoron is a spice mix that gives a distinctive taste to dishes on both sides of the border that divides West Bengal from Bangladesh. The quantities given here make enough for the recipe that follows. As the spices are stored whole, much more can be made and kept for other recipes.

½ teaspoon nigella
½ teaspoon yellow mustard seeds
½ teaspoon cumin seeds

½ teaspoon fennel seeds
½ teaspoon fenugreek seeds

Combine and use whole.

BENGALI PANCH PHORON SPICED VEGETABLES

SERVES 4–6

225g/8oz yellow split peas
1 teaspoon turmeric
200g/7oz pumpkin, peeled, seeded
    and cubed
175g/6oz green beans, topped and
    tailed and cut into 2in/5cm lengths
200g/7oz mooli radishes,
    cut into cubes (if unavailable
    use regular radishes)

150g/5oz okra, topped and tailed
    and cut in half
1 tablespoon ghee
panch phoron (see above)
3 bay leaves
2 green chillies, finely chopped
1 dessertspoon brown sugar
salt to taste

In a large saucepan, combine the yellow split peas, turmeric and 1.25 litres/2 pints water and bring to the boil. Reduce the heat and simmer gently with a lid on until the lentils start to break down. Skim off and discard any scum appearing on the surface. Add the pumpkin, beans, radishes and okra and simmer until they become soft.

In a small pan heat the ghee and crackle the *panch phoron*. Add the bay leaves and chillies and fry until the chillies are soft. Remove from the heat and add to the vegetables and split peas.

Add the brown sugar and salt to taste, stir well and serve with rice.

The wet delta lands of Bengal have always relied on river transport to distribute produce. When there is no wind, the crew resort to poles and oars

CALCUTTA AUBERGINE v

SERVES 4—6

1 large onion, chopped
12 garlic cloves
6 green chillies
6 tablespoons sunflower oil
3 teaspoons ground paprika
½ teaspoon cayenne pepper
1 teaspoon ground turmeric

450g/1lb baby aubergine, cut into
    quarters lengthwise
3 teaspoons tamarind purée
2 teaspoons finely chopped jaggery
    or brown sugar
handful of coriander leaves, chopped

Blend the onion, garlic and chillies in a food processor.

Heat the oil in a large heavy pan and, when hot, fry the mixture with the paprika, cayenne and turmeric for 3 minutes. Add the aubergine and cook for 5 minutes more. Dissolve the tamarind in a little water and stir in, then add the jaggery. Cook until the aubergines become soft.

Serve garnished with lots of fresh coriander, and accompanied by chapatis.

This is one of the dishes we ate regularly in Calcutta, sitting on low wooden benches under one of the huge shade-giving board trees on the pavement beneath our guest-house. The street café, operating out of a typically Calcuttan hole in the wall, had the added bonus of being so popular with taxi drivers that we could always be sure of a cab straight after our meal. The food was so good that we hardly ate anywhere else.

Above **The Calcuttan 'hole-in-the-wall' café**
Right **Calcutta Aubergine**

EGG CURRY

1 onion, roughly chopped

2 garlic cloves, roughly chopped

1in/2.5cm piece of ginger, peeled and roughly chopped

2 teaspoons ground turmeric

½ teaspoon chilli powder

6 free-range eggs, hard-boiled

1lb/450g potatoes, peeled and cubed

4 tablespoons sunflower oil

1in/2.5cm piece of cinnamon, broken into small pieces

6 green cardamom pods, crushed

6 cloves

4 bay leaves

1 red onion, thinly sliced

3 tomatoes, finely chopped

12fl oz/375ml water

1 teaspoon jaggery or brown sugar

salt to taste

Blend the roughly chopped onion, garlic, ginger, turmeric and chilli powder in a food processor until smooth, and set to one side.

Peel the eggs, slash the whites of the eggs a few times, and cut in half. Heat the oil in a wok and when hot, add the eggs and fry until golden. Remove from the pan and set to one side. Add the potatoes to the same pan and fry until brown; then remove from the pan and set to one side.

Add the cinnamon, cardamom, cloves and bay leaves to the remaining oil and fry for a minute or so. Add the sliced red onion, fry until soft and then add the onion spice mix and sauté for 5 minutes, stirring regularly to prevent sticking. Add the chopped tomatoes and fry for a further 5 minutes. Add the water, jaggery or brown sugar and salt to taste, bring to the boil, and then reduce heat. Add the eggs and potatoes, and gently simmer until the sauce has reduced and the potatoes are nice and soft.

Egg Curry

PUMPKIN WITH CHICKPEAS AND PANCH PHORAN

4 tablespoons sunflower oil

4 red chillies, slit down the side

3 bay leaves

12oz/350g peeled and cubed pumpkin

8oz/225g mooli (white radishes), peeled and cubed

8oz/225g carrots, peeled and cubed

1 teaspoon ground turmeric

½ teaspoon chilli powder

1 dessertspoon ground coriander

2 dessertspoons ground cumin

1 tablespoon finely chopped ginger

6fl oz/175ml water

8oz/225g cooked chickpeas

2 teaspoons jaggery or brown sugar

salt to taste

2 tablespoons ghee or butter

1 teaspoon garam masala

For the panch phoran

½ teaspoon black mustard seeds

½ teaspoon fennel seeds

½ teaspoon cumin seeds

½ teaspoon nigella seeds

½ teaspoon fenugreek seeds

Heat the sunflower oil in a wok. When hot, add the panch phoran ingredients, chillies and bay leaves. When they crackle, add the vegetables and fry until golden. Combine the turmeric, chilli, coriander, cumin and ginger with a little of the water to make a paste, and stir into the vegetables with the rest of water. Add the chickpeas, jaggery or sugar and salt to taste. Bring to the boil; then reduce heat, cover the pan and simmer until the sauce has reduced and the vegetables are soft.

Melt the ghee or butter in a small frying pan and pour over the vegetables. Finally sprinkle the garam masala over the top.

TOMATO CHUTNEY V

1 tablespoon sunflower oil

panch phoran (above)

½ teaspoon chilli powder

8oz/225g tomatoes, diced

2in/5cm piece of ginger, peeled and finely chopped

1 tablespoon raisins

2 teaspoons jaggery or brown sugar

salt to taste

Heat the oil in a saucepan and when hot, add the panch phoran. When it crackles, add the chilli powder, followed by the tomatoes, ginger, raisins, jaggery or brown sugar and salt to taste. Cover the pan and simmer until the chutney has thickened.

One of the essential tastes of Bengal is created by use of mustard oil and the spice mixture known as panch phoran or Bengali five spice. The spices – black mustard seeds, fenugreek seeds, cumin seeds, nigella seeds and fennel seeds in equal quantities – are all fried together in oil, into which they release their perfumes. The resulting aroma and flavour is familiar in many vegetable and pulse dishes that accompany the ubiquitous fish dishes of which Bengalis are so fond.

Pumpkin with Chickpeas and Panch Phoran

Even before the British established Calcutta as an international port and the capital of their eighteenth-century Indian possessions, this coast of Bengal attracted traders. Arab dhows arriving on monsoon winds from the Levant brought fenugreek, cumin, nigella and fennel, four spices of panch phoran (page 159). Merchants from Java brought cloves and nutmegs; from the Malabar coast of India came black pepper, turmeric, cardamom and cinnamon. Junks from China delivered ginger and the Portuguese introduced chillies from the Americas. All these flavours have been combined to create one of the most interesting and least exported regional Indian cuisines.

Pages 166–167, clockwise from top right **A lakeside temple at Pushkar oasis; two images of the spa pool at Oberoi Udaivilas in Udaipur, Rajasthan; the Golden Temple in Amritsar; a reflection of the Taj Mahal; the arch of the Charminar mosque in Hyderabad**

Left **Cauliflower and Pea Masala**

CAULIFLOWER AND PEA MASALA

As this is a dry curry, it is important to fit a lid on the wok while the cauliflower cooks, so that it is almost steamed.

7 tablespoons ghee or butter
4 whole dried red chillies
1½ teaspoons black mustard seeds
1½ teaspoons fenugreek seeds
3 teaspoons cumin seeds
1 pinch of asafoetida
1lb 6oz/625g cauliflower, cut into florets
11oz/325g shelled peas, fresh or frozen
1½ tablespoons grated ginger
1½ teaspoons chilli powder
7 teaspoons ground coriander
2½ teaspoons ground turmeric
1½ teaspoons ground cardamom
4fl oz/125ml water
salt to taste

Heat the ghee or butter in a wok. When hot, add the whole red chillies and fry until they become black. Add the mustard seeds, fenugreek seeds, cumin seeds and asafoetida and fry until they crackle; then add the cauliflower, peas and remaining spices. Add the water, cover the pan and cook on a low heat until the cauliflower is cooked. Add salt to taste.

PRUNE AND DATE CHUTNEY

3oz/90g prunes, roughly chopped
3oz/90g dates, roughly chopped
3oz/90g raisins
8fl oz/250ml boiled water
1 tablespoon sunflower oil
½ teaspoon black mustard seeds
½ teaspoon cumin seeds
1 teaspoon fennel seeds
3 red chillies
½ teaspoon ground turmeric
2 tablespoons honey
salt to taste

Soak the prunes, dates and raisins in the boiled water for 1 hour.

Heat the oil in a small saucepan. When hot, add the mustard, cumin and fennel seeds. When they crackle, add the red chillies and turmeric, followed by the prunes, dates and raisins with the water they have been soaking in. Add the honey and salt to taste and gently simmer the chutney, covered by a lid, until it has reduced.

ORISSAN JAGDISH SAAG ALOO V

Serves 4—6

6 tablespoons oil

2 tablespoons dried red chillies

2 teaspoons black mustard seeds

5 medium potatoes, cubed, soaked in
cold water for a few hours, then
drained well

2 tablespoons fresh fenugreek leaves

6 garlic cloves, crushed

1 thumb-sized piece of root ginger,
peeled and finely chopped

3 green chillies, finely chopped

450g/1lb fresh spinach,
finely chopped

Heat the oil in a large heavy pan and, when hot, add the dried chillies, stirring to turn them in the oil. Add the mustard seeds and cook them briefly until they pop. Add the potatoes, a spoonful at a time so as not to lower the heat of the oil too much, and stir-fry for 5 minutes.

Add the fenugreek leaves, garlic, ginger and green chillies. Continue to stir-fry until the potatoes start to break up. Add the spinach and loosen with a little water. Serve when the spinach has wilted.

We rented a house for a few weeks on the coast of Orissa, in the eccentric village of Gopalpur-on-Sea. During our stay there, we passed several jovial evenings in the homes of local minor dignitaries, but most of our meals were enjoyed in the hub of Gopalpur's nightlife, the Jagdish Coffee Hotel.

This was not a hotel at all, but a one-room café open to the street. The kitchen received a constant supply of firewood, water, vegetables and milk, and delivered an equally constant supply of great food.

We grew especially fond of the two dishes on these pages, the spinach and potato dish saag aloo, and vegetable masala.

The Bay of Bengal at Gopalpur-on-Sea

MIXED VEGETABLE MASALA v

This is a basic mixed-vegetable masala, using fried whole spices, chopped vegetables and tomatoes. The vegetables used can vary according to taste and availability.

SERVES 4—6

6 tablespoons sunflower oil

2 teaspoons black mustard seeds

2 teaspoons cumin seeds

2 teaspoons coriander seeds

6 fresh green chillies, chopped

12 garlic cloves, crushed

1 onion, thinly sliced

5cm/2in piece of root ginger, peeled and finely chopped

1 teaspoon ground turmeric

2 medium carrots, cut into quarters lengthwise, then chopped

2 medium courgettes, cut into quarters lengthwise, then chopped

125g/4oz long green beans, cut into thirds

450g/1lb white cabbage, cut into 2.5cm/1in squares

225g/8oz green peas (fresh or frozen)

225g/8oz tomatoes, chopped

handful of chopped coriander stalks, reserving leaves for garnish

2 tablespoons tomato purée

Get the oil very hot in a large heavy pan, then fry — in this order — the mustard seeds, cumin, coriander, chillies, garlic, onion, ginger and turmeric, adding each in rapid succession so the seeds have enough time to pop without burning.

When the onion begins to soften, add all the remaining vegetables except the tomatoes, together with the coriander stalks, and fry for a few minutes, until the cabbage begins to brown and the other vegetables soften.

Add the tomatoes and cook for 1 minute more. Add the tomato purée and reduce the heat, adding a little water to allow the vegetables to simmer until cooked.

Serve with rice and the coriander stalk leaves as a garnish.

WESTERN INDIA

The western states of Rajasthan and Gujarat are, perhaps, the most visually exciting in India. The stark beauty of desert landscapes is offset by brightly dressed women adorned with elaborate jewellery, and fine-featured men with noble moustaches and multicoloured turbans. Fairy-tale palaces and dramatic forts dominate towns of tiny blue, pink and white houses squeezed together in narrow alleys. In the countryside, thatched mud huts have dung-floor courtyards populated with buffalo, camels and goats.

Desert culture is experienced in all its glory at the annual Camel Mela (fair) and Hindu pilgrimage in the oasis village of Pushkar. The ingredients are seductive: tens of thousands of Rajasthanis in all their finery, almost as many camels in theirs, a holy lake surrounded by temples, long days of sunshine, and nights of moonlit skies and festivities. The first time I went, my companion and I left our passports behind for safety in our Delhi hotel — breaching a law that requires foreigners to carry their documents. On being discovered without passports, we were arrested. Thus began a two-week ordeal.

For several days we were kept in an overcrowded cell, manacled hand and foot, and very worried. We were then taken in chains under police escort back to Delhi, an eighteen-hour train journey that we spent locked to the luggage rack. Even once our passports were found to be in order, we were told we had to return to the desert to be sentenced for the crime of not carrying them with us. Meanwhile, we had a day to spend in Delhi. None of our three police escorts had been to the capital before. A bargain was struck. We would give them a day out in the city and buy some presents for their wives, and they would put our chains in a bag. A good day was had by all.

Back in Pushkar we were given a clean cell all to ourselves — and were treated to fine feasts, delivered from the kitchens of our new friends' wives. At our trial we pleaded guilty and were released unconditionally. The policemen now insisted we stay on as guests in their homes. We met their wives, proudly dressed in the saris and bangles from Delhi, and complimented them on their cooking. With a mix of Hindi, English, and much pointing and laughing we gathered some of the recipes in this chapter.

Some of our trips produce pleasures less fraught with excitement. One of the most interesting parts of Rajasthan we visited is Shekhawati — a sand-blown region, home in the fourteenth century to prosperous Muslim merchants who built great mansions, or *havelis*, lavishly decorated with carvings and murals. Later generations abandoned these desert homes for the more sophisticated pleasures of the cities. Today the *havelis* are occupied by caretakers or local families, and most, sadly, are in a serious state of neglect.

The Pushkar Camel Mela (fair)

The Rann of Kutch is a wild district of Gujarat bordering Pakistan. The desert tribes are semi-nomadic, travelling in family groups with camels and goats. The capital, Bhuj, feels like a town from another century, although it is only three hours by air from Bombay. On our way back to Bombay, we stopped in Junagadh to climb the 10,000 stone steps up the temple-strewn Girnar Hill. Our ascent coincided with the festival of Shivaratri and its tens of thousands of pilgrims — many of them naked, ash-covered *sadhus* (holy men) who were not at all keen on being photographed. It was hard even to see a patch of ground in the throng of humanity, and the climb seemed quite effortless as the great crowd swept us with it up the mountain.

173

SAAG PANEER

This spinach and cheese dish is our all-time favourite recipe and we have eaten it in practically every state in India. There are many ways of cooking it, but in our opinion this is the best. The Indian cheese paneer is pretty tasteless in its raw state, but fried and soaked in sauce it is fantastic. Paneer is widely available in good supermarkets or in Indian stores.

SERVES 4–6

- 1kg/2¼lb fresh spinach, shredded
- 3–4 tablespoons ghee or butter (or sunflower oil)
- 400g/14oz paneer, cut into 1cm/½in cubes
- 6 garlic cloves, crushed
- 5cm/2in cube of root ginger, peeled and crushed
- 4 green chillies, finely chopped
- 1 dessertspoon garam masala
- ¼ teaspoon freshly grated nutmeg
- 250ml/9fl oz double cream
- large handful of coriander leaves, chopped
- salt

Cook the spinach with a small quantity of water, just enough to stop it from sticking, until wilted. Remove from heat.

Melt the ghee or butter, or heat the oil, in a heavy-based saucepan and fry the paneer until it is golden brown, turning it occasionally to make sure all sides are cooked.

With a slotted spoon, remove the paneer from the pan. Add the garlic, ginger and chillies to the saucepan (there should be enough ghee, butter or oil left in the pan, if not simply add a little more). Fry for 1 minute, stirring constantly.

Add the cooked spinach and any liquid that has come out of the spinach. Stir and simmer for 10 minutes.

Add the fried paneer back to the pan, together with the garam masala and nutmeg. Simmer for a further 10 minutes.

Finally add the double cream, chopped coriander leaves and salt to taste. Gently simmer for 5 minutes.

Serve with Raita (page 157) and rice cooked with cinnamon, cardamom and cloves (2.5cm/1in piece of cinnamon stick, 3 cardamom pods and 3 cloves for 500g/1lb 2oz of rice).

At the luxurious end of the comfort scale, we photographed royal palaces in Rajasthan and Gujarat that have been converted into Heritage Hotels. Some of these are former residences of undiluted opulence, others more modest ancestral homes.

In the superbly romantic courtyard of Shiv Niwas Palace in Udaipur we ate one of the best saag paneer dishes we tasted in India.

Saag Paneer

AN ALOO GOBI OF RAJASTHAN

Aloo gobi (cauliflower and potato) is one of the ubiquitous dishes of India; it comes in hundreds — probably thousands — of forms. In fact, as the name suggests, cauliflower and potato are the only essential ingredients; beyond these the possibilities are endless.

SERVES 4–6

4 tablespoons ghee or butter
(or sunflower oil)
pinch of hing (asafoetida)
pinch of fenugreek seeds
1 teaspoon fennel seeds
handful of fresh fenugreek leaves,
finely chopped
handful of fresh coriander stalks,
finely chopped

6 fresh green chillies, finely chopped
1 teaspoon ground turmeric
1 medium head of cauliflower,
separated into florets
and parboiled
3 medium potatoes,
cubed and parboiled
salt and pepper

Heat the ghee in a heavy pan and put in the hing, fenugreek seeds and fennel seeds. After 1 minute, add the fresh fenugreek and coriander; the ghee will spit as these fry, so the pan will need to be covered with a lid for a few seconds.

Add the chillies and turmeric with the parboiled cauliflower and potato, and stir around to coat these in ghee. Add salt and pepper to taste and a little water to loosen the mixture enough to simmer on a low heat, covered with a lid, until all is cooked.

Above **Brightly dressed women in a Rajasthani marketplace**
Right **The blue houses of Jodhpur seen through a narrow window in the Red Fort**

ROOT VEGETABLES IN A SPICY MINT SAUCE v

We enjoyed this dish in Udaipur, on the banks of the lake overlooking the Lake Palace. You can use any root vegetable, but plenty of fresh mint is essential. Serve with rice and the Savoury Fruit Salad on page 181.

SERVES 4–6

4 teaspoons coriander seeds

1 teaspoon ground turmeric

2 teaspoons cayenne pepper

5cm/2in cube of root ginger, peeled and roughly chopped

5 tablespoons sunflower oil

6 medium turnips, cubed

4 medium potatoes, cubed

6 medium tomatoes, puréed in a food processor

2 large handfuls of mint leaves, chopped

small handful of coriander leaves, chopped

salt

Dry-roast the coriander seeds in a hot small pan until they start to brown, then grind to a powder.

Place the ground coriander, turmeric, cayenne and ginger in a food processor and blend with a little water until a paste forms.

Heat the oil in a pan. When it is hot, fry the turnips and potatoes until they start to soften. Add the spice paste and stir until the vegetables are coated. Add the tomatoes and a little water to make a sauce. Simmer until the vegetables are nice and soft.

Add the mint and coriander with salt to taste. Stir to combine and serve immediately.

DEEP-RED RAJASTHANI VEGETABLES IN A POPPY-SEED SAUCE v

In this unusual dish red cabbage, pumpkin, beetroot and a spice mixture based on chillies and paprika combine to make a dish of vivid colour, like the colours of Rajasthan itself. Poppy seeds are used to thicken the sauce.

SERVES 4–6

1 teaspoon fenugreek seeds
3 dessertspoons white poppy seeds
1 tablespoon sweet paprika
1 teaspoon ground coriander
1 teaspoon amchoor
1 teaspoon ground turmeric
1 teaspoon ground cinnamon
½ teaspoon ground cloves
5cm/2in piece of root ginger,
   peeled and finely chopped
5 tablespoons sunflower oil
1 red onion, thinly sliced
4 garlic cloves, crushed

4–5 red chillies, thinly sliced
400g/14oz trimmed pumpkin, cut
   into cubes
5 medium raw beetroot,
   peeled and cubed
⅓ small red cabbage,
   thinly shredded
6 medium tomatoes, puréed in a
   food processor
2.5cm/1in square of jaggery or
   1 dessertspoon brown sugar
salt
chopped coriander leaves, to garnish

In a hot pan, dry-roast the fenugreek seeds until they start to brown. Remove from the heat and add to the poppy seeds. Grind these in a spice grinder or using a pestle and mortar. Combine with all the remaining spices and ginger.

Heat the oil in a large pan and, when hot, add the red onion, garlic and chilli. Fry these for a few minutes. Add the pumpkin, beetroot and red cabbage, and fry until they start to soften. Add the spice mix and stir until the vegetables are coated. Add the puréed tomatoes and a little water until the sauce just covers the vegetables. Bring to the boil and simmer until the vegetables are soft and the sauce has reduced. Add the jaggery or brown sugar and salt to taste. Stir to dissolve the sugar.

Garnish with chopped coriander and serve with rice and Banana Raita (page 157).

Deep-red Rajasthani
Vegetables in a Poppy-
seed Sauce

We love khadi, which is a kind of yoghurt soup, but we always imagined it would be difficult to make as the tastes seem to be so complex and intriguing. In fact it's very easy, the secret being the blending of yoghurt with gram flour (*besan*). Khadi makes a good starter or addition to any rice and vegetable meal.

KHADI

SERVES 4–6

500ml / 18fl oz thick yoghurt
1½ tablespoons gram flour
4 green chillies, chopped
2.5cm / 1in piece of root ginger, finely chopped
2 teaspoons salt
2 teaspoons sugar
2 tablespoons ghee or butter (or sunflower oil)

½ teaspoon black mustard seeds
½ teaspoon fenugreek seeds
½ teaspoon cumin seeds
½ teaspoon ground turmeric
6 cloves
1 tablespoon curry leaves
pinch of hing (asafoetida)
handful of coriander leaves, chopped

In a large bowl, whisk together the yoghurt, gram flour, green chillies, ginger, salt and sugar with 1.5 litres / 2¾ pints of water. Pour into a heavy pan, bring to the boil and simmer for 20 minutes on a low heat.

In a small pan, melt the ghee and fry all the seeds until they pop. Add the turmeric, cloves, curry leaves and hing. After 30 seconds, add all this to the yoghurt mixture, together with the coriander leaves. Stir and serve.

SAVOURY FRUIT SALAD V

This is a zingy salad that makes a perfect accompaniment to a sweet, spicy curry.

SERVES 4–6

2 apples, cored and diced
2 carrots, cubed
2 oranges, peeled and cut into small cubes
½ cucumber, cubed
1 papaya, peeled, deseeded and cut into small cubes

juice of 1 lemon
handful of coriander leaves, chopped
1 teaspoon cumin seeds, dry-roasted and ground
½ teaspoon amchoor
½ teaspoon freshly ground black pepper
salt

A camel trader in Pushkar

Simply combine all ingredients and chill for about 30 minutes before serving to allow flavours to combine.

GUJARATI CARROT SALAD v

Hand-thrown village pots
in western India

SERVES 4–6

1 level dessertspoon black mustard seeds	1 teaspoon salt
4 carrots, grated	juice of 2 limes
	handful of mint leaves, roughly chopped

First dry-roast the mustard seeds in a hot pan until they start to 'pop' (cover the
pan with a lid or plate to prevent them jumping out). Remove from the heat
and, when cool, combine with all the remaining ingredients.

GUJARATI PUMPKIN WITH TAMARIND

This Gujarati dish blends the sweetness of pumpkin and jaggery with the sourness of tamarind and amchoor. It works well served with Coconut Cabbage (page 151) and Date and Tamarind Chutney (page 156).

SERVES 4–6 WITH ACCOMPANIMENTS

4 garlic cloves

3 red chillies

1 red onion, roughly chopped

1 heaped teaspoon coriander seeds

1 dessertspoon tamarind paste

1 dessertspoon jaggery or brown sugar

3 tablespoons of boiling water

3 tablespoons ghee or butter
   (or sunflower oil)

1 large onion, thinly sliced

1kg/2¼lb pumpkin, peeled,
   deseeded and cubed

½ teaspoon ground turmeric

½ teaspoon ground black pepper

1 level teaspoon amchoor

salt

large handful of coriander leaves,
   chopped

Place the garlic, chillies and red onion in a blender or food processor and blend to a paste.

In a small pan, dry-roast the coriander seeds until they start to turn golden-brown, then grind to a powder.

Dissolve the tamarind paste and jaggery or brown sugar in the boiling water.

In a large pan, melt the ghee or butter or heat the oil. Add the onion and fry until it starts to soften. Add the pumpkin and fry until it starts to brown, stirring occasionally.

Add the garlic, onion and chilli paste, the ground coriander, turmeric and black pepper. Stir well and fry for a few seconds. Add the tamarind and jaggery water and 250ml/9fl oz more water. Simmer gently, with the lid on, until the pumpkin is soft and most of the water has evaporated (but if it gets too dry at any time, add a little more water).

Add the amchoor, salt to taste and chopped coriander leaves, stir and simmer for 3 more minutes. Serve.

DIU SWEETCORN CURRY

Coconut milk is a perfect accompaniment to corn cobs. This curry is delicious served with Gujarati Carrot Salad (page 182) and fresh mango chutney, or, for a larger meal, with the Gujarati Pumpkin (page 183) as well.

SERVES 4–6

6 corn cobs, cut into 2.5cm/
    1in rounds
2 large handfuls of coriander leaves,
    chopped, plus more to garnish
4 green chillies
5cm/2in piece of root ginger,
    peeled and chopped
2 garlic cloves

2 heaped tablespoons
    desiccated coconut
200ml/7fl oz coconut milk
2 tablespoons ghee or butter
    (or sunflower oil)
1 dessertspoon black mustard seeds
10 curry leaves
salt

Cook the corn cobs in boiling salted water until they start to soften. Drain and place back in the pan.

In a food processor, blend the coriander leaves, chillies, ginger, garlic and desiccated coconut to a paste. Add the paste to the corn cobs with enough water to make a sauce. Bring to the boil, reduce the heat and simmer, covered, for 10 minutes. Add the coconut milk and gently simmer for 5 minutes more.

Meanwhile, melt the ghee in a small pan and add the mustard seeds. When they start to 'pop' (a matter of seconds), add the curry leaves. Remove from heat and pour over the curry – it will make quite a loud crackling noise, so stand back a little. Add salt to taste and garnish with more coriander leaves.

Diu, a small island in the Arabian Sea, is just offshore from India's last 'dry' state, Gujarat, but has a decidedly European taste for the pleasures of beer, wine and spirits bequeathed to it by its long Portuguese history. Diu's pastel houses, narrow cobbled lanes, tavernas and beaches are more reminiscent of the Mediterranean than India.

We discovered this dish while trying to drag ourselves away from the island after a welcome rest. A long-delayed train resulted in the station-master's inviting us to lunch in his home, and we ate with the family in a cobalt-blue courtyard just behind the station. We were quite disappointed when our train eventually arrived.

Diu Sweetcorn Curry, with Gujarati Carrot Salad (page 182)

The spectacular twelfth-century fort of Jaisalmer, perched like a sandcastle on a hill overlooking the vast Thar Desert, was home to Rajput warriors and Jain merchants. The golden yellow citadel is still a living fortress of paved, winding, narrow alleys between palaces, temples and *havelis*. A contemporary trade in tourism has halted the city's long decline, but sadly this has brought new threats with it. The resident population has grown alongside tourism, putting unbearable pressure on the ancient infrastructures of water supply and drainage. Water seepage has penetrated and saturated the sandy foundations of the fort, and the castle has begun to collapse. Homes and palaces are in ruins and some people have been killed. In response to this tragedy, the Indian National Trust for Art and Cultural Heritage (INTACH), Jaisalmer in Jeopardy (a British registered charity) and World Monuments Fund USA have been active in raising funds and instigating programmes to alleviate the problems. In the winter of 1999 I travelled to Jaisalmer to attend and document a fund-raising weekend of festivities associated with this project.

My first visit to the castle had been twenty years earlier, arriving out of the desert after a seven-day camel trek across the Thar Desert from Bikaner. My friend Daniel and I spent these days becoming increasingly saddle-sore and unwashed in the company of our bad-tempered camels, inappropriately named Ladoo and Jelabi, after delicious Indian sweets, and two very good-humoured guides whose genial personalities probably owed a lot to their constant consumption of opium. We foolishly chose to undertake this journey in May, just as the pre-monsoon heat was reaching its zenith and the oases were running dry.

The nights cooking and sleeping under the stars were pleasant enough at first. Our guides cooked fine suppers and sang Rajasthani folk songs to us, often in the company of other desert-crossers sharing our camp. The best we could contribute was an out-of-tune version of 'I've been through the desert on a horse with no name'. To discourage snakes from sharing our bed we were advised to spread crushed onions over our skin every night. As there was never enough water to wash with, the morning sun baked the stale onion juice dry within minutes of rising, and our ability to remain fresh-faced deteriorated rapidly. The days became torture. Increasingly desperate for our adventure to end, we were torn between wanting to ride as much as possible every day and not wanting to ride at all because the camels were so uncomfortable and the sun so hot. Eventually we fell into our guides' habit of numbing ourselves to the hardships with a haze of opium-induced euphoria. By the time we caught our first glimpse of the longed-for Jaisalmer rising majestically out of the desert haze, the romance of the moment was compromised somewhat by our fuddled brains and dilapidated bodies.

Above A water seller waits for business at a stopping point on a desert pathway
Opposite A woman passes designs painted on a wall inside the fort of Jaisalmer

My return could not have been more of a contrast, arriving on a specially chartered plane from Delhi, packed with affluent glitterati all donating fistfuls of rupees to support the Jaisalmer Conservation Initiative. A long weekend of events and entertainments had been organized to reward the donors. By day there were talks and tours, revealing the splendours of the city within the fort and numerous pavilions, temples, *havelis* and cenotaphs in the desert around it. At night there were sumptuous feasts, including one hosted by the Maharaja and Maharani of Jaisalmer at their remote summer palace of Moolraj Sagar. By the light of a full moon (the timing was brilliant), we were treated to a pre-dinner evening raga sung by Shubha Mudgal, in a courtyard of gentle fountains and pools filled with thousands of rose petals, surrounded by hundreds of tiny ghee-burning lanterns.

RAJASTHANI PUMPKIN DHAL

SERVES 4

300g/10oz masoor dhal, washed and soaked for 1 hour
pinch of salt
½ teaspoon sugar
1 teaspoon turmeric
1cm/½ in square of fresh ginger, chopped
½ teaspoon ground cumin

300g/10oz pumpkin chopped into 1cm/½in cubes
juice of a lime
2 tablespoons ghee
1 teaspoon black mustard seeds
pinch of hing
2 garlic cloves, chopped
6 small dried red chillies

Bring 1.7 litres/3 pints of water to the boil, add the soaked dhal, salt, sugar, turmeric, ginger, cumin and pumpkin and boil for 30 minutes. Remove from the heat, add the lime juice and blend in a food processor until smooth.

In a small pan melt the ghee and fry the mustard seeds, hing, garlic and chillies until the seeds have popped.

Stir the spice mixture into the dhal and serve.

An elegant elephant carved in sandstone at the entrance to one of the Jain temples at Palitana in Gujarat

India

After our weekend of partying at Jaisalmer, we accompanied some Jain friends on the flight to Bhavnagar in Gujarat. About an hour by plane from the cosmopolitan bustle of Bombay, this is one of the most sleepy, undeveloped parts of India. Our friends were on a pilgrimage to climb the twin peaks of Mount Shatrunjaya, and perform *puja* (worship) at the beautifully carved white marble temples of Palitana at the summit.

Jains believe in the sanctity of all sentient beings. This necessitates a diet demanding not just strict vegetarianism, but also abstinence from all things that grow beneath the ground, for fear that harvesting them may harm creatures of the earth. White-clad Jain priests and nuns sweep the ground beneath their feet as they walk, and wear face-masks to ensure they cause no accidental harm to insects. Every Jain hopes once in their life to make the climb to visit Palitana and descend Mount Shatrunjaya.

Camels like this bejewelled creature at the Pushkar oasis in Rajasthan are still used for desert transportation, but on nothing like the scale of the heyday of the trade caravans

Hing
(Ferula assafoetida)
The use of hing spread from Iran and Afghanistan to Ancient Greece and Imperial Rome. Today, however, it is used almost exclusively in Indian cookery, where it is famed as an antidote for flatulence, and is particularly popular in dishes using pulses and cauliflower.

It is collected as a sap from the rhizomes of certain giant fennel plants. The pungent, sulphuric smell of hing makes it seem an unlikely flavour enhancer. When sold as a powder it is often mixed with gum arabic and turmeric and referred to as 'yellow powder'. The food enhancement qualities of hing are not dissimilar to those of onion and the spice is popular with Jains, for whom root crops are taboo.

The Jains are a tiny minority among India's population of a billion, but generations of success as traders and merchants, stretching back to the early seafaring days of the spice trade, have elevated many to positions of wealth and influence disproportionate to their number. In expectation of regular demand, *dolleywallas* wait at the foot of the mountain offering, for a fee, to carry any pilgrim disinclined to toil. They do this in groups of four, using bamboo poles with a hammock suspended between them.

We did it the hard way as usual, setting off half-asleep at 4.30am to try and beat the heat. We failed: by the time we reached the summit five hours later we were nearly defeated. It was still the tail end of the monsoon in Gujarat, which is a quiet season for pilgrims, on account of increased insect activity on the paths. This meant no food or drink stalls at the top. By the time we got down again anything would have tasted delicious. First we drank copious glasses of fresh lime sodas with kal nemak (black salt), which is an excellent rehydration aid and surprisingly palatable in small quantities. Then we joined the *dolleywallas*, tucking into a Gujarati favourite, pau bhaji. Pau bhaji is like an Indian version of bubble and squeak. On a big round disc of steel heated by a naked flame, a mixture of mashed potato and vegetables sizzles away in ghee and spices. Around the outside are bread rolls cut in half and toasting, absorbing the spicy butter. It makes a sensational lunch for hungry pilgrims, although sadly our Jain friends could not join in, as they cannot eat potatoes.

PAU BHAJI SPICE MIX v

A garam masala with the addition of amchoor and caraway seeds. This recipe gives enough to make both the pau bhaji and the pau bhaji chutney on page 192.

3 bay leaves	2 star anise seeds
1 dessertspoon coriander seeds	1 teaspoon caraway seeds
1 dessertspoon cumin seeds	1 teaspoon ground chilli
2.5cm / 1in piece of cinnamon stick	½ teaspoon ground ginger
½ teaspoon black peppercorns	1 teaspoon amchoor
	¼ teaspoon hing

In a small pan dry-roast the bay leaves, coriander, cumin, cinnamon, peppercorns, star anise and caraway until aromatic. Remove from the heat and grind to a powder. Combine with the remaining spices.

Above **Ideally suited to harsh desert environments, camels have been known to survive for seventeen days without water**
Opposite **Pau Bhaji**

PAU BHAJI v

SERVES 4

450g/1lb new potatoes, peeled and cubed

½ a medium cauliflower, cut into small florets

3 medium carrots, diced

150g/5oz fresh peas, shelled

150g/5oz green beans, topped and tailed and cut into 1cm/½in lengths

5 tablespoons sunflower oil

2 medium red onions, chopped

4 garlic cloves, finely chopped

3 tablespoons pau bhaji spice mix (see page 191)

450g/1lb tomatoes, pulped in a food processor

150g/5oz fresh spinach leaves, roughly chopped

2 handfuls of coriander leaves, chopped

6 soft bread rolls

In a saucepan boil the potatoes until soft. Remove from the heat and drain, then mash them with 85ml/3fl oz of water. Boil the cauliflower, carrots, peas and beans until soft, drain and set to one side.

In a large wok, heat the oil and fry the onion and garlic until the onion softens. Add the pau bhaji spice mix and stir well for 1 minute. Add the pulped tomatoes and spinach, bring to the boil then reduce heat. Simmer gently until the sauce reduces and the oil returns. Add the mashed potatoes, drained vegetables and salt to taste. Stir well to combine all the ingredients and gently cook on a low heat for 5 minutes.

Garnish with fresh coriander leaves and serve with tomato chutney (below) and the soft bread rolls halved, toasted and buttered.

TOMATO CHUTNEY FOR PAU BHAJI v

2 garlic cloves, roughly chopped

2 green chillies, roughly chopped

2 large tomatoes, roughly chopped

handful of coriander leaves

1 heaped teaspoon pau bhaji spice mix (see page 191)

1 dessertspoon brown sugar

salt to taste

Place all the ingredients in a blender. Blend to a smooth purée.

GUJARATI DHOKLA v

This is a recipe for an unusual snack which could be served with drinks or as a starter. It is easy to make and quite delicious; whenever we serve it, it becomes a conversation piece. It is made with chickpea (gram) flour which is easily available in Asian/Middle Eastern shops and many supermarkets. In India, dhokla *is usually made by mixing the gram flour with curds and allowing the batter to ferment in the sun for nine hours. Luckily there is a quick and easy alternative method using bicarbonate of soda and lemon juice.* Dhokla *is cooked by steaming. If you don't have a big enough steamer, you can improvise using a wok with a lid.*

SERVES 4–6

125g/4oz gram flour, sieved

1 teaspoon sugar

½ teaspoon salt

juice of a lemon

1 heaped teaspoon bicarbonate of soda

2 tablespoons sunflower oil

3 green chillies, finely sliced

2 teaspoon black mustard seeds

1 dessertspoon curry leaves

1 tablespoon desiccated coconut

handful of coriander leaves

1 teaspoon desiccated coconut

Grease a 23cm/9in cake tin. In a bowl mix the gram flour, sugar, salt and lemon juice. Gradually add 175ml/6fl oz of water, stirring well to prevent lumps forming. Now prepare the steaming vessel; pour water into the bottom of the steamer or the wok, cover with a lid, bring to the boil, then reduce the heat to a simmer and place a stand in the water in the middle of the steamer or the wok.

Sift the bicarbonate of soda into the batter, stir well and pour immediately into the greased cake tin. Carefully lower the cake tin on to the stand, cover with a lid and steam for twenty minutes. Remove the cake tin and allow to cool for ten minutes, then cut the dhokla into 5cm x 2.5cm/2in x 1in diamond shapes.

Now make the spice tempering. In a small pan, heat the sunflower oil. When the oil is hot, add the sliced green chillies, followed by the black mustard seeds and curry leaves. Fry for one minute, add the desiccated coconut and continue frying until the coconut begins to turn brown. Remove from heat and pour evenly over the surface of the cooked *dhokla*.

Garnish with the coriander leaves and desiccated coconut. Lift out of the tin to serve.

Gujarati Dhokla

NORTHERN INDIA

The far north of India has more in common with Tibet than it does with the rest of the subcontinent. The Himalayan peaks and snowfields of Ladakh form a backdrop to Buddhist monasteries and shrines; most of the people are Tibetan rather than Indian in origin, a fact reflected in the style of the food. The lake district of Kashmir is distinctive in a different way, owing more to the Islamic traditions of Central Asia than to the plains of India. Kashmiri-inspired dishes crop up all over India but there is no better way to try them than home cooked while staying in one of the grand old wooden houseboats moored on the tranquil waters of Dal Lake, surrounded by a vista of Himalayan mountains.

Water taxis like this elegant yellow *shikara* are used to ferry tourists and Kashmiris around Dal and Naki lakes

Located in the foothills of the Himalayas along the flood-plain of the Ramganga River, the Corbet National Park is only few hours north of Delhi, yet it could not be a more serene and peaceful place. The first time we went there we had unrealistic expectations of seeing a wild tiger. The dawn and dusk elephant-rides through the forest, the sightings of deer, monkeys and other wildlife, the great natural beauty, and the fine evening meals in the forest lodge were all very enjoyable, but we still felt frustrated by the lack of tiger. When we left I filled in the visitors' book and was asked to list all the animals I had seen. I cheekily ended by writing 'BUT NO TIGER' — and was left looking slightly ridiculous when the bus to the park gates had to stop to wait for a fine, full-grown tigress and her cubs to stroll across the road and off into the jungle.

Dal and rice form the staple diet across India. The recipe for dal fry given here is less refined than some in this chapter, yet the dish is utterly delicious.

DAL FRY

Lentils are cooked until they form a creamy soup; the spices are fried and added at the end of the cooking. Serve the dal simply with rice or as an accompaniment to any curry.

SERVES 4–6

250g/9oz yellow split peas
5cm/2in piece of root ginger, peeled and grated
½ teaspoon ground turmeric
2 tablespoons ghee or butter (or sunflower oil)

4 garlic cloves, thinly sliced
1 dessertspoon black mustard seeds
1 teaspoon cumin seeds
6 small red chillies
salt
chopped coriander leaves, to garnish

Rinse the yellow split peas until the water runs clear. Place in a saucepan and cover with 700ml/1¼ pints water. Bring to the boil; a foam will rise to the top of the pan, simply scoop this off and discard.

Add the ginger and turmeric and simmer until the split peas become very soft and break up. The dal should be smooth and like a thick soup. Lentils do absorb a lot of water, so you may need to add more during the cooking time.

Melt the ghee in a small frying pan, add the garlic slices and fry until they are golden brown. Add the mustard seeds, cumin seeds and chillies; when they start to 'pop' (after just a few seconds), remove from heat and pour over the dal. Stand back slightly as it will crackle and spit.

Finally add salt to taste and garnish with chopped coriander leaves.

KASHMIRI GOBI v

This is a northern Indian way of cooking cauliflower, using cashew nuts and cayenne pepper, together with an aromatic creamed tomato sauce. It makes a good main dish, along with Nalagarh Brinjal (page 200) and orange rice (page 201).

SERVES 4—6

1 large onion	1 teaspoon ground cinnamon
4 garlic cloves	½ teaspoon ground cloves
5cm/2in piece of root ginger, peeled	1 teaspoon ground cardamom seeds
3 medium tomatoes	4 bay leaves
6 tablespoons oil	1 teaspoon sugar
1 large cauliflower, separated into florets	1 teaspoon salt
1 teaspoon ground turmeric	*For the garnish*
1 teaspoon cayenne pepper	30g/1oz cashew nuts, toasted
	30g/1oz raisins

Purée the onion, garlic, ginger and tomatoes together in a food processor.

Heat the oil in a large heavy pan and, when hot, fry the cauliflower until it is beginning to brown and soften, then remove.

Fry the purée with the turmeric and cayenne for 3 minutes. Then add the cinnamon, cloves, cardamom, bay leaves, sugar and salt.

Return the cauliflower to the mixture and turn to coat well and heat through.

Serve garnished with the toasted cashew nuts and raisins.

Kashimiri Gobi, Nalagarh Brinjal and Narangi Pulao were among the many dishes we ate while photographing Nalagarh Fort, the ancestral home of the maharaja Vijayendra Singh, situated in the foothills of the Himalayas. We went there just before it was opened as a hotel; the cooks were old family retainers, and must by now be cooking some of these recipes for the hotel guests. Kashmiri Gobi is a recipe brought into the family by the Maharani, who came from the western side of Kashmir, which is now part of Pakistan.

Kashmiri Gobi

NALAGARH BRINJAL

This side-dish of aubergine in yoghurt is quite luxurious, as is appropriate for the table of a maharaja.

SERVES 4–6

1 large aubergine, cut into rounds
   1cm / ½in thick
1 teaspoon ground turmeric
salt
5 tablespoons sunflower oil
450g / 1lb Greek-style yoghurt
125ml / 4fl oz double cream

3 garlic cloves, crushed
2.5cm / 1in cube of root ginger,
   peeled and crushed
2 green chillies, finely chopped
handful of fresh coriander leaves,
   chopped, for garnish

Sprinkle the aubergine slices with the turmeric and some salt. Get the oil very hot in a frying pan and fry the aubergine slices, a few at a time, until well browned, then drain on kitchen paper.

In a food processor, blend the yoghurt, cream, garlic, ginger and chillies. Place the aubergine slices on a flat dish and pour over the mixture.

Serve garnished with coriander.

Above left **Narangi Pulao and Lassi (page 155)**
Above right **A man smokes a hookah at dusk on Dal Lake**

NARANGI PULAO

SERVES 4–6

450g/1lb potatoes, cut into
   small cubes
4 tablespoons oil
1 onion, puréed
4 garlic cloves, puréed
3 cloves
3 cardamom pods, split
1 cinnamon stick, broken up
1 teaspoon cayenne pepper
4 bay leaves
250g/9oz full-fat yoghurt
juice of 1 lemon
rosewater

For the orange rice
3 oranges, preferably unwaxed
450g/1lb basmati rice, washed,
   soaked and drained
3 tablespoons oil
1 tablespoon sugar
2 onions, very thinly sliced
8 cloves
8 cardamom pods, split to release
   the seeds
salt
12 cashew nuts
12 whole almonds

Narangi pulao can be eaten as a side-dish with almost any curry or dal. The traditional way to serve it at Nalagarh is with a layer of fried potato-and-yoghurt mixture sandwiched between the rice, making it into a whole meal.

The dish is similar to the rice we ate in Oman (see page 68), cooked in an essentially Persian style: the similarity again reflects the historical family connections with lands farther to the west in the days before the partition of India.

To make the orange rice: peel the oranges and cut the rind into thin strips. Chop the oranges into cubes, discarding pips and pith. Put the rind with 6 cups of water, 1 tablespoon of oil and the sugar into a pan and boil for 5 minutes.

Meanwhile, fry the onion, cloves and cardamom seeds in the remaining oil until brown. Season with salt to taste, then add the drained rice. Stir to coat the rice, then add the orange rind with the boiling water. Cook until the rice is tender, about 12 minutes.

To serve as a side-dish, garnish with the cubes of orange and the cashews and almonds lightly fried in butter.

To make the main-course dish: fry the potatoes in half the oil until crispy and set aside. Fry the puréed onion and garlic in the remaining oil until brown. Add the cloves, cardamom, cinnamon, cayenne and bay leaves, and cook for a minute. Add the yoghurt and lemon juice, and cook slowly for 10 minutes, then stir in the potatoes.

To complete the dish, place half the rice on a flat dish, pour on the yoghurt and potato mixture, then put the other half of the rice on top.

Serve garnished with the fried almonds and cashews and the orange pieces as above, then sprinkle with a little rosewater.

POTATO BONDAS v

These potato fritters are particularly good served with Green Coconut Chutney (page 156).

SERVES 4–6

oil for deep-frying
1kg/2¼lb potatoes, cooked
   and mashed
2 tablespoons sunflower oil
½ teaspoon salt
2 teaspoons sugar
4 teaspoons desiccated coconut
5–10 green chillies, finely chopped
2 pinches of hing (asafoetida)
5cm/2in piece of root ginger, very
   finely chopped

1 teaspoon sesame seeds
1 teaspoon garam masala
juice of 1 lime
handful of coriander leaves, chopped

For the batter
6 tablespoons gram flour
pinch of salt
pinch of hing (asafoetida)
1 teaspoon ground turmeric
1 teaspoon chilli powder

Mix all the batter ingredients together in a bowl, adding a little water a spoonful at a time until a thick paste forms.

Heat the oil for deep-frying.

Mix all the rest of the ingredients together and mould by hand into balls about the size of a golf ball.

When the oil is hot enough to cause a drop of the batter to sizzle and bubble rapidly, dip each ball of mixture in the batter and deep-fry in 2–3 batches, turning regularly until golden brown all over, 5–10 minutes. Drain on kitchen paper and serve hot or cold.

For convenience, the balls may instead be flattened out a bit and shallow-fried, turning once.

Potato bondas make a wonderful snack or starter and keep for several days, so it's worth making quite a lot at a time. We made a whole tinful to take skiing in Kashmir, filling our ski-jacket pockets with them at the beginning of each day so that we could snack on them during ski-lift rides. As the balls are quite fragile they also provided an extra incentive not to fall over.

The bondas are supposed to be very spicy, so they are particularly good to eat on the cold snow slopes. When I offered one to a Scandinavian skier sharing my chair lift, he found it excessively hot and, as soon as we got off, grabbed mouthfuls of snow to relieve his burning mouth. This recipe has been considerably toned down to make a milder version – if you want to spice it up again just add more chilli.

Potato Bondas, with Green Coconut Chutney (page 156)

Pakistan &

Nepal

PAKISTAN

When the overnight flight from London delivered us to the steamy summer heat of Islamabad at dawn, making the connection with a 0615 flight on a little Fokker Friendship to whisk us up to the Gilgit was only half the uncertainty: if any bad weather is suspected, the flight can be cancelled at a moment's notice and it has even been known to turn back halfway through the journey if the weather closes in, which it often does during the summer monsoon. But our timing was perfect and the sky was clear.

This is one of the most spectacular flights in the world. We could see the Karakoram Highway below, fighting its way through the foothills of Kashmir and then up into the deep valleys of the mountains. The plane flies past Nanga Parbat, the world's ninth-highest peak at 23,347 feet/8,125 metres, which towered above us.

After the sweatbox of the plains, Gilgit was pleasingly cool, the sun reassuringly still warm in the thin clear air. At the 'Foreigners' Registration Booth' a man with a deeply chiselled face and a thick beard dyed red with henna, who looked like a fierce Pathan warrior apart from his warm smile, welcomed us and entered our details in an antique ledger, which looked as though it had been recording the occupations, intentions and mothers' maiden names of travellers for decades.

Our final destination was the Hunza valley, which we reached by jeep along the Karakoram Highway. At Hunza a deep canyon between the mountains opens out into a broad valley and there is a sudden abundance of fertility. Orchards of apricots, apples, pears, mulberries and cherries among terraced fields of wheat and potatoes and wooded glades of deodar or Himalayan cedar are all watered by ancient systems of water channels fed by melting glaciers nestled among the snowy peaks around the valley. Dominating the whole valley are the white walls and wooden pillars of Baltit fort. Arriving there felt like entering a hidden paradise.

The food in Hunza was excellent. Local specialities include lots of *chamus*, apricot juice; *haneetze daudo*, a noodle and vegetable soup with crushed apricot kernels, on one of which I broke a tooth; *burus berakutz*, a cheese and fresh herb filled chapatti spread with apricot kernel oil; and *garma*, a spinach-like vegetable, served with *phitti*, a robust wholemeal bread.

It was during our stay in Hunza that we learnt many of the recipes in this chapter. Others come from Lahore, capital of the Punjab and a city rich in contemporary and historic culture and fine cuisine. Lahore also has a wealth of sensational Mughal-built mosques, fortifications, mausoleums and gardens, and an old city packed with bustling bazaars.

Pages 204–205 **The Hunza valley in the Karakoram moúntains of Pakistan**

Right, clockwise from top right **The Badshahi mosque in Lahore; an apple seller in Azad, Kashmir; the Baltit fort of Karimabad; Punjabi boys in Lahore; a farmer in the Hunza valley; a girl in the Rawalpindi bazaar**

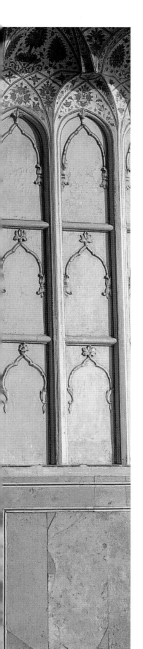

LAHORE BUTTER SAAG

This is a great side dish to serve with dhal and chapatti.

2oz/60g ginger, peeled
2¼lb/1kg spinach, washed, stems
   removed and roughly chopped
6 green chillies, slit down the side
1¼ pints/750ml water

1½ tablespoons cornflour
½ teaspoon chilli powder
5oz/150g butter
salt to taste

Roughly chop two-thirds of the ginger and cut the remaining ginger into fine matchsticks. Put the spinach, 3 green chillies, roughly chopped ginger and water in a pan, bring to the boil and gently simmer for 40 minutes. Drain the spinach, retaining the water. Place the spinach in a food processor with the cornflour and blend until it becomes a coarse purée. Return to the pan along with the chilli powder, remaining green chillies, two-thirds of the butter, salt to taste and retained cooking water. Gently simmer for a further 15 minutes.

Meanwhile prepare the tempering by melting the remaining butter in a small frying pan. Add the ginger matchsticks and sauté for 2 minutes. When the spinach is cooked, pour the tempering over the top and serve immediately.

Left The Badshahi mosque in Lahore; *below left* a young vegetable seller in the Lahore bazaar; *Below right* three Ismaili women in the Hunza valley

DHAL MAKHANI

Urid dhal, also known as black dhal, is available from Indian stores. The lentils have dark skins and a white interior.

6oz/175g split black urid dhal,
   soaked overnight
2 pints/1.25 litres water
5 tablespoons red kidney beans, cooked
2½in/6cm piece of ginger, peeled and
   finely chopped

5 garlic cloves, crushed
4 tablespoons tomato purée
1 teaspoon chilli powder
3oz/90g butter
4fl oz/125ml double cream
salt to taste

Drain the soaked lentils and place in a saucepan with the water. Bring to the boil, cover the pan, and then reduce the heat and gently simmer until the lentils are cooked. Lightly mash with a potato masher and then add the kidney beans, ginger, garlic, tomato purée, chilli powder, butter and salt to taste. Cook for a further 20 minutes. Finally add the cream and gently simmer for 5 minutes.

Serve with Lahore Butter Saag (page 209), rice and chapatti.

Below **The Badshahi mosque in Lahore**
Right **Women off to harvest apricots in the Hunza valley below the Karakoram mountains**

PANEER, CASHEW NUT AND HUNZA APRICOT MASALA

This recipe uses ajwain, a seed with a thyme-like flavour. You can buy it from any Indian store. First you make a gravy, and then you add this to the paneer and spices.

For the gravy
1lb/450g tomatoes, diced
1 teaspoon grated ginger
2 garlic cloves, crushed
4 green chillies, slit down the side
8 cloves
8 green cardamom pods, crushed
8fl oz/250ml water
2oz/60g butter
2fl oz/60ml double cream
2 teaspoons honey
½ teaspoon ground fenugreek
1 dessertspoon ginger, peeled and cut
  into matchsticks
salt to taste

3 tablespoons ghee or butter
2 teaspoons ajwain seeds
1 medium onion, sliced
1in/2.5cm piece of ginger, peeled and
  finely chopped
15oz/425g paneer, cut into
  ½in/1cm cubes
3oz/90g cashew nuts
6oz/175g Hunza or unsulphured
  dried apricots, cut in half
½ teaspoon chilli powder
1 teaspoon ground coriander
2 teaspoons garam masala
large handful of chopped
  coriander leaves

To make the gravy, place the tomatoes, grated ginger, garlic, chillies, cloves and cardamom in a saucepan with the water, bring to the boil, reduce the heat and then cover the pan and gently simmer until the gravy reduces to a sauce consistency. Stir in the butter, cream, honey, fenugreek, ginger matchsticks and salt to taste, and continue cooking for a minute or so.

Heat the ghee or butter in a wok. When hot, add the ajwain seeds and, when they crackle, add the sliced onion and ginger. Sauté until the onions soften. Add the paneer, cashew nuts and chopped apricots and fry until the paneer starts to brown. Stir in the chilli powder and ground coriander, followed by the gravy. Gently simmer until the gravy coats the paneer. Finally stir in the garam masala and chopped coriander leaves.

Not only is the scenery of Hunza stunning but the people are particularly friendly and hospitable. They are followers of the Aga Khan and the Ismaili style of Islam. Women are unveiled and comfortable about talking to foreigners, including men.

There have been lots of romantic stories about Hunza and how its people live to exceptionally old age in fine health. They inspired James Hilton to write his novel *Lost Horizon* about a lost kingdom of Shangri-La. In reality Hunza's history has been one of tribal conflicts and power struggles to control the trade route between China and the Indian subcontinent. Nevertheless our stay there was one of the closest experiences to visiting a Shangri-La we have found anywhere in the world.

Paneer, Cashew Nut and Hunza Apricot Masala

NEPAL

As Buddha Air Flight 200 from Kathmandu reached its climax, I just happened to be the passenger taking a turn at spending a couple of minutes squeezed between the pilots to admire the view. 'Complete top of the world,' said one of them, pointing through the perfect clarity of a Himalayan morning. Right in front of us was the distinctive pyramidal peak of Everest, all around us a vast snowscape of other peaks, valleys, glaciers and ridges of unparalleled dramatic grandeur. This was a once-in-a-lifetime's experience.

On my last trip to Nepal over twenty years ago, these Everest flights weren't an option. I experienced Everest the hard way, trekking with all my possessions on my back, sleeping in primitive teahouses and living off dhal and rice: it took weeks. That trek had also been a lifetime experience, although it didn't get me nearly quite so close to the summit. Flight 200 was cheating really. In fact our whole trip to Nepal this time round was a bit like cheating compared to my first. But we weren't here for the physical challenge; we had come to find Nepalese cuisine beyond dhal bhaat, among the mustard fields of the foothills.

Nepal grows 80,000 tons of mustard seed a year, supplying much of the vast demand across the border in India. The mustard fields are all far south of the Kathmandu Valley between the plains of the Terai and the Himalayas. The first interesting recipe we came across was a Newari dish we ate in a restaurant while still in Kathmandu. Newari food is traditionally very complex, reflecting the regal past of the Newars. Historically it has been a long way removed from the simple diet of most Nepalese. The emergence of a more affluent middle class around the Kathmandu Valley has inspired the inclusion of some of the less eccentric examples of Newari cuisine on Kathmandu menus. This one, called *panch kol*, is a spicy curry using five vegetables. In its spiciness it is typically Newari, but less typical for being meatless: the Newars have a tradition of cooking every part of a buffalo, as well as pork and venison.

The peak of Mount Everest, 8,848m/29,028ft above sea level. Despite the extreme terrain, an ancient trade route was forged not far from here, linking La-sa in Tibet with Kathmandu

PANCH KOL

Panch kol is a combination of five vegetables — cauliflower, carrots, spinach, peas and radish — with a rich garlic and spiced-tomato gravy tempered with mustard seeds and sprinkled with an aromatic garam masala.

SERVES 4

For the garam masala
4 green cardamoms, skins removed
1 strand of mace
2 star anise
2.5cm/1in piece of cinnamon stick
4 cloves

1 large onion, roughly chopped
5 garlic cloves, roughly chopped
5cm/2in piece fresh ginger, peeled
    and roughly chopped
2 green chillies, roughly chopped
350g/12oz cauliflower, cut into
    small florets
200g/7oz carrots, diced
2 tablespoons mustard oil or ghee

1 dessertspoon sesame seeds
3 dried red chillies, chopped
½ teaspoon turmeric
400g/14oz tomatoes, pulped in a
    food processor
200g/7oz mooli, cut into cubes
    (or radishes, if unavailable)
150g/5oz fresh peas, shelled
175g/6oz fresh spinach,
    roughly chopped
1 dessertspoon brown sugar
1 dessertspoon mustard oil or ghee
1 tablespoon black mustard seeds
salt to taste
handful of chives, chopped
handful of fresh coriander leaves

Above **A village in the Gorkha region of Nepal, perched on a hilltop in the morning sun**
Opposite **A Gorkha woman on the terraced hillsides of Nepal**

Prepare the garam masala by dry-roasting the ingredients in a small frying pan and grinding to a powder.

Pulp the onion, the garlic, the ginger and the green chillies to a purée in a food processor. Parboil the cauliflower and carrots and set aside. In a large wok heat the mustard oil and fry the sesame seeds, dried red chillies and turmeric until the sesame seeds crackle. Add the onion purée and fry for a further 5 minutes, stirring regularly. Add the pulped tomato, bring to the boil, reduce heat and simmer gently until the oil returns and the sauce reduces.

Add the mooli, the peas, the spinach and the brown sugar and simmer gently for 10 minutes more; add the drained parboiled vegetables and simmer for another 5 minutes.

Meanwhile, heat the mustard oil in a small frying pan. Add the mustard seeds and fry them until they crackle, then pour them on to the curry.

Finally, add salt to taste and sprinkle with garam masala, stir well and serve garnished with the chopped chives and coriander.

Pakistan & Nepal

On our journey south from Kathmandu we visited Bhagwati Mandir, a favourite destination of Nepalese Hindus seeking divine favour. This temple, in the hilltop village of Manakamana, is dedicated to the goddess Bhagwati, who rewards pilgrimage and animal sacrifice with the granting of wishes. Until very recently this pilgrimage meant a long, hard trek up steep paths, with all the family, luggage and sacrificial beast in tow. As in many places of pilgrimage around the world, the effort required to get to Bhagwati Mandir would appear to have been part of the bargain of gaining merit through toil. The Nepalese, however, still find the journey meritorious enough, in spite of the recent construction of a gleaming new Austrian-built cable car. The overnight hike has been replaced by an easy two-hour round trip from the main road in the valley. Not only do more Nepalese make the pilgrimage now, but the temple also attracts coach- and carloads of Hindus from India and even a few foreign tourists.

The operation looks just like a ski resort in the Alps until it becomes apparent that in between some of the glass bubble capsules are special open ones for animals with one-way tickets. At the top there are more goats and chickens for sale for anyone who is still not equipped for the ritual. The Indian Hindus do not sacrifice animals, so there are stalls selling kits of coconut, rice, flowers and sweets for their own version of appeasing Bhagwati. The pilgrims queue in family groups around the temple waiting for their time to enter the inner sanctum.

Those with animals, which on festival days or for big favours can include buffalo, are sure they are giving their victims a privileged departure from this world. A better chance for next time. They fondly stroke and whisper to the animals right up to the time a *sharki* caste temple butcher dispatches them with a swift decapitating stroke of his *khukhiri* knife. They are all going to be eaten anyway, and there is a thriving sub-industry around the temple in keeping braziers burning and in preparing dispatched animals for a family feast. Apart from the animals, the main victims of this modern style of pilgrimage are the empty teashops, food stalls and hostels that ran along the old trails.

The next stage of our trip took us away from the cool air of the mountains down to the humid jungles of southwest Nepal. Here, the only places to stay are jungle lodges associated with wildlife conservation parks like Chitwan and Bardia. These parks are beautiful areas of natural habitat for some of the last tigers, wild elephants, rhinoceroses and bears in the subcontinent, as well as many other less spectacular species. Much of the surrounding farmland is carpeted in vivid yellow mustard flowers.

There is a significant conflict of interests between the parks and the farmers. Wild animals can be deadly and may easily be tempted to help themselves to neat rows of healthy crops or domesticated farm animals. Many villagers have suffered the consequences of this uneasy equation. Possibly because of this, the villagers of the Terai, mostly poor farmers, are not as openly hospitable as the inhabitants of Nepal's mountain villages. The only places to eat were the kitchens of the lodges. Sadly, most of these attempt to provide a range of international dishes that takes them down some disastrous paths; but when the cooks produce their own food it is invariably excellent.

A ranger in the Chitwan National Park crossing a river in the pre-dawn mists that rise out of the jungle as the temperature climbs

Pakistan & Nepal

In the the flatlands of Nepal's Terai, most of the forest has been cleared to make room for carpets of yellow mustard flowers

From our vantage point, high up on an elephant in Chitwan, the mountains were still visible as a wall of snow beyond the forest. Elephant rides give the unusual experience of fording deep rivers without getting wet, and passing through dense jungle getting very close to wild animals such as tigers, sloth bears and rhinoceroses, without getting killed. In the evening we were taken to see the elephants sleeping. There were twenty or so, all snoring, lying on their sides and looking like giant grey boulders. From time to time each of the elephants in turn would rise to its feet and, hardly bothering to wake, grab a mouthful of straw, then settle down again on its other side. These massive creatures have to turn over at regular intervals throughout the night to save their organs from being crushed under their immense weight.

In Bardia we saw a tiger kill a small deer right in front of us; the tiger's roar was blood-curdling. We had imagined that our elephant would keep us safe from anything, so were somewhat alarmed when it turned and fled, apparently motivated by the same primaeval fear as the roar awoke in us.

Mustard Seeds

(Brassica nigra)

There are three main varieties of mustard, two of them native to Europe and the other to Asia. While the European varieties are traditionally ground with water to make a paste, the Asian brown mustard seeds are usually dried and added whole to dishes. The seeds are either fried in oil at the beginning of cooking vegetable dishes, dry-roasted and added at the end to salads and chutneys, or fried separately and added at the end to give a nutty flavour to dhals.

Most of the trade in these brown mustard seeds is confined to distribution within the Indian subcontinent from the carpets of yellow-flowered fields in the foothills of the Nepalese Himalayas. Mustard seeds are a particular feature of the dishes of Gujarat and the south.

NEPALESE BREAKFAST POTATOES

One morning at the Narayani Safari Lodge on the edge of Chitwan we were served this wonderful Nepalese dish of potatoes cooked in a sweet mildly spiced tomato sauce. It made a perfect accompaniment to the fried eggs and locally grown forest mushrooms on offer. Even guests suspicious of the idea of 'curry for breakfast' enjoyed it.

SERVES 4

750g/1½lb new potatoes, cut into small cubes	5cm/2in cube of jaggery or 1 tablespoon brown sugar
½ teaspoon turmeric	2 dessertspoons coriander seeds and
3 teaspoons ghee or butter	2 dessertspoons cumin seeds,
2 dessertspoons black mustard seeds	dry-roasted until aromatic and ground to a powder
3 garlic cloves, finely chopped	1 dessertspoon ghee or butter
225g/8oz tomatoes, pulped in a food processor	2 dessertspoons cumin seeds
	salt to taste
	handful of coriander leaves, chopped

In a large saucepan, boil the potatoes along with the turmeric until they are soft. Drain and set to one side.

In a large wok, heat the ghee and add the mustard seeds. When they start to crackle, add the garlic, and fry until it browns. Add the pulped tomatoes, the jaggery and 350ml/12fl oz of water, bring to the boil, then simmer gently until the oil returns and the sauce reduces. Add the ground coriander and cumin, plus the drained potatoes, stir well and simmer gently for 5 minutes.

Meanwhile, in a small frying pan, heat 1 dessertspoon of ghee and fry 2 dessertspoons of cumin seeds until they crackle. Remove them from the heat and pour on to the potatoes.

Finally, add salt and pepper to taste and garnish with the chopped coriander leaves. Serve for breakfast with fried eggs and mushrooms.

Southeast Asia

Southeast Asia

All the countries of this region have a strong tradition of creative cooking using vegetables, nuts, spices and soya bean products. The results are quite different from the dishes that dominate Indian cooking. Pulses are used much less, and soya beans appear in the guise of tofu, tempeh and of course soy sauce. Lemon grass, galangal and lime leaves are the dominant spices. When travelling through most of this region vegetarians can enjoy a great variety of dishes to accompany the ubiquitous staple of steamed white rice.

In some parts of the region travel is very easy. Our journeys around Bali and Lombok were made in the comfort of a private jeep, and we were never far from a luxury hotel. By contrast, in Burma, hours of travelling in overcrowded jeeps down forest tracks and mountain paths were rewarded by the sight of exquisite landscapes and encounters with some of the most welcoming people in Asia. Similarly in China, although it seemed that every day another complex negotiation was needed to enable us to continue our journey down the Li River, the beauty of the mountainous country compensated for any frustration. We were less fortunate in Laos, where all our attempts to travel beyond the capital were defeated by bureaucracy. But then in Borneo I was granted the ultimate privilege of travelling deep in virgin rainforest, where no human race has ever lived.

Not unexpectedly, of the countries in this chapter, it is Burma, bordering India, whose cuisine is most clearly influenced by the style of its larger neighbour, with its blending of Indian and Oriental styles. China can be the hardest of all these countries for a vegetarian to travel through. Its most interesting vegetarian dishes are from Buddhist cooking traditions, which are most easily accessible in the cosmopolitan environment of Hong Kong. Conversely, in Thailand, Malaysia and Indonesia it is rarely a problem to find sound vegetarian meals, although a tolerance of (or even a liking for) shrimp paste and fish sauce is a big bonus when it comes to enjoying street food. We have omitted such ingredients from the recipes in this chapter and used soy sauce instead. The complex flavours of all the other ingredients combine to make such exciting tastes that the fish flavours are hardly missed. The ingredients for Southeast Asian cooking are increasingly easy to find in European and North American supermarkets, and often in health-food stores as well, although it's always worth stocking up on the basics when in a Chinese or Thai shop.

Pages 222–223 **The Huang Shan Mountains**

Right **Fresh vegetables piled high in a vegetable market in Burma**

BURMA

Burma is populated by a variety of different ethnic and cultural groups, including the Shans, the Mons, the Chins, the Karens and the Burmans. Each group has its own culinary style prevalent in their particular area, however, there are some dishes that have become ubiquitous throughout the country. Most Burmese dishes are influenced by the cuisine of it's five terrestrial neighbors; India, Bangladesh, China, Thailand and Laos. The spice mixtures used by Burmese cooks are often referred to as either Indian curry powder, based on the classic garam masala mix of ground spices such as cardamom, cumin, pepper and fenugreek, or Chinese curry powder, made up of fennel, star anise, cinnamon, Sichuan pepper and cloves. The Indian version is most prevalent as an aromatic seasoning in wet curries, while the Chinese mix is usually used to flavour rice and noodle dishes which often include other Chinese ingredients like dried shitake mushrooms and soya sauce.

CUCUMBER AND SESAME SEED SALAD

SERVES 4–6

1 heaped tablespoon sesame seeds
1 tablespoon sunflower oil
2 red onions, thinly sliced
2 garlic cloves
1 large cucumber, peeled and cubed

For the dressing
2 tablespoons cider vinegar
½ teaspoon ground turmeric
1 generous teaspoon brown sugar
  or honey
2 tablespoons sesame oil
salt

Dry-roast the sesame seeds in a heavy pan until they start to 'pop', then set aside. Heat the sunflower oil in a frying pan and, when hot, fry the onions and garlic until caramelized and brown.

Make the dressing by slowly mixing the vinegar with the turmeric and sugar or honey, then stir in the sesame oil. Season to taste with salt.

Pour the dressing over the diced cucumber and top with the fried onions and garlic and toasted sesame seeds.

Shadowy boat traffic
haunts Rangoon
harbour at dawn

LEMON GRASS RICE v

Serves 4–6

1 small red onion, roughly chopped
2 garlic cloves
2 red chillies, roughly chopped
500g/1lb 2oz basmati rice

salt
2 lemon grass stalks, cut down the middle and hit with a rolling pin
juice of 1 lime

Blend the onion, garlic and chillies in a food processor until a paste forms.

Rinse the rice until the water runs clear. Place it in a pan which has a tight-fitting lid and add enough water to cover by 1 cm/½ inch, with salt to taste. Add the lemon grass and bring to the boil. Cover, reduce the heat and simmer gently until all the water is absorbed.

Fluff the rice with a fork, at the same time stirring in the onion paste. Cook over a very low heat for a further 5 minutes. Squeeze over the lime juice and adjust the seasoning if necessary.

STIR-FRY IN TAMARIND GRAVY

SERVES 4–6

1 red onion, roughly chopped

3 garlic cloves

3 fresh red chillies

2.5cm/1in cube of root ginger, peeled and roughly chopped

2 lemon grass stalks, thinly sliced

2 teaspoons cumin seeds, dry-roasted and ground

1 teaspoon dark soy sauce

2 tablespoons tamarind paste

3 tablespoons sunflower oil

bunch of spring onions, cut into 2cm/¾in slices

2 carrots, cut into fine matchsticks

450g/1lb Chinese leaf, cut into 2.5cm/1in strips

300g/10oz pak choy, coarsely cut

200g/7oz fine asparagus, cut into 7.5cm/3in pieces

2 red peppers, deseeded and thinly sliced

1 dessertspoon brown sugar or honey

2 tablespoons shoyu or light soy sauce (optional)

salt

For the garnish

large handful of coriander leaves, chopped

large handful of beansprouts

In a food processor, blend the red onion, garlic, chilli, ginger, lemon grass, cumin and dark soy sauce until a paste forms. Dissolve the tamarind paste in 300 ml/½ pint of hot water.

In a wok, heat the sunflower oil until hot. Add the onion paste and fry briskly for a few seconds, stirring to avoid sticking. Add the spring onions, carrots, Chinese leaf, pak choy, asparagus and red pepper. Stir-fry on a high heat until the vegetables are all coated in the paste and they start to soften. Gradually add the tamarind water, a little at a time, until the vegetables are just cooked.

Add the brown sugar or honey, shoyu or soy sauce if necessary and salt to taste. Garnish with coriander and beansprouts piled on top of the dish.

Pagan, on the flood plain of the Irrawaddy River, is like a setting for a fairy tale. Majestic temple ruins in their hundreds are scattered over the plains along the meandering river. When we were there only the most basic accommodation was available. After a long, hot, dusty day's cycling around the ruins we really enjoyed the Stir-Fry in Tamarind Gravy served by the family who ran our rustic guest-house.

After dinner the women of the house offered us a local-style massage, which involved their walking over our backs with animated vigour. They giggled so much as they did this that we half-suspected it to be a joke they played on passing foreigners.

Stir-fry in Tamarind Gravy

CHINA

Our one experience of China was a boat-journey down the Li Xian and Pearl rivers from Yangshuo to the South China Sea at Hong Kong – perhaps one of the most beautiful river journeys in the world. The Huang Shan Mountains around Yangshuo form the round-topped, sheer-sided shapes familiar from classical Chinese paintings. One night we slept in a cave near the summit of one of the hills so that we could photograph the dawn mists rising through the extraordinary landscape. During the day we hired bicycles to explore the rice paddies and villages between the peaks.

Southern China is a bit of a horror show for vegetarians. Most villages we stopped in had drab cafés where surly waiters threw frightening bowls of gruel down on dirty tables. Sometimes the 'menu' was a stack of cages stuffed with all kinds of animals, including rats, cats and owls. Some days we lived off boiled rice and raw peanuts.

We were relieved to get back to Hong Kong, one of the world's most interesting cities in which to discover unusual food. Some dishes use extraordinary ingredients such as tree moss and fermented gluten, while others are simple but enticing combinations of mushrooms or mixed vegetables in light sauces.

**A rice paddy
near Yangshuo**

Several of Hong Kong's islands offer an almost rural escape from the intensity of the city. Lantau is not the quietest, but it is one of the most rewarding to visit. There is a good walk up to the hill-top monastery of Po Lin, where the monks invite visitors to eat lunch with them; it was at Po Lin that I first ate this dish of 'Buddhist meat' with shiitake mushrooms.

'BUDDHIST MEAT' AND SHIITAKE MUSHROOMS v

'Buddhist meat' is a popular name for seitan or wheat gluten, which can be found in health-food stores and Chinese shops. If there is a problem getting hold of seitan, tofu can be used instead; the dry pre-cooked style works better than the more common wet style.

SERVES 4

5 tablespoons sunflower oil
2.5cm/1in piece of root ginger, peeled and thinly sliced
3 garlic cloves, thinly sliced
250g/9oz shiitake mushrooms, quartered
4 medium carrots, cut into matchstick strips
bunch of spring onions, cut into 2.5cm/1in pieces

salt and pepper
300g/10oz seitan or tofu, cut into strips
1 tablespoon hoisin sauce
1 tablespoon light soy sauce
1 tablespoon rice wine
1 teaspoon sesame oil
toasted sesame seeds, to serve

Heat 3 tablespoons of the sunflower oil in a wok and, when hot, fry half the ginger and half the garlic for about 20 seconds. Add the mushrooms, the carrots and most of the spring onions and toss in the hot oil for 2 minutes. Remove these vegetables, sprinkle with salt and set aside.

Wipe out the wok and heat the remaining oil. When hot, fry the seitan or tofu with the remaining garlic and ginger, until it begins to go brown on the outside.

Combine the hoisin sauce, soy sauce, rice wine, sesame oil and a little salt and pepper in a bowl with 4 tablespoons of water, then pour into the wok, returning the vegetables at the same time. Simmer gently for a few minutes.

Serve with steamed rice, the rest of the spring onions and toasted sesame seeds.

SOUTH CHINA STIR-FRY v

This is a simple, healthy, clean-tasting combination of fresh vegetables cooked quickly in a little oil and flavoured with fresh ginger and rice wine. Any vegetables can be used.

SERVES 4–6

125g/4oz fresh asparagus

125g/4oz cauliflower florets

125g/4oz broccoli florets

4 tablespoons sunflower oil

7.5cm/3in piece of root ginger, cut into fine matchstick strips

60g/2oz shiitake mushrooms

225g/8oz straw mushrooms (canned are fine)

125g/4oz sugar snap peas

125g/4oz baby sweetcorn, cut in half lengthwise

4 red chillies, cut into strips

2 teaspoons cornflour, mixed to a paste with a little water

2 tablespoons rice wine

2 tablespoons soy sauce

1 teaspoon salt

1 teaspoon sugar

finely chopped spring onions, to finish

Boil the asparagus, cauliflower and broccoli in salted water for 1 minute, then refresh in cold water and drain.

Heat the oil in a large wok until smoking, then add the ginger, all the vegetables and the chillies. Cook over a high heat, stirring continuously for 5 minutes.

Stir in all the remaining ingredients and serve with finely chopped spring onions sprinkled over, accompanied by rice.

In southern China we were 'slightly' arrested for being slightly off limits. It was a genuine mistake on our part, and a nervous provincial policeman decided that instead of putting us in the cells he would invite us to be guests in his home for the night, before sending us back to a town 'on limits'.

We managed to convey our desire for a meatless meal in time to save any embarrassment during the evening meal with his family. This stir-fry turned out to be the best meal we ate in China. The vegetables are simply those the policeman's wife found in the local market that day.

The distinctive peaks of the Huang Shan Mountains

LAOS

In the late 1980s Laos began to open up after decades of isolation and, as we were in Thailand anyway, we decided to go and have a look. We specially wanted to visit the temple sites of the first Lao kingdom and the old French colonial mansions in Luang Phabang. The Laotian Embassy in Bangkok refused us visas, but we booked a two-week 'package', including visas, through a scruffy little tourist agency. We crossed the Mekong on a small ferry at dawn. The immigration officers seemed happy with our visas which, written in Lao script, meant nothing to us, and we struck up an acquaintance with a couple returning to Laos for the first time since escaping as refugees fifteen years

Detail from a Buddhist temple in Vientiane

We first ate this stir-fry on the banks of the mighty Mekong River, at the village wedding feast we had been invited to by our new friends. The thickening of puréed aubergines is characteristic of Laotian dishes — aubergines are abundant in Laos.

before. They were on their way to a village near Vientiane, the capital, for a family wedding, and with typical Asian hospitality they invited us to accompany them. We spent several enjoyable hours at the feast, sharing in the double celebration of the reunion and the wedding festivities, and eating vast quantities of delicious food.

That was the good bit. The next day, having reluctantly spent a night in our sombre pre-paid hotel in Vientiane, a compulsory part of the package, we tried to organize a flight or a boat-journey to Luang Phabang, only to find, to our dismay, that our visas were good only for Vientiane and, moreover, expired that day. There was no way of getting to Luang Phabang 'with visas like this'; we had no option but to return to the ferry. And that was all we saw of Laos.

MEKONG STIR-FRY WITH PURÉED AUBERGINE v

SERVES 4–6

2 aubergines
3 tablespoons sunflower oil
6 spring onions, cut into
  2cm/¾in slices
3 garlic cloves, crushed
3 red chillies, thinly sliced
1 teaspoon fennel seeds, crushed
250g/9oz shiitake mushrooms,
  thickly sliced

250g/9oz fine green beans,
  cut in half
225g/8oz spinach, shredded
225g/8oz sugar snap peas
5cm/2in piece of galangal,
  peeled and thinly sliced
handful of fresh mint leaves
handful of fresh sweet basil leaves
salt

Make the aubergine purée: cut away the top of the aubergines and slice the rest in half lengthwise. Immerse these in boiling salted water and simmer until the flesh is soft. Remove from the pan and scoop the flesh from the skin using a spoon. Either mash the flesh using a potato masher or purée in a food processor. Set aside.

Heat the oil in a wok and, when hot, flash-fry the spring onions, garlic and chillies. Follow these with the fennel seeds, then add the shiitake and green beans, and stir-fry for a further minute or two. Add the shredded spinach and sugar snap peas, stirring constantly. Add the aubergine purée, galangal and enough water to make a sauce. Simmer until the vegetables are just cooked.

At the last minute, stir in the fresh mint and sweet basil leaves with salt to taste. Serve with noodles and Crunchy Sweet-and-Sour Salad (page 236).

CRUNCHY SWEET-AND-SOUR SALAD

SERVES 4–6

⅓ small head of Chinese leaves,
   thinly sliced
bunch of watercress
large handful of spinach leaves,
   sliced, or young leaf spinach
200g/7oz beansprouts
85g/3oz mange-tout peas, cut into
   strips lengthwise
4 spring onions, cut into strips
85g/3oz skinned shelled peanuts,
   dry-roasted in a pan and crushed

small handful of fresh mint
small handful of sweet basil leaves

For the dressing
2 tablespoons oil
3 garlic cloves, sliced
2 tablespoons lime juice
2 tablespoons light soy sauce
1 dessertspoon brown sugar
   or honey
2 red chillies, thinly sliced

Crunchy Sweet-and-Sour Salad is another of the dishes we sampled at the wedding, sitting on the floor among a hundred happy people, with most of whom we didn't share a word of language.

Mix the Chinese leaves, watercress, spinach, beansprouts and mange-touts in a bowl.

Make the dressing: in a heavy-based pan heat the oil and fry the garlic until brown and crunchy. Remove the pan from heat and add the lime juice, soy sauce, brown sugar or honey and the chillies. Stir until all ingredients are combined. Allow to cool slightly, then pour over the salad.

Finally, sprinkle the spring onions, peanuts and herbs on top.

Left **Detail from a Buddhist temple in Vientiane**
Right **Crunchy Sweet-and-Sour Salad**

CAMBODIA

Cambodia has emerged from its appalling recent history with a renewed enthusiasm for the traditions of its ancient past, including some very fine Khmer cuisine. Cambodians are now welcoming visitors to the wonderful jungle temples of Angkor in Siem Reap Provence and their capital Phnom Penh without a hint of the cynicism that can so easily creep in to better-worn destinations. You don't even need to haggle with pedallers of the city's cyclo-rickshaws: the fares they charge are so embarrassingly low that when you give them a well-deserved tip they shake your hand in warm thanks. As the volume of tourists increases, the warmth of this welcome may reduce, so now is the perfect time to visit Cambodia. There is a great choice of hotels to suit most budgets and it's still possible to find yourself alone among the ancient temples and grand palaces.

At its height the Khmer kingdom, centred on Angkor, ruled an empire that included most of South East Asia. The Khmer recipes being revived today go back to this time, before chillies arrived in Asia from Mexico. Consequently dishes are much milder than those of most Asian countries.

There are plenty of places to try delicious traditional Khmer food in Siem Reap, the town closest to the ruins of the Khmer kingdom's greatest relics around Angkor wat. Simple and incredibly inexpensive food is on sale from food stalls around the bustling Psar Chas market. In the pavement cafés near by, equally delicious food is served at tables in the open air. Salads are popular starters, made with ingredients such as banana flower blossom, lotus roots, green mango or green papaya, served with finely chopped roasted peanuts and shrimps, and all doused in lively dressings of lime juice, palm sugar and lots of fresh coriander leaves. Wherever you eat it, *amok* – an aromatic dish of chicken, fish or tofu – is a good choice. Many Khmer dishes include fish sauce or fresh-water shrimps but we have adapted our recipes to exclude these.

Phnom Penh is located at the confluence of the Mekong, Tonla Sep and Bassac rivers. The city's social life is concentrated in the cafés, bars and markets along its attractive riverside promenade. Every afternoon, just before sunset, hundreds of hawkers set up stalls along it, selling an extraordinary choice of snacks and fast food to strolling residents. It's hard to believe that so recently, for three years, this charming city was a ghost town, forcibly evacuated by the Khmer Rouge. The residents who survived those terrible years, when a third of Cambodia's population perished, began repopulating the city only twenty-five years ago. It's taken most of that time for it to recover. At last food production and supplies are well established again and the city's cafés and markets thrive once more.

Right, clockwise from top right **An offering of incense at the feet of a Buddha in Angkor wat; a monk at Siem Reap monastery; Ta Prohm temple, Angkor; Buddhist shrine in Angkor; a stone face at the Bayon temple, Angkor; a monk at Angkor wat**

AMOK WITH SPINACH AND TOFU

The most essential ingredient in most Khmer dishes is a herb paste known as kroeung, a blend of lemon grass, galangal, rhizome (or lesser galangal), turmeric and garlic. Sometimes shallots or kaffir lime zest are added.

Amok is an extremely popular steamed curry, served all over Cambodia. Cambodians like it best with fish or chicken but this vegetarian-style version with tofu often appears on menus. Don't bother to deep fry the tofu yourself – you can buy it. The curry is thickened with egg and flavoured with the classic Khmer spice paste *kroeung*. The resulting dish is solid but moist. Although the traditional *amok* does not include chillies, we prefer this dish to be spicy. To make a milder dish, just leave the chillies out of the *kroeung*.

The *amok* is usually then steamed in a banana leaf but we steam it in bowls. We wouldn't recommend cooking this for large groups, as steaming lots of bowls could be a fiddle, so this recipe serves 2 people.

For the kroeung
1 lemon grass stem, thinly sliced
1in/2.5cm piece of galangal, sliced
½ teaspoon ground turmeric
2 garlic cloves, roughly chopped
2 dried red chillies, soaked until soft
    and then roughly chopped (optional)
2 shallots, sliced

For the amok
5fl oz/150ml coconut milk
1 tablespoon dark soy sauce
1 teaspoon palm sugar or honey

1 small egg, beaten
salt to taste
1oz/30g spinach leaves, washed,
    stems removed and sliced
3oz/90g Chinese broccoli, chopped
2oz/60g deep-fried tofu, sliced
    ¼ in/½ cm thick

For the garnish
1 large red chilli, finely sliced
1 dessertspoon sliced lime leaves
2 tablespoons coconut cream or thick
    coconut milk

First make the kroeung by blending all the ingredients together in a food processor until a paste forms.

Pour half the coconut milk into a bowl and stir in the kroeung, soy sauce, palm sugar or honey, beaten egg and salt to taste; then add the remaining coconut milk. Choose the bowls in which you are going to serve the amok, making sure that they are heatproof, and divide the sliced spinach, chopped broccoli, sliced deep-fried tofu and coconut spice mix between the bowls. Steam the amok in a steamer for 30 minutes. If you don't have a steamer, you can simmer water in a wok, place the amok on a steamer stand in the bottom and cover with the lid.

Remove the bowls from the steamer and garnish with the sliced red chilli, sliced lime leaves and coconut cream or milk.

Amok with Spinach and Tofu

KAPI SAUCE

4 tablespoons lime juice

2 tablespoons light soy sauce

1 teaspoon honey

4 garlic cloves, crushed

2 shallots, finely chopped

2 red chillies, finely chopped

½ teaspoon crushed
  black peppercorns

1 tablespoon peanuts, dry roasted
  until toasted and then crushed

Combine all the ingredients and serve.

A taste for chillies hasn't entirely passed Cambodia by: often a powerful side dish of *kapi*, chillies mixed with honey, soy sauce, garlic and peanuts, is provided, for those who want to spice things up a bit. *Kapi* sauce is a spicy, thin condiment. There are many versions but this is our favourite. If you don't want heat, leave out the chillies.

GREEN MANGO SALAD

This is great as a light meal, appetizer or accompaniment to a main meal.

2 green mangoes, cut into thin strips

6oz/175g shredded cabbage

2 carrots, grated

For the dressing

2 tablespoons sliced shallots

2 garlic cloves, crushed

1 tablespoon finely sliced lemon grass

1 teaspoon finely chopped galangal

1 red chilli, finely chopped

2fl oz/60ml coconut milk

2fl oz/60ml tamarind water
  (1 teaspoon tamarind paste
  dissolved in water)

1 tablespoon lime juice

2 dessertspoons honey

2 tablespoons light soy sauce

For the garnish

2 tablespoons sliced shallots, fried
  until brown

1 tablespoon sliced garlic, fried until
  brown

2 heaped tablespoons peanuts,
  dry roasted until toasted and
  then crushed

handful of chopped coriander leaves

handful of chopped Thai sweet basil
  or basil

Combine the green mangoes, cabbage and carrots in a bowl. In a separate bowl, combine all the dressing ingredients. Pour the dressing over the salad and mix well. Finally sprinkle the garnish ingredients over the top.

A window of a monastery
in Siem Reap

CAMBODIAN YELLOW CURRY

This is another dish based on the flavour of a kreoung. In this one the added quantity of turmeric lends a distinctly yellow colour to the curry. Pea aubergines are small, round green aubergines available from Thai supermarkets. You can substitute peas if they are not available.

For the kreoung
grated zest of 2 kaffir limes or limes
2 lemon grass stalks, sliced
1 tablespoon sliced galangal
5 shallots, sliced
4 garlic cloves, chopped
3½oz/100g peanuts, dry roasted
    until toasted
1 teaspoon ground turmeric

For the curry
4 tablespoons sunflower oil

1 medium onion, diced
10oz/300g aubergine, cut into cubes
12oz/350g sweet potatoes, peeled
    and cut into cubes
12oz/350g cauliflower,
    cut into florets
4oz/115g pea aubergine
14fl oz/400ml coconut milk
2 tablespoons dark soy sauce
1 dessertspoon honey
8fl oz/250ml water
salt to taste

First make the kreoung by blending all the spice paste ingredients in a food processor until smooth.

Heat the oil in a wok. When hot, add the onion, fry until soft and then add the other vegetables, sprinkling with a little salt to prevent the aubergine from drying out. Fry until the vegetables start to soften, and then add the kreoung, stirring to coat the vegetables with the spice paste. Add the coconut milk, soy sauce, honey, and salt to taste, bring to the boil and then reduce the heat, cover the pan and gently simmer until the vegetables are soft.

Serve with Savoury Pineapple Salad (page 248), rice and popadums.

**Cambodian
Yellow Curry**

SAMLA SOUP

Samla is thin soup that is served alongside the main meal. Alternatively you can have it, as we do, for supper with tofu – added at the same time as the spinach – and rice noodles on the side.

2 tablespoons sunflower oil
4 garlic cloves, crushed
1¾ pints/1 litre vegetable stock
1 teaspoon chopped parsley root
2 teaspoons tamarind paste
1 tablespoon dark soy sauce
1 teaspoon honey
1 teaspoon crushed black
   peppercorns
3 carrots, cut into strips

7oz/200g baby sweet corn,
   sliced diagonally
3 small tomatoes, cubed
6oz/175g spinach, washed, stems
   removed and sliced
4 spring onions, thinly sliced
handful of chopped coriander leaves
10 sweet basil leaves, chopped
2 red chillies, finely chopped
salt to taste

Heat the oil in a wok. When hot, add the garlic and fry until brown and crunchy. Turn down the heat and allow to cool for a few minutes. Then add the stock, parsley root, tamarind paste, soy sauce, honey and black pepper. Cover the pan and bring to the boil, add the carrots, baby sweet corn and tomatoes, and simmer until the vegetables are just soft. Add the spinach, spring onions, chopped herbs, chillies and salt to taste. Serve as soon as the spinach has wilted.

TEMPEH STUFFED AUBERGINES

This is a recipe from the Cambodian royal household, the cuisine of which includes dishes to celebrate key events during a reign, offerings to the gods and dishes to mark births, weddings and deaths. We use Chinese aubergines, which are thinner and paler purple than regular aubergines. If you can't get them, don't worry: use regular aubergines, but try to pick small, slender ones. Tempeh (fermented soya bean curd) is available from health food or Asian stores; however, if you find it hard to buy, tofu or vegetables work just as well.

3 medium Chinese aubergines,
   cut in half lengthways
6 tablespoons cooked Thai rice
6 oz/175g tempeh, finely chopped
2 free-range eggs, beaten
1 dessertspoon vegetarian oyster sauce
3 tablespoons sunflower oil
spring onions, finely sliced,
   to garnish

For the kroeung
3 tablespoons finely sliced lemon grass
3 teaspoons grated galangal
1 teaspoon finely chopped parsley root
5 garlic cloves, chopped
7 shallots, chopped
4 red chillies, finely chopped
2 tablespoons dark soy sauce
½ teaspoon coarsely ground
   black peppercorns
salt to taste

First make the kroeung by blending all the ingredients in a food processor until smooth.

Blanch the aubergines in a large saucepan of boiling water for 4 minutes. Remove from the pan, dry with kitchen paper and scoop out the centres, leaving enough flesh to keep the shells firm. Chop up the flesh and mix it with the rice, tempeh, eggs, vegetarian oyster sauce and kroeung, and stuff the aubergines with the mixture. Heat the sunflower oil in a non-stick frying pan. When hot, fry the aubergines, stuffing sides down, over a moderate heat until soft and brown. Carefully turn the aubergines and fry until the other sides are brown.

Serve garnished with the sliced spring onions. Serve with Kapi Sauce (page 242).

Far left **Monks at a monastery in Phnom Penh**
Left **A huge stone face above a gateway to Angkor thom**

SAVOURY PINEAPPLE SALAD

A perfect balance of sweet, savoury and spicy.

10oz/300g fresh pineapple, cut
    into cubes
small handful of chopped Thai
    sweet basil leaves, or basil
small handful of chopped mint leaves

For the dressing
2 garlic cloves, crushed
2 shallots, crushed
2 tablespoons light soy sauce
2 dessertspoons honey
2 red chillies, finely chopped

Mix the pineapple and the chopped herbs in a bowl. In a separate bowl, combine the dressing ingredients. Pour the dressing over the salad and mix well.

PHNOM PENH STIR-FRY WITH HOLY BASIL

3 tablespoons sunflower oil
6 garlic cloves, crushed
2 red chillies, finely chopped
6 shallots, sliced
1 red pepper, sliced
1 yellow pepper, sliced
9oz/250g fine green beans
9oz/250g Chinese broccoli or
    broccoli, chopped

2 tablespoons vegetarian
    oyster sauce
1 tablespoon soy sauce
1 teaspoon honey
4fl oz/125ml water
9oz/250g bean sprouts
4 large handfuls Thai holy basil,
    chopped

Heat the oil in a wok. When hot, add the garlic, chillies and shallots, and sauté until soft. Add all the vegetables except the bean sprouts and fry for a few minutes. Add the vegetarian oyster sauce, soy sauce, honey and water, cover the wok, reduce the heat and cook until vegetables are soft but retain some bite. Stir in the bean sprouts and the chopped holy basil, and fry until the basil wilts.

Serve immediately with Samla Soup (page 246), Kapi Sauce (page 242) and rice noodles.

Phnom Penh is an easy-going capital with a wealth of excellent street markets and exotic temples, one of the best museums in the world just packed with immense antique Buddhas and a royal palace that rivals any in Asia for opulent splendour. The perfect way to end any day in the city is sipping a cold Angkor beer looking out over the Tonle Sap river from the balcony of the Foreign Correspondents' Club of Cambodia on the promenade.

**Savoury
Pineapple Salad**

THAILAND

Thailand is one of the easy countries of Asia for foreign tourists. It has an abundance of natural beauty, from the jungly hills of the north to the forests and rivers of the centre and the tropical paradises of the southern peninsula. Visitors can explore the spectacular ruins of past Siamese kingdoms and colourful living temples, ride an elephant or trek to a tribal village in the hills, and enjoy idyllic beaches, bargain-shopping, great-value accommodation and efficient public transport. The country has developed a massive tourist industry, the downside of which is that it is all too easy to spend a trip almost entirely in the company of other tourists. Thailand demands so little in return for all it offers that travelling there almost seems like cheating.

Despite providing such a generous holiday destination, Thais have kept much of the traditional grace and elegance of their way of life, together with a unique cuisine. Never having been invaded or colonized (a singular history in southern Asia), they have food that is undiluted Thai and very good. Fresh ingredients are cooked in heavily spiced pastes and flavoured with lemon grass, lime leaves, galangal root, black pepper, sweet basil, ginger, tamarind, coconut milk, peanuts and coriander leaves. Being completely vegetarian can be complicated by the fish and shrimp sauces that are much used in Thai cooking, but these can easily be excluded when cooking at home. Anyone who enjoys eating fish and seafood will be well satisfied, especially in southern Thailand. There are some excellent vegetarian restaurants in Bangkok and in larger towns such as Chiang Mai. Some are smart and relatively expensive; others, including those set up by the Theravada Buddhists, indicated by a large green sign with a Thai numeral on it, are incredibly cheap.

One of our first experiences of travel in Asia was several weeks spent living for a few pence a night in palm-thatched beach-huts on various islands in the Gulf of Thailand. Our budget was so tight that we didn't want to use any of it buying the food on sale in the tourist cafés along the beach, so we cooked every night on a paraffin stove outside our hut, using whatever we found in the local market. We didn't know much about Thai cooking at the time, but simply enjoyed experimenting with all the ingredients we came across. Since then we have learnt far more about how to use these ingredients to create more traditional and much tastier Thai dishes.

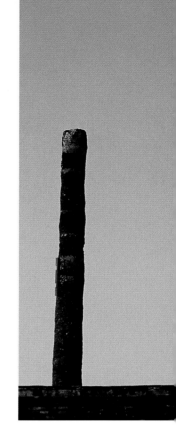

A huge statue of the Buddha in the ruins of Sukhothai, the ancient Siamese capital

BANGKOK STIR-FRY v

This stir-fry is a dish we ate on the street in Bangkok after watching a film in an open-air street cinema. The film was projected on to a sheet suspended between two trees. It cost a few bhat to sit in front of the trees, while to watch the film back to front behind the sheet was free. Both sides of the sheet drew large crowds, as did the street-food stalls which produced this feast in just a few minutes.

SERVES 4

4 tablespoons sunflower oil
8 baby aubergines,
    cut into quarters lengthwise
salt
300g/10oz deep-fried tofu,
    cut into 1cm/½in slices

225g/8oz fine green beans
4 fresh red chillies, cut into strips
good pinch of crushed dried red chilli
2 teaspoons brown sugar
400ml/14fl oz coconut milk
handful of chopped coriander leaves

Make sure you have all ingredients prepared and at hand ready to throw in.

Heat the sunflower oil in a wok. When hot, fry the aubergine, sprinkled with a little salt to avoid it absorbing too much oil and drying out, until the aubergine starts to soften.

Add the tofu and the green beans and flash-fry for a few minutes. Add the fresh chillies, the crushed chillies and the brown sugar, stirring constantly to avoid sticking.

Reduce the heat and add the coconut milk. Simmer for 5 minutes. Season with salt to taste. Serve with noodles and garnished with coriander leaves.

JUNGLE CURRY v

This curry is made with a red curry paste that can be made in advance and stored in the fridge.

SERVES 4–6

4 tablespoons sunflower oil

150g/5oz baby sweetcorn, cut down the middle lengthwise

2 small red peppers, deseeded and thinly sliced

225g/8oz green beans, cut in half

225g/8oz button mushrooms, cut in half

2 small heads of broccoli, broken into florets

350ml/12fl oz stock

1 tablespoon dark soy sauce

4 kaffir lime leaves, rolled and thinly sliced

1 dessertspoon brown sugar

salt

For the red curry paste

4 hot red chillies

4 garlic cloves

2 lemon grass stalks, thinly sliced

5cm/2in cube of galangal or ginger, peeled and chopped

1 red onion, roughly chopped

½ teaspoon salt

1 dessertspoon coriander seeds, dry-roasted and ground

For the garnish

coriander leaves, chopped

red chillies, thinly sliced

First make the red curry paste simply by blending all ingredients in a food processor.

Heat the sunflower oil in a wok and, when it is hot, add the red curry paste. Fry for a few seconds, stirring constantly. Now add the vegetables, still stirring constantly until they are well coated with the paste and starting to soften.

Pour over the stock and the soy sauce. Add the lime leaves and sugar. Simmer until the vegetables are just soft but retain a little bite, adding more water if necessary.

Finally add salt to taste. Garnish with chopped coriander leaves and thinly sliced red chillies. Serve with rice or noodles and Beancurd and Beansprout Spicy Salad (page 255).

'Jungle curries', from the northern part of Thailand, are characterized by strong flavours and the absence of the sweet coconut milk so favoured in the south. The most memorable jungle curry we tasted was one that we ate while staying in a forest guest-house among the great Buddha statues that are scattered around the ruins of Sukhothai.

Jungle Curry

THAI GREEN CURRY v

SERVES 4–6

4 tablespoons sunflower oil

6 baby aubergines, cut into quarters,
    or 8 Thai aubergines, cut in half

⅔ head of a medium cauliflower,
    cut into small florets

150g/5oz fine green beans, cut in half

175g/6oz oyster mushrooms, sliced

150ml/¼ pint stock

4 kaffir lime leaves, rolled up and
    thinly sliced

2 dessertspoons dark soy sauce

1 dessertspoon brown sugar

400ml/14fl oz coconut milk

large handful of sweet basil leaves

salt

chopped coriander leaves, to garnish

For the green curry paste

1 teaspoon coriander seeds

1 teaspoon cumin seeds

1 dessertspoon black peppercorns

large handful of coriander stalks,
    chopped

6 shallots or 1 red onion,
    coarsely chopped

4 garlic cloves

5cm/2in cube of galangal or root
    ginger, peeled and roughly chopped

2 lemon grass stalks, thinly sliced

4 green chillies

1 tablespoon dark soy sauce

grated zest and juice of 1 lime

Thai Green Curry with its aromatic coconut milk sauce is typical of the south, and is our favourite Thai curry. It is actually not very green, but most of the ingredients of the paste that forms the basis of the curry are. You can use almost any vegetable, but aubergine works particularly well. If you can get small round Thai aubergines, all the better; baby aubergines are a good substitute and are available from most good supermarkets.

First make the green curry paste: dry-roast the coriander and cumin seeds in a small pan, then mix them with the peppercorns and grind using a spice grinder or pestle and mortar. Add to a food processor with all remaining ingredients and process until a paste forms. Store in the fridge if making in advance.

Heat the sunflower oil in a wok. When hot, fry the aubergines (sprinkled with a little salt to prevent them absorbing all the oil and drying up too much) until it starts to soften. Add the cauliflower, green beans and oyster mushrooms.

When the cauliflower starts to brown, add the green curry paste, stirring well to avoid sticking. When this is well combined, add the stock, kaffir lime leaves, dark soy sauce and sugar. When the vegetables are just starting to soften, add the coconut milk and sweet basil. Cook for a further 5 minutes, ensuring the sauce doesn't boil. Season with salt to taste, if necessary.

Serve with rice or noodles, garnished with chopped coriander leaves.

Fried beancurd (tofu) makes a lovely side-dish to be served with any of the Thai curries in this chapter. Deep-fried tofu can be bought from any health-food or oriental shop, or from good supermarkets – much easier than frying it yourself.

BEANCURD AND BEANSPROUT SPICY SALAD

SERVES 4–6

1 cucumber, grated
1 red pepper, cut into fine strips
200g/7oz beansprouts
300g/10oz deep-fried tofu, cut into
   1cm/½in slices
1 tablespoon sunflower oil
1 garlic clove, crushed
1–2 green chillies, thinly sliced

1–2 red chillies, thinly sliced
juice of 1 lime
2 tablespoons light soy sauce
1 dessertspoon brown sugar or honey
125g/4oz skinned shelled peanuts,
   dry-roasted in a pan and
   then crushed
handful of coriander leaves, chopped

Combine the grated cucumber, red pepper and beansprouts in a salad bowl.

Fry the tofu slices in hot oil until they are brown and crunchy. Place to one side and allow to cool.

Using the same pan, fry the garlic and chillies for a few seconds, then add the lime juice, soy sauce and brown sugar or honey. Stir until all these dressing ingredients are combined.

Arrange the fried tofu slices on top of the salad, sprinkle with the crushed peanuts, pour on the dressing and garnish with lots of coriander leaves.

The Buddha's hand — a detail from one of the statues around the ruins of Sukhothai

CHU CHEE RED CURRY

Pad Thai (opposite) is a good accompaniment to this creamy red curry.

7oz/200g baby aubergines, cut into
    quarters, lengthways
7oz/200g mooli (white radishes),
    cut into thick matchsticks
4oz/115g button mushrooms
3½oz/100g oyster mushrooms, sliced
4oz/115g deep-fried tofu, cut into
    ¼ in/½ cm slices
2 tablespoons dark soy sauce
juice of ½ a kaffir lime or lime
1 tablespoon chopped palm sugar
    or honey
6 kaffir lime leaves, thinly sliced
salt to taste
2 large red chillies, thinly sliced,
    to garnish

For the red curry paste
1 dessertspoon coriander seeds, dry
    roasted until aromatic and ground
5 dried red chillies, soaked in hot
    water until soft
3½ garlic cloves, chopped
1 lemon grass stalk, sliced
1 tablespoon chopped kaffir lime peel
4 coriander roots
1 tablespoon chopped galangal
5 shallots, chopped
2 tablespoons sunflower oil
2 garlic cloves, thinly sliced
16fl oz/500ml coconut milk
8fl oz/250ml vegetable stock

Blend all the curry paste ingredients in a food processor until smooth.

Heat the oil in a wok. When hot, add the garlic and fry until brown, reduce the heat a little and stir in the curry paste; then add the coconut milk and vegetable stock. Add the vegetables, tofu, soy sauce, lime juice, palm sugar or honey and half the sliced lime leaves, and bring to the boil. Cover the pan, reduce the heat and gently simmer until the vegetables are cooked.

Add salt to taste and serve garnished with the remaining sliced lime leaves and the sliced large red chillies.

Above **The food market in Chaing Mai**
Right **A rice farmer with a buffalo at Dhara Dhevi, Chaing Mai**

PAD THAI

This is a one-dish meal that you can buy in street stalls all over Thailand. It's great for a quick lunch or as a side dish for a larger meal.

4 tablespoons sunflower oil
8 shallots, thinly sliced
4 garlic cloves, finely chopped
3 red chillies, thinly sliced
4 eggs, beaten
6oz/175g deep-fried tofu cut into
½in/1cm cubes
8oz/225g dried flat rice noodles
½ teaspoon chilli powder
½ teaspoon ground white pepper
4 tablespoons dark soy sauce

1 teaspoon tamarind paste, dissolved
in 3 tablespoons of water
3 tablespoons lime juice
1 heaped tablespoon brown sugar
8 spring onions, sliced diagonally
10 tablespoons peanuts, dry roasted
until brown and then ground
until fine
12oz/350g bean sprouts
large handful of chopped coriander
leaves, to garnish

Soften the rice noodles according to the directions on the packet. Heat the oil in a wok. When hot, add the sliced shallots, garlic and chillies, and fry until brown. Add the eggs, cook for a moment and then stir well. Add the tofu and fry for a minute or so. Add the softened noodles along with the chilli powder, white pepper, soy sauce, tamarind water, lime juice and brown sugar. Finally add half the spring onions, peanuts and bean sprouts. Place the rest of the spring onions, peanuts and bean sprouts on the table in bowls, along with the chopped coriander leaves to garnish and Sweet and Sour Dipping Sauce (page 264).

MALAYSIA & INDONESIA

Peninsular Malaysia, Borneo and all the Indonesian islands share an essentially common language and cuisine. The language, Bahasa, is very easy to learn, and with little variation the spoken language is understood all the way from the air-conditioned office blocks of Kuala Lumpur and Jakarta to the most remote longhouse in the jungles of Sarawak or Irian Jaya. Numerous regional languages, and Chinese dialects and Tamil, are spoken through the region, but a knowledge of Bahasa will enable a tourist to communicate with most people, most of the time.

As far as food is concerned there are regional variations too, and rather more of a difference between Malaysia and Indonesia than with language. The ingredients themselves remain more constant. Vegetarian food is easy to find. A street food classic is the delicious satay sauce made from roasted peanuts blended with spices, into which barbecued chicken or red meat is usually dipped. Luckily for vegetarians, a raw vegetable and beancurd dish, gado gado (page 275), served with a similar sauce, is common throughout Indonesia. There are also numerous fried rice, beancurd and egg dishes, as well as vegetable concoctions in coconut milk curries, to choose from.

Peninsular Malaysia, like Thailand, is so undemanding of the tourist that it makes for a perfect holiday destination. The east coast is less developed than the richer, more urban west; some of the offshore islands are sensationally beautiful, and a train journey from Gemas to Kota Bharu through the centre passes through some impressive rainforest. My real jungle experience came on a Royal Geographical Society assignment to the Batu Apoi Forest Reserve in the remote Temburong district of eastern Brunei on the island of Borneo. Thanks to its phenomenal oil wealth, Brunei's tropical rainforests have largely escaped felling for profit. In this, as in much else, it differs sharply from the rest of Borneo.

To reach the reserve I had to travel from the capital, down the Brunei River, across open sea, through mangrove swamps and up the Temburong River to the sleepy settlement of Bangar. A Land Rover then took me cross-country to an Iban longhouse at Batang Duri on the Kuala (river) Belalong. From here the journey was by motorized canoe, negotiating rocks and rapids all the way up to the riverside jungle clearing where a collection of wooden huts on stilts was to be home for the next six weeks.

A highlight of my trip was a four-day trek to Bukit Belalong, the topmost point in the reserve. Sleeping out in the forest on stretchers suspended above the forest floor, so as to escape the worst of the leeches, was much more cosy than I had imagined it would be. Bed was the only place to be dry, and we carefully preserved a spare set of

The dense rainforest of the remote Batu Apoi Forest Reserve

dry clothes to sleep in, changing back into our damp daytime clothing in the morning. There was no point in trying to stay dry: within seconds of setting off into the forest, perspiration and damp from the regular rainfall soaked everything. Putting on wet clothes isn't the most pleasant way to start a day — but the dawn chorus of gibbon calls above the mutterings of a million birds and insects made up for a lot. In fact, I have found that one way of conveying how amazing it is to be in the rainforest is to relate the hardships — which include constant thirst, complete exhaustion, fear of getting lost (and dying), sliding painfully down steep muddy banks, and finding leeches in one's underclothes. For, despite all this, it is still an unforgettable experience in an entirely positive way.

TOFU WITH CRISPY FRIED BASIL AND CHILLI SAUCE

This recipe makes a good side dish to Stir-fried Vegetables with Green Peppercorns and Shitake Mushrooms (page 263).

5 tablespoons sunflower oil
1 cup Thai sweet basil leaves, or basil
14oz/400g tofu, cut into
 ½in/1cm slices
6 garlic cloves, sliced
6 red chillies, finely sliced

3 tablespoons vegetarian oyster sauce
3 tablespoons dark soy sauce
2 tablespoons chopped palm sugar
 or honey
3 teaspoons cornflour mixed with
 8 tablespoons water

Heat 2 tablespoons of the sunflower oil in a wok. When hot, fry the basil leaves until crispy and set to one side. In the oil remaining in the pan, fry the tofu until brown on both sides. Remove the tofu from the wok and then add the remaining oil. When hot, fry the garlic and chillies until brown. Reduce the heat and add the vegetarian oyster sauce, soy sauce and palm sugar or honey; then gradually stir in the cornflour mixed with water. Spoon this sauce over the fried tofu and garnish with the crispy basil leaves. Serve immediately.

On our last night in Kuala Lumpur we were taken out to dinner in the revolving restaurant at the top of a tower that looks out over the whole city, with a spectacular view of what was then the tallest building in the world, the Petronas towers. I made the classic mistake of putting my camera bag down on the floor next to the table. As the slowly rotating restaurant brought our table level with the Petronas towers I went to grab my camera, only to find that the whole bag had disappeared. After a moment of panic I realized that it was exactly where I had left it while we had travelled to the other side of the restaurant.

Tofu with Crispy Fried Basil and Chilli Sauce

HERB AND NOODLE SALAD

For this salad, mung bean noodles, available from Asian food stores, are dressed with a sweet and sour sauce and mixed with lots of fresh herbs. It can be served on its own or as a side dish. Don't bother to deep fry the tofu yourself — you can buy it.

6oz/175g deep-fried tofu, cut into
¼ in/½ cm slices

3oz/90g dried mung bean
vermicelli noodles

6oz/175g wing beans or flat green
beans, diagonally sliced and
blanched for 1 minute

½ cucumber, cut into matchsticks

3 celery stalks, cut into matchsticks

5 spring onions, diagonally sliced

large handful of Thai sweet basil leaves,
or basil

large handful of chopped mint leaves

8 tablespoons lime juice

3 tablespoons light soy sauce

3 red chillies, finely chopped

2 garlic cloves, crushed

2 tablespoons chopped palm sugar
or honey

4 Chinese leaves, thinly sliced

For the garnish

5oz/150g bean sprouts

2 heaped tablespoons peanuts,
finely chopped

1 tablespoon sesame seeds,
dry roasted until brown

handful of chopped coriander leaves

Toast the tofu in an oil-free frying pan until brown on each side and set to one side.

Place the noodles in a bowl of boiling water for 10 minutes, and as they become pliable spread them out and cut into thirds with a pair of cooking scissors. Drain in a colander and rinse with cold water, place in a bowl and combine with the blanched wing beans or flat green beans, cucumber, celery, spring onions, basil and mint. In a separate bowl, mix the lime juice, soy sauce, chillies, garlic and palm sugar or honey until dissolved, pour over the noodles and mix well.

Serve individually on a bed of sliced Chinese leaves, topped with the noodles and garnished with the bean sprouts, chopped peanuts, sesame seeds, coriander and tofu slices.

STIR-FRIED VEGETABLES WITH GREEN PEPPERCORNS AND SHITAKE MUSHROOMS

Green peppercorns are young peppercorns; they are sold on their stems and available from good supermarkets or Asian stores. We use dried shitake mushrooms; however, you can use fresh instead if it's easier — just double the quantity.

4 tablespoons sunflower oil

3 large red chillies, sliced diagonally

6 spring onions, sliced diagonally

10 strings green peppercorns, broken in half

4oz/115g dried shitake mushrooms, soaked in hot water for 30 minutes and then sliced

9oz/250g fine green beans, cut in half

9oz/250g baby sweet corn, sliced lengthways

12oz/350g cauliflower florets

3 tablespoons dark soy sauce

1 tablespoon chopped palm sugar or honey

14fl oz/425ml vegetable stock

2 large handfuls of Thai sweet basil leaves, or basil

salt to taste

coriander leaves, to garnish

For the spice paste

4 dried red chillies, soaked in water until soft

4 garlic cloves, chopped

1 lemon grass stalk, sliced

3 shallots, sliced

4 coriander roots, chopped

1 teaspoon grated kaffir lime zest

½in/1cm galangal, grated

½ teaspoon coarsely ground black peppercorns

Blend the ingredients for the spice paste in a food processor until smooth.

Heat the oil in a wok. When hot, add the spice paste and sauté for a couple of minutes; then add the sliced large red chillies, spring onions and green peppercorns, stir into the paste and fry for 3 minutes. Add the mushrooms, green beans, baby sweet corn and cauliflower, and fry, stirring constantly until the vegetables start to soften. Then add the soy sauce, palm sugar or honey and vegetable stock. Cover the wok and simmer until the vegetables are just soft.

Add the basil and salt to taste, and serve with rice and Tofu with Crispy Fried Basil and Chilli Sauce (page 260).

Stir-fried Vegetables with Green Peppercorns and Shitake Mushrooms

TEMPEH AND SHITAKE RICE PAPER ROLLS v

2 tablespoons sunflower oil

2 garlic cloves, thinly sliced

2in/5cm piece of ginger, peeled and
cut into thin strips

3 large mild red chillies, cut into long
thin strips

1 teaspoon chopped coriander root

½ teaspoon coarsely ground
black peppercorns

2oz/60g dried shitake mushrooms,
soaked in boiling water for ½ hour
and then sliced

3oz/90g tempeh, cut into
large matchsticks

4 kaffir lime leaves, cut into
thin strips

4 spring onions, shredded

small handful of chopped mint leaves

handful of bean sprouts

2 tablespoons lime juice

2 tablespoons light soy sauce

12 rice paper wrappers

Heat the oil in a wok. When hot, add the garlic, ginger, chillies, coriander root
and black peppercorns, and fry until brown. Add the sliced shitake mushrooms,
tempeh and lime leaves, and fry until the tempeh is crunchy and the mushrooms
are browned. Turn out into a bowl and allow to cool; then stir in the spring
onions, mint leaves, bean sprouts, lime juice and soy sauce.

Soak a rice paper wrapper in a bowl of hot water until soft, remove and dry
with kitchen paper. Place a twelfth of the filling down the centre, fold one end
over and roll. Repeat until you have used up all the sheets.

Serve with Sweet and Sour Dipping Sauce (below).

SWEET AND SOUR DIPPING SAUCE v

6 tablespoons rice wine vinegar

4 tablespoons brown sugar

1 tablespoon lime juice

1 red chilli, finely chopped

1 green chilli, finely chopped

salt to taste

Gently heat the rice wine vinegar and sugar until the sugar is dissolved, and allow
to cool. Stir in the remaining ingredients.

Rice paper wrappers,
available dried from
Asian stores, are used to
roll the tempeh and
shitake mushroom filling.
The rolls are then served
with a spicy sweet and
sour dipping sauce.

Right Tempeh
and Shitake Rice
Paper Rolls
Below Ingredients for
Tempeh and Shitake
Rice Paper Rolls

VEGETABLES IN A LEMON GRASS AND HERB-SCENTED BROTH

Fresh vegetables and dried mushrooms are combined in a tasty broth made with a curry paste packed with typical Thai flavours of lemon grass and galangal. The end result is a vegetarian version of an Oriental bisque.

For the curry paste
4 dried red chillies soaked in water
    until soft and then drained
2 lemon grass stalks, finely sliced
1 tablespoon finely chopped galangal
1 tablespoon chopped garlic
1½ oz/40g shallots, sliced
1 tablespoon ground turmeric

For the broth
2 pints/1.25 litres vegetable stock
½ oz/15g dried black fungus
    mushrooms or cloud ears, soaked
    in boiling water for 15 minutes
6oz/175g baby sweet corn,
    sliced lengthways

4oz/115g thin asparagus, cut into
    2in/5cm lengths
8oz/225g pak choi, cut into ¼in/1cm
    slices lengthways
8oz/225g bean sprouts
2 teaspoons chopped palm sugar
    or honey
3 tablespoons dark soy sauce
2 tablespoons lime juice
6 kaffir lime leaves, finely sliced
large handful of Thai sweet basil leaves,
    or basil
large handful of chopped coriander
    leaves
salt to taste

Make the curry paste by blending the ingredients in a food processor until smooth.

Heat the vegetable stock in a pan, and add the curry paste, drained black fungus, baby sweet corn and asparagus. Cover the pan and simmer until the vegetables are *al dente*. Add the pak choi, bean sprouts, palm sugar or honey, soy sauce, lime juice, lime leaves, basil and coriander leaves, simmer for a further minute and add salt to taste. Serve immediately.

CRISP VEGETABLE AND COCONUT SALAD

For this dish, fresh coconut is toasted and mixed with a crunchy salad. If you cannot get a fresh coconut, you can use desiccated coconut instead.

½ a small fresh coconut, finely grated, or 4 heaped tablespoons desiccated coconut
7oz/200g bean sprouts
½ medium cucumber, cut into matchsticks
7oz/200g sugar snap peas, sliced diagonally
5 spring onions, finely sliced

handful of chopped coriander leaves
handful of finely chopped Asian mint leaves
4 red chillies, finely chopped

For the dressing
3 tablespoons lime juice
3 tablespoons light soy sauce
1 dessertspoon honey

Toast the finely grated coconut or dessicated coconut in a small frying pan until golden, set to one side and allow to cool.

Combine the bean sprouts, cucumber, sugar snap peas, spring onions, coconut, coriander, mint and red chillies in a bowl. Mix the dressing ingredients, pour over the salad and mix well.

Allow the flavours to combine for 15 minutes before serving.

SAMBAL SAUCE

Sambal, a spicy sauce, usually accompanies every meal in Malaysia.

2 red chillies, finely chopped
1 tablespoon dark soy sauce
1 teaspoon tamarind paste
1 tablespoon lime juice

2 teaspoons honey
4 shallots, finely chopped
1 tomato, finely chopped

Blend all the ingredients in a food processor until finely chopped but not too smooth.

The Petronas towers of Kuala Lumpur at night

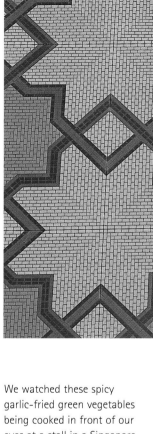

SPICY GARLIC-FRIED GREEN VEGETABLES

Black bean paste is available at most supermarkets or oriental stores; if you can't find it, simply use finely chopped salted black beans.

SERVES 4–6

4 tablespoons sunflower oil
8 shallots or 2 red onions,
    thinly sliced
4 garlic cloves, sliced
4 red chillies, thinly sliced
4 small courgettes, cut into
    fat matchsticks
150g/5oz okra, cut in half
    lengthwise
200g/7oz sugar snap peas

1 small head of Chinese leaves,
    cut into 2.5cm/1in slices
250g/9oz spinach, shredded
2 tablespoons black bean paste (or
    1 tablespoon salted black beans,
    finely chopped and mixed with
    1 tablespoon water)
2 tablespoons brown sugar or honey
2 tablespoons dark soy sauce

Heat the oil in a wok and, when hot, stir-fry the shallots or onions, garlic and chillies.

Add the courgettes, okra, sugar snap peas and Chinese leaves, stirring constantly. When the vegetables start to soften, throw in the spinach and when it starts to wilt add the black bean paste or chopped salted black beans, the brown sugar or honey and the soy sauce. Stir well.

Finally add 5 tablespoons of water to help soften the vegetables and fry until all the ingredients are well combined. Serve immediately.

We watched these spicy garlic-fried green vegetables being cooked in front of our eyes at a stall in a Singapore food market. As with most stir-fries, the recipe relies on a hot wok and all the ingredients being at hand ready to throw in. It can be served as a side-dish or as a full meal.

The view down from
the minaret on to the
geometrically patterned
floor of a mosque in
Bandar Seri Begawan,
the capital of Brunei

MALAYSIAN FRUIT AND VEGETABLE SALAD

SERVES 4–6

1 small firm mango, peeled and cubed

1 firm pear, cored and cubed

½ pineapple, peeled, cored and cubed

2 carrots, cubed

125g/4oz beansprouts

1 red pepper, deseeded and cut into
    thin slices

1 tablespoon crushed roasted skinned
    peanuts, for garnish

handful of coriander leaves, chopped,
    for garnish

For the dressing

2 tablespoons light soy sauce

2 teaspoons honey or brown sugar

1 red chilli, finely chopped

1 tablespoon tamarind paste

juice of 1 lime

Combine all the vegetable and fruit salad ingredients in a salad bowl.

Make the dressing by simply combining all the ingredients with 2 tablespoons
of water until the sugar has dissolved.

Pour the dressing over the salad and sprinkle with crushed peanuts and
chopped coriander leaves to serve.

MALAY SAMBAL

SERVES 4–6

2 small red onions, roughly chopped

4 garlic cloves

4 red chillies

45g/1½oz ground almonds

2 lemon grass stalks, thinly sliced

5cm/2in cube of galangal or root
 ginger, peeled and chopped

400g/14oz tomatoes,
 roughly chopped

4 tablespoons sunflower oil

2 medium sweet potatoes, cubed

4 carrots, cut into matchsticks

½ small white cabbage,
 finely shredded

200g/7oz baby sweetcorn,
 halved lengthwise

bunch of spring onions, cut into
 2.5cm/1in strips

4 kaffir lime leaves, rolled up and
 thinly sliced

200ml/7fl oz coconut milk

1 generous dessertspoon sugar
 or honey

juice of 1 lime

salt

For the garnish

125g/4oz beansprouts

⅓ cucumber, grated

2 red chillies, thinly sliced lengthwise

handful of coriander leaves, chopped

good shake of soy sauce

juice of 1 lime

60g/2oz crushed roast peanuts

The island of Tioman on Malaysia's east coast can be reached by fishing boat from Mersing. From the jetty a footpath climbs into the rain-forest, past giant monitor lizards and waterfalls, over a ridge, then steeply down to the refreshingly clear water of the South China Sea at Kampung Juara. We stayed here, sleeping a few metres from the sea in a simple A-frame hut and eating each day in one of the two beach cafés, where we discovered the Malay sambal dish that we describe here.

In a food processor, blend the red onion, garlic, chillies, ground almonds, lemon grass, galangal and tomatoes. Set aside.

Heat the sunflower oil in a wok and, when hot, fry the sweet potato until it starts to brown. Add the carrots and fry for a few minutes. Then add the cabbage and fry until it starts to wilt.

Add the corn and spring onions with the lime leaves and the spice/tomato mixture. Stir until the vegetables are coated. Add enough water to make a thickish sauce and gently simmer until the vegetables are just soft but retain some bite.

Add the coconut milk, sugar and lime juice, with salt to taste. Simmer for a further minute or two. The sambal is now ready to serve.

Garnish with the mixed beansprouts, cucumber, chilli, coriander, soy sauce, lime juice and crushed peanuts. Serve with rice.

KUCHING TAMARIND AND COCONUT MILK CURRY v

This curry, which is very popular across southern Malaysia and Kuching, works particularly well with noodles.

SERVES 4–6

1 red onion or 6 shallots,
   roughly chopped
3 garlic cloves
4 red chillies
2 teaspoons tamarind paste
1 tablespoon dark soy sauce
scant ½ teaspoon ground turmeric
4 tablespoons sunflower oil
6 baby aubergines, cut into quarters
salt
½ small white cabbage,
   finely shredded

1 large red pepper, thinly sliced
300g/10oz pak choy,
   roughly broken up
400ml/14fl oz coconut milk
200g/7oz beansprouts

To garnish
2 shallots, thinly sliced
large handful of coriander leaves,
   chopped
2 red chillies, thinly sliced

Chinese lettering on a shop front in Malaysia

Whizz the onion, garlic, chilli, tamarind paste, soy sauce and turmeric in a food processor until they form a paste.

Heat the sunflower oil in a wok and, when hot, fry the baby aubergine, sprinkled with a little salt to prevent it from absorbing too much oil.

Add the flavouring paste and stir well until the aubergine is coated with it. Add the shredded cabbage and sliced red pepper, stirring constantly. Pour on some water to loosen the spices and make a sauce. Cook until the vegetables are tender but not too soft.

Add the pak choy, coconut milk and beansprouts. Simmer for a further 3 minutes, but do not allow to boil. If necessary, add salt to taste.

Serve in bowls with a generous garnish of thinly sliced shallots, chopped coriander leaves and thinly sliced red chillies.

BORNEO RAINFOREST VEGETABLES v

SERVES 4–6

1 teaspoon ground coriander seeds
1 teaspoon crushed dried red chillies
1 teaspoon ground turmeric
2 teaspoons ground almonds
1 large onion
4 garlic cloves
3 tablespoons sunflower oil
300g/10oz tempeh, cut into strips
3 tablespoons cashew nuts
1 lemon grass stalk, cut into short
    lengths and bruised
5cm/2in piece of galangal, chopped
    and bruised

200g/7oz baby sweetcorn,
    halved lengthwise
200g/7oz cauliflower florets
200g/7oz green beans,
    cut in half lengthwise
1 can (400g/14oz) of coconut milk
1 tablespoon coconut milk powder,
    mixed to a paste with water

For the garnish
thin strips of fresh red chilli
coriander leaves
roasted peanuts

In a food processor, blend the coriander, chillies, turmeric, almonds, onion and garlic to a paste.

Heat the oil in a heavy pan and fry the tempeh and cashew nuts until they turn brown. Add the garlic paste, the lemon grass and the galangal, and cook for 2 minutes.

Add all the vegetables and toss to coat in the paste. Add the coconut milk and simmer until the vegetables are soft.

Remove the lemon grass and galangal, and stir in the coconut milk paste to thicken.

Serve with rice, garnished with thin strips of fresh red chilli, coriander leaves and roasted peanuts.

One of the most pleasant surprises during my stay at the Batu Apoi Forest Reserve in Brunei was the presence of two excellent and entertaining Indonesian cooks; another was the location of an Iban 'short house' on the edge of the camp to accommodate the Iban guides and porters. Between cooking and language lessons and Iban hospitality there was never a dull evening. By day the rainforest, awesome in its scale and mystery, provided countless photographic delights and an unparalleled feeling of disregard for anything that might exist beyond it. This tempeh and cashew-nut dish that I ate there is one of the best reminders of that time.

**Borneo Rainforest
Vegetables**

BALINESE GADO GADO

SERVES 4—6

3 carrots, cut into matchstick strips
200g/7oz beansprouts
125g/4oz fine green beans
125g/4oz sugar snap peas
½ cucumber, cut into thickish matchstick strips
1 small head of Chinese leaves, thinly sliced

For the peanut sauce
1 large red onion, coarsely chopped
3 garlic cloves
3 fresh red chillies
175g/6oz skinned peanuts
2 tablespoons sunflower oil
1 tablespoon soy sauce
1 dessertspoon tamarind paste, dissolved in 2 tablespoons water

150ml/¼ pint coconut milk
1 tablespoon smooth peanut butter
1 dessertspoon brown sugar
2 lemon grass stalks, cut down the middle and bashed with a rolling pin
salt

For the garnish
4 hard-boiled eggs, cut into wedges
4 tomatoes, cut into wedges
200g/7oz tempeh, cut into strips and fried (if not available use 1cm/½in slices of deep-fried tofu, fried until crunchy)
large handful of spinach, shredded
1 large onion, dry-fried (page 277)
handful of coriander leaves, chopped

First make the sauce: blend the onion, garlic and chillies in a food processor until they form a paste. Gently dry-roast the peanuts in a pan, stirring to avoid burning. Allow to cool, and crush them in a food processor until finely ground. Heat the oil in a wok. When hot, add the onion paste and fry, stirring constantly, for a minute. Add the ground peanuts and stir until all the ingredients are combined. Add the soy sauce, tamarind, coconut milk, peanut butter, sugar and lemon grass. Gently cook until all the flavours are combined and a thickish sauce has formed (add a little water if necessary). Finally, take out the lemon grass and season with salt to taste.

Combine all the salad ingredients (you can serve this dish either in individual portions or in one big bowl). Pour the warm sauce over the salad, then arrange the egg, tomato, tempeh or tofu around the edge and pile the spinach and dry-fried onions in the centre. Sprinkle with coriander leaves.

Balinese Gado Gado

TEMPEH GORENG AND BEANSPROUTS V

SERVES 4–6

4 garlic cloves, crushed

1 teaspoon ground coriander seeds

225g/8oz tempeh, cut into
chunky sticks

4 tablespoons sunflower oil

200g/7oz beansprouts

3 tablespoons soy sauce

Mix the crushed garlic and coriander with 2 tablespoons water to make a paste.

Fry the tempeh sticks in the oil until brown, moving them around gently. Then add the garlic paste. After 30 seconds, add the beansprouts. Mix well, add the soy sauce and serve.

Tempeh goreng is real bus-station food. In Bali, even in small towns, bus stations encourage fast-food street stalls. At night they are entertaining, even romantic places to eat, all lit up and full of animated bustle. By day, however, the illusion is swiftly shattered by the number of flies and the state of the kitchens.

Left The spectacularly located Than Lot shore temple in Bali
Right A typical Malaysian food stall in a Penang street

The thin, spicy sauces known as sambals form part of most meals in Malaysia and Indonesia.

Usually a table will be laid with sambals and a variety of other accompaniments, all served in small dishes. We list a few suggestions here:
Dry-fried onions (thinly sliced and gently fried in a hot dry pan until brown)
Thinly sliced red onions
Sliced chillies
Sliced spring onions
Crushed roasted peanuts
Prawn crackers
Sliced cucumber
Grated coconut
Tempeh, broken up into individual grains, then fried in oil until brown.

MALAYSIAN SAMBAL

SERVES 4–6

2 green chillies, finely chopped
2 red chillies, finely chopped
2 spring onions, finely chopped
½ teaspoon salt

juice of 1 lime
2 teaspoons honey or brown sugar
1 tablespoon cider vinegar

Mix all the ingredients together and allow to stand for 15 minutes before serving.

INDONESIAN SAMBAL

SERVES 4–6

2 garlic cloves, very finely chopped
2 red chillies, finely chopped
juice of ½ lime

1 teaspoon sugar or honey
2 tablespoons dark soy sauce

Mix all the ingredients together and allow to stand for 15 minutes before serving.

THE STRAIT OF MALACCA

The settlements at either end of the Strait of Malacca have both played an important role in the history of the Asian spice routes. At the northern end is Malacca itself, now known as Melaka, which was once the most strategically important port in the international spice trade between east and west. Today it is a small provincial town of little significance to the rest of the world. At the southern end is Singapore, a pirate- and malaria-infested swamp town during Malacca's heyday, which is now one of the most powerful and wealthy ports in the world.

The Strait offers the fastest sea route between the South China Sea and the Indian Ocean. Early spice traders from China, India, Siam and Indonesia all used it as a regular route between sources and markets. The port stood conveniently halfway between China and India, and the Strait linked the Spice Islands with the Malabar Coast of India.

Malacca was more than just a wealthy port. Founded in 1400 by the Sumatran Hindu prince Paramesvara, it became a powerful trading state and home to a large expatriate Chinese community. Islam came to Malacca from the Middle East, via Gujurati spice merchants, and the port was soon the centre of Islam in Southeast Asia.

Afonso d'Albuquerque's Portuguese fleet sailed into the Strait in 1511, seeking the first European trade route to the sources of nutmeg and cloves. Malacca was conquered and occupied by Portugal for a hundred years. The Portuguese language was established among the resulting Eurasian population, but attempts to spread Catholicism mostly failed and led to a boycott of Malacca by Muslim sailors. The decline in Malacca's importance was reversed when the Protestant Dutch ousted the Portuguese and concentrated on incorporating the port into their Southeast Asian empire.

During the Napoleonic Wars in Europe, Britain stepped in to protect the Dutch territories from French occupation. Following the French defeat, the British, not wanting a return to Dutch domination of the spice trade in the region, negotiated the ceding of Malacca to their own crown. The key player in these 1824 negotiations was Sir Stamford Raffles, who had established a free port on the island of Singapore the previous year, giving Britain control of both ends of the Strait. Malacca and Singapore, together with Penang to the north, became known as the Straits Settlements. They became key ports in the British trade of Indian opium to China and Chinese tea to Europe. Penang and Singapore attracted huge migrant populations of Cantonese and

The Strait at sunset. These waters are the gateway to the Far East

Hakkas from China and Tamils from India, but Malacca was soon the least significant of the three ports.

Singapore's boom followed the opening of the Suez Canal in 1869, when it became an important stopover between London and the Far East. By the time Singapore was declared an independent country in 1965, the expatriate Chinese dominated Singapore, bringing their cuisine and spices with them. Singapore remained a free port and prospered, and by the 1970s it was the richest country in Asia after Japan.

Architecture in Melaka today is similar to that of Singapore, dominated by high-rise glass, steel and concrete. The old town, however, still has remnants of a more colourful past, including the Dutch church

Eating out is a serious part of daily life. The easiest and cheapest way to enjoy Chinese food is at one of the Hawkers' Centres, where dozens of stalls provide steaming dishes of fresh food with a flurry of chopping and sizzling woks.

Today, old Melaka is a romantic and atmospheric enclave of crumbling colonial Dutch and Portuguese churches and streets of migrant Chinese merchant houses. We found the 'devil's curry' featured below in a café along Medan Portugis.

MELAKAN DEVIL'S MUSHROOM CURRY v

This recipe has a sixteenth-century Portuguese origin. Aubergines, Asian mushrooms and water chestnuts are combined with Indian and Southeast Asian spices to produce a robust dish.

SERVES 4

4 tablespoons sunflower oil

1 heaped teaspoon black mustard seeds

1 heaped teaspoon fenugreek seeds

2 large red onions, finely chopped

3 garlic cloves, finely chopped

5cm/2in piece of ginger,
    cut into strips

6 red chillies, finely sliced

225g/8oz baby aubergine,
    cut in half lengthwise

salt to taste

200g/7oz shiitake mushrooms,
    cut into quarters

200g/7oz oyster mushrooms,
    thickly sliced

115g/4oz water chestnuts

8 ground candlenuts or macadamia
    nuts or cashew nuts

1 teaspoon ground turmeric

2.5cm/1in piece galangal, grated

2 lemon grass stalks, finely sliced

300ml/10fl oz vegetable stock

1 tablespoon dark soya sauce

175g/6oz bean sprouts

handful chopped coriander leaves

Mace is the red cage that encases the nutmeg kernel. It is native to just a few islands of Indonesia

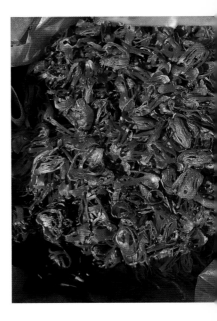

In a large saucepan, heat the oil and add the mustard seeds and fenugreek seeds. When they crackle, add the onion, garlic, ginger and chillies, and fry until they start to soften. Add the baby aubergine, sprinkle with a litle salt to prevent from drying, and fry until golden brown, stirring regularly.

Add the shiitake and oyster mushrooms and fry for a further few minutes. Add the water chestnuts, ground candlenuts, tumeric, grated galangal and lemon grass and fry for 30 seconds, stiring well. Add the vegetable stock and soya sauce, and bring to the boil. Cover the pan and simmer gently for 10 minutes with salt to taste.

Serve garnished with bean sprouts and coriander leaves.

MALACCAN LAKSA v

For the garnish
1lb 5oz/600g fresh laksa rice noodles
    or 10oz/300g dried thick
    rice vermicelli
12oz/350g deep-fried tofu,
    cut into ½in/1cm slices
½ cucumber, cut into matchsticks
9oz/250g bean sprouts
large handful of chopped
    coriander leaves
large handful of roughly chopped
    Asian mint leaves
6 spring onions, finely sliced

For the paste
2 tablespoons coriander seeds
1 level teaspoon ground turmeric
4 red chillies, roughly chopped
3 stalks of lemon grass, thinly sliced
thumb-sized piece of galangal,
    peeled and thinly sliced
2 garlic cloves
15 small shallots, peeled
5 candlenuts or 10 skinless almonds
2 tablespoons dark soy sauce

For the soup
3 tablespoons sunflower oil
28fl oz/800ml coconut milk
8fl oz/250ml water
8oz/225g sugar snap peas
7oz/200g fine green beans, cut in half
salt to taste

To prepare the garnish ingredients, first cook the laksa noodles. If you are using fresh noodles, plunge them in boiling water for a few minutes and then drain. If you are using dried, boil a saucepan of water and add the noodles, cook for 5 minutes until the noodles are soft, drain and rinse with cold water, and place in a bowl. Put the remaining garnish ingredients in bowls and place on the table.

Next make the paste. Dry roast the coriander seeds in a small frying pan until aromatic, remove from the pan and grind to powder. Combine with all the remaining paste ingredients and grind to a paste in a food processor.

Now make the soup. Heat the oil in a wok. When hot, stir in the paste mix and fry for a few minutes. Add the coconut milk and water, bring to the boil and then reduce the heat and gently simmer for 5 minutes. Add the sugar snap peas, fine green beans and salt to taste, and cook for a couple of minutes.

Take the wok to the table. Put some of the noodles into your bowl, add the garnish ingredients you like the look of, and then ladle the soup over them.

Laksa is a meal in a bowl. It is bought from street stalls and eaten as a mid-morning snack, and it is also a very sociable meal to serve for friends: the garnish ingredients are placed in the middle of the table so that people can help themselves and the thick spicy coconut soup is poured over the top. *Laksa* noodles are made of rice and look like thick spaghetti. They are available from Asian food stores; however, you could substitute them with thick rice vermicelli.

Malaccan Laksa

French Polynesia

French Polynesia

As soon as we arrived, we had an overwhelming feeling that we were in a good place. Nuka Hiva, the largest of the French Polynesian Marquesas Islands, right out in the middle of the vastness of the Pacific Ocean, is one of the most hospitable, beautiful destinations we have visited. Hidden in the tropical vegetation and dramatic mountainous landscape are many ancient sites, such as Koueva, a vast clearing with ancient stone platforms, sacrificial altars and statues overgrown with creepers and vines. Tourism is still a novelty.

The drive to Taiohae was a wonderful introduction to the island. We climbed up a track through pine forests and ravines to a pass between jagged mountain peaks. Ahead mountains stretched like a massive amphitheatre around the Toovii plateau. Once across the plain, we descended through a landscape of towering round-topped hills in forested valleys reminiscent of a Chinese scroll painting. Then a great vista revealed a scattering of buildings around a bay of blue water dotted with yachts.

Taiohae is an easy-going town, spread out along the beach. Everyone knows each other and they soon get to know you. Traditional sculpture, carving and tattooing are still part of everyday life. Invitations to people's homes to see these activities come easily, blissfully free of any hard sell. Many of the men of Nuka Hiva have heavily tattooed muscular bodies yet avoid being intimidating by wearing flowers in their hair and offering broad smiles at every meeting. Many of the women share their good looks and confidence. It was the natural beauty of the Marquesas and their people that attracted Paul Gauguin to make his final home on neighbouring Hiva Oa.

We set off east over the mountains to the lush river valley of Taipivai, which leads up to a high pass, looking down on waterfalls cascading out of the forest on one side and the sandy bay of Hatiheu on the other. Inland from the north shore are two archaeological sites, larger and even more atmospheric than Koueva: Hikokua and Kamuihei, where there are extensive remains of temples, pyramid altars, platforms, tikis and pits used to fatten up sacrificial victims for cannibal feasts. In the past warring tribes practised cannibalism as a symbol of victory.

We had a much more palatable introduction to traditional cuisine at a beachside café. Chez Yvonne served us a Marquesan feast of coconut and sweet potato soup, then an *ahimaa* of breadfruits, sweet potatoes and plantains accompanied by various salads. We took a very necessary rest after this on the beautiful white sand beach at Anaho Bay. Like the food, we found that the beauty of Nuka Hiva is both more delicate and dramatic than the more obvious charms of Tahiti, Bora Bora and Rangiroa. It was well worth the extra effort needed to get there.

Pages 284–285 **Hatiheu Bay on Nuku Hiva, one of the Marquesas Islands**

Right, clockwise from top right **Leg tattoo on Nuku Hiva warrior; a tiki statue; a young would-be warrior at Taiohae; the church at Hatiheu; a Polynesian girl in Taipivai; the Tohua Koueva ruins of Pakoko's jungle capital on Nuku Hiva**

This dish takes its name from the Polynesian style of cooking food in an *ahimaa*. This is a hole dug in the ground and lined with kindling and stones. The kindling is lit and banana leaves are placed on top of the stones. Food is placed on the leaves – usually a suckling pig, fish or vegetables. The hole is then covered with leaves and sand and the food allowed to cook for several hours. Today this time-consuming method is frequently replaced by marinating ingredients and cooking them on a barbecue.

The marinade is a traditional one, using the tropical French spice mix *quatre épices*, a mixture of black pepper, nutmeg, ginger and clove. We think this works well with tempeh (fermented soya bean curd), which is available from health food or Asian stores; however, if you find it hard to buy, tofu or vegetables work as well.

Polynesian Maa Tahiti Tempeh with Sweet Peppers and Haricot Beans

POLYNESIAN MAA TAHITI TEMPEH

1lb/450g tempeh, cut into
    ½ in/1cm slices

For the marinade
1 medium onion, chopped
2 garlic cloves, chopped
1 tablespoon olive oil
2 tablespoons thick coconut milk
grated zest of 1 lime

2 tablespoons lime juice
1 dessertspoon honey
1 teaspoon coarsely ground
    black peppercorns
½ teaspoon ground cloves
½ teaspoon grated nutmeg
1 teaspoon ground ginger
½ teaspoon cayenne pepper
salt to taste

Blend all the marinade ingredients until smooth and then coat the tempeh with the marinade and allow to stand for 1 hour. You can then cook the tempeh under the grill, on a griddle, in the oven or on a barbeque – take your pick.

Serve with Sweet Peppers and Haricot Beans (below), green salad and freshly baked baguette.

SWEET PEPPERS AND HARICOT BEANS

4 tablespoons butter
2 medium onions, cubed
3 garlic cloves, finely chopped
2 red peppers, sliced
1 teaspoon ground cinnamon
½ teaspoon cracked black peppercorns
½ teaspoon cayenne pepper

5 medium tomatoes, chopped
1lb/450g cooked haricot beans
4fl oz/125ml white wine
1 tablespoon chopped sage leaves
1 handful chopped parsley
salt to taste

Melt the butter in a thick-bottomed pan, add the onions, garlic and red peppers, and sauté until soft. Stir in the spices and cook for 1 minute. Add the chopped tomatoes, haricot beans, white wine and herbs, and bring to the boil; then cover the pan, reduce the heat and gently simmer until the sauce reduces and the oil returns.

Season to taste and serve with Polynesian Maa Tahiti Tempeh (above), green salad and freshly baked baguette.

COCONUT AND SWEET POTATO SOUP

3 tablespoons butter
2 medium onions, diced
2 garlic cloves, finely chopped
1½lb/750g sweet potato
½ teaspoon ground cinnamon
½ teaspoon coarsely ground
    black peppercorns
½ teaspoon grated nutmeg

½ teaspoon ground cloves
½–1 teaspoon cayenne pepper
1½ pints/750ml vegetable stock
½ pint/250ml coconut milk
salt to taste
handful of chopped coriander leaves,
    to garnish

Melt the butter in a saucepan, add the onions and garlic, and sauté until soft. Add the sweet potato and fry until it starts to soften. Stir in the spices and fry for 1 minute. Add the stock and bring to the boil; then reduce the heat, cover the pan and simmer until the sweet potato is soft. Add the coconut milk and simmer for 5 minutes or so. Blend the soup until smooth. Return it to the heat and gently heat until hot enough to serve, adding extra water if necessary.

Add salt to taste and serve garnished with chopped coriander leaves and warm baguette.

Above Taiohae Bay on Nuku Hiva; *right* Bora Bora lagoon in the Society Islands

POLYNESIAN SALAD WITH COCONUT MILK DRESSING

3 medium carrots, grated
2 red peppers, diced
3 medium tomatoes, diced
1 tablespoon sunflower oil
1 plantain, peeled and sliced into oval
   shapes ¾ in/2cm thick
1 medium red onion, diced
4 large free-range eggs, hard-boiled
   and then crushed

For the dressing
2 garlic cloves, crushed
juice of 2 limes
3½ fl oz/115ml coconut milk
1 teaspoon red wine vinegar
1 teaspoon coarsely ground
   black peppercorns
handful of parsley, finely chopped
Tabasco to taste
salt to taste

Combine the grated carrots, red peppers and tomatoes in a bowl.

To make the dressing, mix the garlic, lime juice, coconut milk, red wine vinegar, black pepper, parsley, Tabasco and salt to taste.

Heat the oil in a frying pan. When hot, fry the plantain until it begins to brown on the outside and soften. Pour the dressing over the salad and top with the fried plantain, red onion and crushed egg.

BAKED PAPAYA AND BANANA POE v

We ate this dish, accompanied by Polynesian Salad with Coconut Milk Dressing (above), as a communal meal with all the other guests at a simple pension on Rangiroa Island on our way to Nuku Hiva. Together the two dishes make a good outdoor meal for a summer evening.

2 medium papayas, peeled, deseeded
   and cut into cubes
2 medium plantains, peeled
   and cubed
cayenne pepper, to taste

½ teaspoon coarsely ground
   black peppercorns
1 vanilla pod, split down the middle
salt to taste
4fl oz/125ml coconut milk

Place all the ingredients except the coconut milk in baking foil and fold to make a sealed parcel. Bake in an oven, preheated to 400°F/200°C, for 25 minutes or so, until soft. Remove from the oven, open the parcel and sprinkle the coconut milk over the top. Reseal and allow to sit for 10 minutes before serving.

Left **The interior of Nuku Hiva**
Above **A Tiki statue on Hiva Oa**

Central &

Southern America

MEXICO

The cuisine of modern Mexico is dominated by indigenous ingredients. Hundreds of chilli varieties provide a great range of colours, tastes and shapes, and are included in almost every Mexican meal, either as a main ingredient or in a salsa. They come stuffed, fresh, dried, sliced as a garnish, fried in batter, smoked and pickled. Some are ferocious and others so tame they are sweet; not all Mexican food need be hot but some is, extremely. The tomato is equally ubiquitous, both as the main ingredient of the salsas that accompany every meal and as a common component of soups, sauces, stews and salads.

Corn (maize) is the daily staple, soaked, dried and ground into flour to make toasted tortillas; wrapped, as a dough mixed with spices and meat or vegetables, in a banana leaf and steamed as tamales; fried into corn chips, or sometimes just eaten off the cob. Beans are boiled and mashed then fried with spices to make refries. Avocados are puréed into guacamole, chocolate into mole sauce and peanuts ground into butter. Vanilla and pecan nuts are baked into pies and puddings.

Many of Mexico's earliest European settlers were Andalucians from southern Spain, and many of the imported ingredients used are a legacy of the Arab Moors' 700-year residence in that area. Rice is served steamed as a side dish or mixed with beans. Limes make regular appearances in salsas as well as in guacamole and in one of Mexico's favourite drinks, margarita. Olives, olive oil, oregano, saffron, garlic and cheese are also found in Mexican recipes. Coriander, originally from the eastern Mediterranean, has become the most used spice after chilli, finding its way into salsas, soups and stews. Cheese became popular with the introduction of Spanish domestic cattle. *Queso anejo* resembles parmesan, and a stringy style of cheese made in Oaxaca is similar to mozzarella.

Mexicans love to eat out and cities are full of cafés and restaurants serving fine food, often with live musicians. Main plazas are usually lined with alfresco eating places and there is always plenty of cheap and often good street food down the alleys.

There are lots of regional variations in Mexican cooking, so travelling round the country is never dull in terms of eating out. Two of the best dishes we discovered were the nutty stuffed *chillies en nogada* –

Pages 294–295 **The Pan–American Highway making its way north along the Pacific coast of Peru**

Left **Straw hats in a Oaxaca market**

freshened with tangy pomegranate seeds – from the cool colonial hill town of Puebla, and a barbecue of marinaded giant Caribbean prawns with a spicy orange, coriander and olive sauce which we had on the steamy Yucatan coast.

CHILLIES EN NOGADA

This recipe is traditionally associated with the Central Mexican city of Puebla, although versions of it turn up all over Latin America. Fist-sized mild green poblana peppers are ideal for stuffing, but any good-sized red or green pepper is suitable. The stuffing is a delicious creamy, nutty, spicy concoction, finished off perfectly by the pomegranate seeds.

SERVES 4

8 poblana peppers or similar
2 tablespoons sunflower oil
1 large onion, finely chopped
2 garlic cloves, finely chopped
1 jalapeño chilli, finely chopped
30g/1oz almonds, finely chopped
60g/2oz walnuts, finely chopped
75g/2½ oz raisins

2 celery sticks, cut into small cubes
4 medium tomatoes, cut into
    small cubes
salt and freshly ground black pepper
250ml/16fl oz double cream
4 tablespoons flat-leaf parsley,
    chopped
seeds of a pomegranate

Above **The unusual fruit of the cashew tree has a very short shelf life, so it needs to be eaten the day it is picked. The tree is more famous for its nuts, which like the chilli have been exported from the Americas to every corner of the planet** *Opposite* **Chillies en Nogada**

Remove the skins from the poblana peppers. To do this, roast them under a hot grill, turning frequently, until the skins blister. Place in a bowl and cover with clingfilm for 5 minutes. The skins should then peel off easily. Slice the peppers down one side and remove the seeds and veins.

Make the stuffing in a frying pan. Heat the oil and fry the onion, garlic and jalapeño chilli until soft and golden. Add the chopped nuts and raisins and fry for 1 minute, then add the celery and fry for another 2 minutes. Add the chopped tomato, half a teaspoon of black pepper and salt to taste. Gently cook until the moisture of the tomatoes has been absorbed.

Stuff the peppers with the nutty mixture and place in a heatproof dish. Combine the cream with 75ml/2½fl oz of water, the parsley, salt and black pepper to taste, and pour over the stuffed peppers.

Grill the peppers until the cream is hot and the peppers are browned. Serve sprinkled with the pomegranate seeds.

YUCATAN RECADO MARINADE V

This combination of marinade and sauce typical of Mexico's Yucatan Peninsula can be used with anything from vegetables and tofu to chicken and meat or fish. The ingredients of choice can be marinaded while the sauce is being made then cooked on a barbecue or grill and served sizzling hot with plenty of the spicy orange and olive sauce.

SERVES 4–6

2 medium red onions, sliced	4 tablespoons olive oil
6 garlic cloves with skins on	juice of two limes
9 whole allspice seeds	1 habañero chilli, seeded and
10 cloves	roughly chopped
2.5cm/1in piece of	2 teaspoons dried oregano
cinnamon stick	1 teaspoon salt
1½ teaspoons cumin seeds	1 heaped teaspoon ground
1½ teaspoons coriander seeds	black pepper

Under a pre-heated grill, heat the onion and garlic until brown and set to one side. In a small pan, dry-roast the whole spices until aromatic and grind to a powder. Place in a food processor with the roasted onion, garlic, olive oil, lime juice, chilli, oregano, salt and black pepper. Blend until smooth.

Coat chosen ingredients with half the blended marinade and leave for one hour. Keep the other half for use in the recado sauce recipe, right.

Chilli *(Capsicum spp.)*
Despite being the most recent spice to join international spice routes, chilli has become the superlative spice. Chillies are all originally native to Mexico and were cultivated more than six thousand years before Columbus arrived in the Caribbean looking for Indian pepper. Many different cultivars of chilli developed in different conditions, giving a huge variety of colours, size and strength. The Spanish and Portuguese introduced them to India and Southeast Asia in the sixteenth century and the popularity of chillies spread rapidly across the globe.

Today, chilli is the most cultivated spice in the world, with hundreds of varieties available. The hottest varieties tend to grow in the tropics and milder ones in temperate climates. Some of the hottest varieties are the Mexican 'Habañero', the Caribbean 'Early Scotch Bonnet', the Thai 'Bird's Eye', and the Indonesian 'Lombok'. A new cultivar has recently been developed in India that is so much hotter than all of these that its main use is in anti-attack pepper sprays.

The effect when eaten is to stimulate the palate, aid digestion, increase blood circulation and cause perspiration. This has a cooling effect on the body, which may be one reason why hotter chillies are popular in countries with tropical climates. However, many people – and not just in hot countries – derive an almost euphoric pleasure from eating the hottest chillies in their food. There is a theory that the brain releases endorphins to combat the irritation of hot chilli in the mouth and

Red chillies

stomach and that these induce mild states of euphoria. Once 'addicted' to the pleasure of chilli, larger quantities are needed to repeat the sensation. Strangely, however, it is by no means a universal passion and other people find the sensation thoroughly disagreeable.

Paprika is a mild capsicum that is dried and made into a powder with the seeds and membranes removed. It is popular in Hungary and most cuisines around the Mediterranean. Cayenne is another chilli used as a powder. It is considerably hotter when seeds and membrane are included.

Vanilla
(Vanilla planifolia)
Vanilla is a tropical orchid native to Mexico. Sun-dried for several months, the pod and tiny fragrant seeds produce an exotic and intense flavour that is now popular all over the world.

Early attempts to grow vanilla away from Mexico as a commercial spice failed, as pollination relies exclusively on a single species of hummingbird or on melipona bees, both of which are unique to Mexico. All vanilla had to be shipped from its source until the nineteenth century, when French botanists developed artificial methods of pollination on Indian Ocean islands. Today, Madagascar is a major producer, with smaller industries in the Comoro Islands, Réunion and the Seychelles.

Pure vanilla extract can be used instead of fresh pods, but avoid synthetic chemical substitutes.

Green chillies

YUCATAN RECADO SAUCE V

Serves 4–6

2 red peppers
1 yellow pepper
3 tablespoons olive oil
recado marinade (see left)
1lb/450g plum tomatoes, pulped in a blender until smooth

zest and juice of a large orange
about 30 green olives
2 handfuls of coriander leaves, chopped
ground black pepper
salt to taste

First remove the skins from the peppers. Roast them under a pre-heated grill, turning frequently, until blackened on all sides, then place them in a bowl, cover in clingfilm and leave for 5 minutes. The skins should peel away easily. Cut the peppers in half and remove the seeds and stalks, then thinly slice. Set to one side.

In a large frying pan, heat the oil and add the recado marinade, stirring constantly for 1 minute. Pour on the pulped tomatoes and simmer gently for 5 minutes. Next, add the peppers, orange zest and juice, olives and coriander, and simmer until the sauce reduces and the oil returns. Add black pepper and salt to taste.

Barbecue or grill the chosen ingredients and serve with the sauce on the side.

GUACAMOLE v

Smooth Guacamole
Serves 4–6

4 large ripe avocados (preferably Hass)
1 jalapeño chilli, roughly chopped
small handful of coriander leaves,
   chopped, plus more for garnish

juice of 1 lime
salt
tortilla chips, to serve

Halve the avocados and stone them. Scoop out the flesh and put it into a food processor. Add all the remaining ingredients and blend until smooth.

Serve garnished with chopped coriander leaves, accompanied by tortilla chips.

Chopped Guacamole
Serves 4–6

3 large ripe avocados (preferably Hass)
2 medium tomatoes, finely diced
1 small red onion, finely chopped
juice of 1 lime

salt
chopped coriander leaves,
   for garnish
tortilla chips, to serve

Peel and stone the avocados. Chop the flesh, place in a bowl and mush slightly with a fork. Now add all the remaining ingredients and mix well.

Serve garnished with chopped coriander leaves, accompanied by tortilla chips.

There are many different versions of guacamole, a delicious avocado salsa. It can be served smooth or with chopped avocado, so we've given you both options. You can serve it either as an appetizer or as an accompaniment.

Chopped Guacamole

This truly original dish combines chocolate and spices to make a rich, dark, savoury sauce. We were taught this recipe by a woman from Oaxaca market. She cooked everything on open fires in her courtyard, which her husband and sons also used as a mechanic's workshop. From tins and jars on shelves above dismantled engines and buckets of sump oil she produced the dried ingredients, which she blended with the chocolate and other items to create the mole. We thanked her so enthusiastically for her trouble that she invited us to join her and the grinning mechanics for lunch. As our cookery lesson had been conducted next to an evil-smelling pot containing a boiling pig's head we politely declined.

Oaxacan Mole

OAXACAN MOLE

It is best to use a chocolate with a high cocoa content.

SERVES 4–6

500g/1lb 2oz sweet potatoes, cut into 2.5cm/1in cubes
2 sweetcorn cobs, cut into 2.5cm/1in rounds
salt
4 tablespoons sunflower oil
2 plantains, peeled and cut into 1cm/½in rounds
1 red and 1 yellow pepper, deseeded and cut into 2.5cm/1in squares
125g/4oz green beans

For the mole sauce
30g/1oz roasted shelled peanuts
30g/1oz sesame seeds

30g/1oz pumpkin seeds
5cm/2in piece of cinnamon stick
60g/2oz ground almonds
1 level teaspoon ground allspice
½ teaspoon ground cloves
1 teaspoon dried thyme
1 level tablespoon dried oregano
1 onion, roughly chopped
3 garlic cloves
2 jalapeño chillies
60g/2oz raisins
1 medium banana, peeled and roughly chopped
3 tablespoons sunflower oil
300ml/½ pint stock
125g/4oz plain chocolate

First make the mole sauce: grind the peanuts, sesame seeds, pumpkin seeds and cinnamon in a food processor. Add the ground almonds, allspice, cloves, thyme and oregano, onion, garlic, chillies, raisins and banana. Blend to a thick paste.

Heat the sunflower oil in a large pan and, when hot, add the paste and fry for 2 minutes, stirring constantly. Slowly add the stock, stirring well.

Break up the chocolate and add to the sauce. Stir well until the chocolate has melted. Simmer gently for 10 minutes. The sauce will be quite thick.

Now prepare the vegetables: parboil the sweet potato and sweetcorn in boiling salted water for about 1–2 minutes. Drain well.

Heat the sunflower oil in a pan. When it is hot, add the plantains and fry until they start to brown. Add the sweet potato, sweetcorn and peppers, and fry until they all start to brown.

Stir the fried vegetables into the mole sauce, then add the green beans and 200ml/7fl oz water. Simmer gently for 10 minutes. Season with salt to taste.

REFRIED BEANS V

When cooking pulses it is important not to add salt until the end as salt stops the pulses from softening properly.

SERVES 4–6

425g/15oz pinto beans, soaked in
    water overnight
1 level tablespoon cumin seeds
1 level tablespoon coriander seeds

4 tablespoons sunflower oil
1 large onion, finely chopped
salt

Drain and rinse the beans. Place in a large saucepan with enough fresh water to cover. Bring to the boil. A foam will rise to the surface of the pan – simply scoop off and discard. Cover the pan and simmer until beans are nice and soft.

Meanwhile, dry-roast the cumin and coriander seeds in a hot frying pan for 1 minute, stirring constantly. Grind in a grinder or using a pestle and mortar. Set aside.

Heat the sunflower oil in a frying pan and, when hot, fry the onion gently until soft (but not brown or it becomes bitter). Add the ground spices and fry with the onion for 1 minute, stirring constantly.

Add the onion mixture to the pan of soft pinto beans. Remove from the heat and mash with a potato masher until the beans are broken down and viscous. If necessary, add more water to get a thick porridge-like consistency. Finally add salt to taste.

Beans are the staple of most Mexican meals. Refried beans are the most common and can be served with almost anything — the options are endless. They can be made with various beans, but pinto or black beans are the most common. We prefer to use pinto beans. In the café we would serve refried beans in a flour tortilla and as part of a mixed Mexican plate.

Above left A colourful Oaxacan street
Above Hats for sale in the town of Mérida

REFRIED BEANS WITH FLOUR TORTILLA

Serves 1

1 serving of Refried Beans (opposite)
1 soft flour tortilla
handful of grated mature Cheddar
    cheese
blob of sour cream

For the salad dressing
lime juice
olive oil

For the mixed salad
finely shredded lettuce
grated carrot
finely shredded red cabbage
finely shredded white cabbage
coriander leaves, chopped, to garnish

Reheat the refried beans. Combine all the salad ingredients and dress with the lime juice and olive oil. Sprinkle with the coriander.

Toast the soft flour tortilla on a hot griddle or in a hot dry frying pan until it starts to puff up. Turn and cover with grated cheese. When the cheese starts to melt, transfer to a plate dressed with the salad. Spoon the beans on the tortilla and fold it in half. Place a blob of sour cream on top and serve immediately.

MEXICAN PLATE WITH REFRIED BEANS

Serves 1

mixed salad as above
Fresh Tomato Salsa (page 310) or
    Salsa Ranchera (page 309)
Smooth Guacamole (page 302)
blob of sour cream

1 serving of Refried Beans (opposite)
handful of grated mature Cheddar
    cheese
coriander leaves, chopped, to garnish
tortilla chips, to serve

Arrange the salad over half of each plate and top it with servings of salsa, guacamole and sour cream. Cover the remaining side of the plate with refried beans and top these with grated Cheddar cheese.

Garnish with chopped coriander leaves and place lots of tortilla chips around the edge of the plate. Serve immediately.

CHAYOTE IN A CINNAMON-SPICED TOMATO SAUCE

The chayote or chow chow, a vegetable enjoyed right across Mexico, is now available in many supermarkets and specialist shops. Resembling a large green pear, it is similar to the marrow in texture. The seed in the middle is considered a delicacy so, when chopping the chayote, use it all. If you cannot find chayote, use marrow instead. When chayote is in season, we like to serve this dish garnished with courgette flowers lightly fried in butter together with mashed sweet potato to soak up the sauce.

SERVES 4–6

3 chayote, peeled with a potato peeler and chopped into cubes, or 675g/1½lb peeled and cubed marrow
5 baby courgettes, halved lengthwise
salt and pepper

For the tomato sauce
4 tablespoons olive oil
1 large onion, diced
3 garlic cloves, crushed
1 teaspoon ground cinnamon

¼ teaspoon ground cloves
1 tablespoon tomato purée
450g/1lb tomatoes, finely diced
handful of raisins
large handful of coriander leaves, chopped
2 jalapeño chillies, chopped

For the garnish (optional)
12 courgette flowers
butter, for frying

First make the tomato sauce: heat the olive oil in a saucepan and, when hot, fry the onion and garlic gently until soft. Stir the cinnamon and cloves into the onions, then add the tomato purée, diced tomatoes, raisins, chopped coriander and chillies, together with a little water to loosen the sauce. Simmer for 10 minutes.

Now prepare the vegetables: parboil the chayote or marrow and the courgettes in salted water until they start to soften. Drain and stir them into the sauce. Simmer gently for 15 minutes. Add salt and pepper to taste.

If courgette flowers are in season, gently fry them in butter until they start to brown. Season to taste.

Serve the dish garnished with the courgette flowers, if you have them, and accompanied by sweet potato mashed with olive oil and chopped fresh thyme.

On Saturdays the streets and alleyways around the *mercado* in Oaxaca fill with Zapotec Indians from the surrounding countryside selling their produce from the pavement. As well as everyday goods, there are numerous Indian crafts on sale, including hundreds of blankets and rugs woven with traditional geometric patterns and coloured with dyes such as cochineal and indigo.

Best of all, there's plenty of street food freshly prepared between the stalls to feed hungry shoppers. As well as lots of warm Oaxaqueño tortillas with various salsas, we ate a very good dish made with chayote, or chow chow, in a tomato, clove and cinnamon sauce spiced with jalapeños and garlic.

SALSA RANCHERA v

SERVES 4—6

1—2 tablespoons sunflower oil
1 red onion, finely chopped
1 garlic clove, crushed
1—2 jalapeño chillies, finely chopped

handful of fresh coriander, chopped
6 medium tomatoes, finely diced
salt

Heat the oil in a small pan and, when hot, fry onion and garlic until starting to soften. Stir in the chillies and coriander and cook for a further few seconds. Now add the chopped tomatoes and gently simmer until all the ingredients are soft and well cooked down. Season to taste with salt.

This salsa can be stored in the fridge for up to 2 weeks.

HUEVOS RANCHEROS

Basically fried eggs served on a flour tortilla and covered in spicy ranchera sauce, this makes not only a delicious breakfast dish but also a wonderful lunch.

SERVES 1

1—2 soft flour tortillas
1—2 eggs
1 tablespoon olive oil
Salsa Ranchera, as much or as little
    as you like, but enough to cover
    the egg

handful of grated mature hard
    cheese, such as Cheddar
coriander leaves, chopped,
    to garnish

On a hot griddle or in a hot dry frying pan, cook the soft flour tortillas until they start to puff up. Flip them over and toast the other side.

Meanwhile, fry the eggs in the oil, keeping the yolk soft. Heat the ranchera sauce.

Now assemble the dish. Place a fried egg on top of each toasted tortilla and cover with the ranchera sauce. Sprinkle with the grated cheese and chopped coriander leaves. Serve immediately.

When you order your food in Mexico you will generally be asked if you would like red or green salsa. These are cooked salsas and are used to sauce your food. Take as little or as much as you like, but no meal is complete without one.

Our favourite is the red salsa known as salsa ranchera. A green version can be made by replacing tomatoes with tomatillos, which look like green tomatoes and are occasionally available in good supermarkets or specialist shops. Salsa ranchera is also an ingredient in a favourite recipe of ours, Huevos Rancheros.

FRESH TOMATO SALSA v

This fresh tomato salsa is often eaten with tortilla chips as an appetizer. It is also good served with refried beans.

SERVES 4–6

1 small red onion, roughly chopped
1–2 jalapeño chillies
large handful of coriander, chopped,
    plus more to garnish
5 medium ripe tomatoes, roughly
    chopped

juice of 2 limes
salt
tortilla chips, to serve

Blend the onion, chillies and coriander in a food processor until finely chopped (you can do this by hand if you prefer). Now add the tomatoes, lime juice and salt to taste, then briefly blend again until the tomato is finely chopped and blended with all ingredients – but not turned to tomato juice.

Serve garnished with more chopped coriander leaves and accompanied by tortilla chips, or as an accompaniment to any meal.

FRESH TOMATO AND RADISH SALSA v

This is a chunkier salsa, which again may be served with tortilla chips or to accompany any meal.

SERVES 4–6

4 medium tomatoes, finely diced
1 small red onion, finely diced
1 bunch of radishes, sliced
small handful of coriander leaves,
    chopped

juice of 1 lime
salt
1 small green chilli, finely chopped

Mix all the ingredients with salt to taste.

As well as the cooked salsas served as condiments, there are various fresh salsas made with raw ingredients, which may be served as an appetizer or as an accompaniment to the main dish.

Fresh Tomato and Radish Salsa

FRESH FRUIT SALSA V

Surfers in the sunset at
Puerto Escondido

*In Oaxaca city, market stalls are piled high with the most beautiful fruits — papaya,
watermelon and cantaloupe melon are but a few — and these are often used to make a
spicy salsa.*

SERVES 4–6

60g/2oz pumpkin seeds
450g/1lb papaya, watermelon, galia
   melon or cantaloupe melon, or a
   mix of all four, peeled, deseeded
   and cut into small cubes

juice of 2 limes
handful of coriander leaves
1 jalapeño chilli, finely chopped
salt

Toast the pumpkin seeds in a hot dry frying pan until they become golden,
stirring constantly. Set aside to cool.

   Mix your choice of fruit with the lime juice, coriander and chilli. Season with
salt to taste and cover with the toasted pumpkin seeds.

MEXICAN WEST COAST PEPPERS v

SERVES 4—6

5 tablespoons olive oil

300g/10oz tempeh, cut into
   1cm/½in cubes

2 red onions, thinly sliced

4 garlic cloves, sliced

2 red chillies, chopped

2 tablespoons coriander seeds,
   crushed

2 red peppers, 2 yellow peppers and
   1 green pepper, deseeded
   and sliced

350g/12oz cooked pinto beans

24 black olives, stoned and halved

soy sauce

large handful of coriander leaves,
   chopped

Heat half the oil in a large pan and, when hot, fry the tempeh until brown.
Remove from pan and set aside.

Add the remaining oil to the pan and, when hot, fry the onion until it starts
to soften. Add the garlic, chilli and crushed coriander seeds. Fry for a couple
of minutes.

Add the peppers and fry, stirring regularly, until they start to soften. Add the
pinto beans and olives. When the beans are heated through, return the tempeh to
the pan and stir well.

Add soy sauce to taste and the chopped coriander. Serve immediately with
Fresh Fruit Salsa (opposite) and rice.

In Puerto Escondido New Age
Californian culture blends
with local Oaxacan youth
culture on the surf beaches
and in their cafés. This blend
has crept into the food. The
beach cafés open at dawn to
serve surfers as much with
muesli, fresh fruit and
yoghurt as with huevos
rancheros. By midday the
choice expands to all manner
of vegetarian, fish and meat
dishes. Many cafés serve
Indonesian tempeh. The recipe
given here combines tempeh
with colourful peppers, olives
and that Mexican staple,
pinto beans.

GUATEMALA & BELIZE

On this visit to Central America we went in search of recipes in Guatemala and Belize. As well as a huge choice of suitable local cuisine, both countries had plenty of other attractions to make them well worth a visit.

The faded charm of Antigua's sixteenth-century Spanish colonial architecture and its dramatic setting between three volcanic peaks make it one of the most beautiful cities in the Americas. The descendants of the Maya who live here have incorporated the religion of the conquistadors into their culture in some unique ways. The night we arrived people were gathered in the town's plazas and cobbled streets to burn giant effigies of the devil. Outside La Merced church a life-like doll of St Diego Juan was being paraded, while a cacophony of exploding fireworks echoed through the streets. The next morning a breakfast of refried beans, scrambled eggs, guacamole and other dishes – our first introduction to Guatemalan food – offered good hope for our quest.

In the colourful, chaotic city market, traders from mountain villages mingled with locals selling fabrics, food and fireworks. Guatemala is one of the world's few sources of jade, which can be found here at bargain prices. But we searched in vain for recipes.

We travelled north to Tikal to visit the great Mayan pyramid temples that tower above the canopy of Guatemala's northern jungle. Climbing to the top of the highest pyramid and looking down over the summits of the other temples poking out above the forest below, alive with the eerie screeching of howler monkeys and squawking of parrots, was unforgettable. The vegetarian options unfortunately were few.

We had more success in Mountain Pine Ridge, a short drive over the border into Belize. Here we found a great vegetable stew flavoured with *achiote*, a combination of allspice, cumin, cinnamon and annatto seeds. We joined an excursion to some local river caves, entering them in canoes and using lamps to see human skulls left in ancient Mayan burial sites. Sometimes we were in cathedral-sized chambers; at others we had to negotiate places where the cave roof was only inches above us. The next day, we canoed in fresh air and sunshine on the Macal river at Chaa creek, where giant iguanas lazed around on rocks along the bank, and then headed for the coast.

We found Placencia, perched on a narrow peninsula of white sand stretching out into the Caribbean, a laid-back, barefoot seaside town of brightly painted wooden houses on stilts. The local 'green and clean committee' sponsors signs along its narrow car-free main street which encourage people not to drop litter that might harm its shoeless residents. They are written in the Creole dialect of English spoken by the Afro-Caribbean people who dominate coastal Belize. Here we ate a very interesting and unusual version of cauliflower cheese.

Right, clockwise from top right **A doorway in Antigua, Guatemala; San Pedro island in Belize; a doorway in Guatemala; one of the Mayan pyramids on Tikal; a window in Antigua; a street in Antigua**

PLACENCIA COCONUT CAULIFLOWER WITH MELTED CHEESE

This unusual take on cauliflower cheese works surprisingly well. Coconut milk, ginger, cashew nuts, chillies and cheese are combined to make a uniquely Belizean dish.

2¼lb/1kg cauliflower florets
2 tablespoons chopped ginger
15fl oz/450ml coconut milk
salt and freshly ground black pepper
    to taste
4–6 green chillies, thinly sliced
2oz/60g cashew nuts, ground in a
    food processor or pestle and
    mortar to make a powder

10 shallots, peeled and cut in half
large handful of chopped
    coriander leaves
2oz/60g ghee or butter
6oz/175g grated strong hard cheese,
    such as mature cheddar, or you can
    use sheep's cheese if you prefer

Place the cauliflower, ginger, coconut milk, and salt and pepper to taste in a large saucepan. Cover the pan and gently simmer until all the liquid has reduced – at this point the cauliflower should be half cooked. Stir in the chillies, ground cashew nuts, shallots, coriander and ghee or butter, cover with the grated cheese and bake in the oven, preheated to 400°F/200°C, for about 15 minutes or until the cheese is melted and nice and brown. Serve with new potatoes and salad.

MOUNTAIN PINE RIDGE STEW v

In this recipe a spicy roux is made and then vegetables are added to make a traditional stew that is eaten in most homes. Annatto seeds are red seeds that give dishes a characteristic ochre colour. They are the principal ingredient of *achiote*, which is a combination of cinnamon, cumin and allspice. If you can't find them, use paprika instead and slightly reduce the amount of allspice, cinnamon and cumin.

12oz / 350g new potatoes, cubed
2 red peppers, sliced
2 green peppers, sliced
4 tablespoons olive oil
1 red onion, thinly sliced
5 celery sticks, thinly sliced
3 garlic cloves, crushed
3 green chillies, thinly sliced
1 heaped teaspoon ground annatto
   seeds or paprika

1 teaspoon allspice
1 teaspoon ground cumin
½ teaspoon ground cinnamon
3 tablespoons chopped oregano leaves
3 tablespoons fine cornmeal
24fl oz / 750ml vegetable water
2 large handfuls of baby spinach leaves
salt and freshly ground black pepper
   to taste
handful of chopped coriander leaves

Boil the potatoes and peppers until just soft, drain and retain the vegetable water, and set to one side.

Heat the olive oil in a large heavy-bottomed pan. When hot, add the onion, celery, garlic and chillies, and sauté until soft. Add the spices and oregano. Stir in the cornmeal, fry for a couple of minutes and then gradually add 3 cups of the retained vegetable water, stirring constantly until a sauce forms. Add the potatoes, peppers, spinach, salt and pepper to taste, and simmer for a further 5 minutes.

Serve garnished with chopped coriander leaves with Corn and Black Bean Salsa with Toasted Pumpkin Seeds (page 318), sour cream and flour tortillas.

Mayan pyramids rising out of the jungle at Tikal in Guatemala

CORN AND BLACK BEAN SALSA WITH TOASTED PUMPKIN SEEDS v

9oz/250g sweet corn kernels, fresh,
   frozen or tinned
9oz/250g cooked black beans or
   kidney beans
1 large red pepper, diced
1 red onion, diced
1 jalapeño chilli or 2 hot green
   chillies, finely chopped

1 teaspoon ground cumin
large handful of chopped
   coriander leaves
juice of 2 limes
salt and freshly ground black pepper
   to taste
2 handfuls of pumpkin seeds

Combine all the ingredients, except the pumpkin seeds. Pour into a bowl and chill in the fridge.

Dry roast the pumpkin seeds in a small frying pan until golden, add a little salt and then sprinkle over the salsa just before serving.

GUATEMALAN BREAKFAST

The dishes eaten at breakfast in Guatemala have the same names as the Mexican equivalents; however, they are completely different in flavour. They are spread out on the table and eaten buffet style. Of course you don't have to eat these dishes only for breakfast: they make a great sociable lunch or dinner.

SALSA v

Unlike Mexican salsa, this contains no tomato or tomatillo, and uses carrot and red onion.

Left **Corn and Black Bean Salsa with Toasted Pumpkin Seeds**
Below **Antigua, Guatemala**

4 medium carrots, grated
1 large red onion, cubed
2 garlic cloves, crushed
2 habanero chillies or 2 hot red chillies, roughly chopped

large handful of chopped coriander leaves
juice of 2 limes
salt to taste
4 dessertspoons olive oil

Place all the ingredients in a food processor and blend until smooth. Chill in the fridge until required.

GUACAMOLE v

Fresh basil and celery are mashed with avocado, cayenne pepper and lime juice.

3 ripe Hass avocados
4 celery sticks, diced
handful of basil leaves, chopped
2 garlic cloves, crushed

juice of 2 limes
¼ teaspoon cayenne pepper
salt to taste

Scoop the avocado flesh into a bowl and mash with a fork until roughly chopped. Stir in the remaining ingredients and chill until required.

REFRIED BEANS

15oz/425g black turtle beans,
   soaked in water overnight
2 large red onions, cubed
6 cloves garlic, chopped

3oz/90g butter, cut into cubes
4 tablespoons olive oil
salt to taste
coriander leaves, to garnish

Drain and rinse the soaked black beans, place in a saucepan and pour in enough water to just cover the beans. Add the onions, garlic and butter, bring to the boil, cover the pan and gently simmer until the beans are soft and nearly all the water has been absorbed. Allow to cool a little, and then blend in a food processor along with the olive oil and salt to taste until a smooth thick purée forms.

Serve garnished with chopped coriander leaves and a drizzle of olive oil.

SCRAMBLED EGG

10 free-range eggs
small handful of oregano leaves,
   chopped
½ teaspoon allspice

salt and freshly ground black pepper
   to taste
2oz/60g butter
2 garlic cloves, crushed

Lightly beat the eggs in a bowl and stir in the oregano, allspice, and salt and black pepper to taste. Heat the butter in a large heavy-bottomed frying pan. When melted, add the crushed garlic and fry until golden. Add the beaten eggs and stir constantly until the eggs are cooked but still soft, as they will continue cooking when you remove them from the heat. Serve immediately.

SERVING THE BREAKFAST

Arrange the above dishes along with: feta cheese, cut into cubes, sour cream, black and green olives, and flour tortillas, toasted on a griddle or in a heavy frying pan.

At our first breakfast in Guatemala, a tray arrived with some refried beans cooked with garlic butter; scrambled eggs laced with oregano leaves and allspice; a carrot, onion and coriander salsa; some guacamole flavoured with basil, celery and cayenne; cubes of feta cheese, olives and sour cream; and a basketful of warm flour tortillas.

Guatemalan Breakfast

BRAZIL

The first time I visited Brazil was for a Royal Geographical Society project in the far north-east, on a remote island called Ilha de Maraca. The island, surrounded by tributaries of the Rio Branco, is covered in dense rainforest. Trails were being cut with machetes by local guides to facilitate the team of scientists due to arrive; I was to photograph the environment in its original state before research began. Apart from the trails, dugout canoes provided the only way of getting around. My second trip to the rainforest was less demanding. In the Itatiaia Reserve between Rio de Janeiro and São Paulo the hilly terrain gives better views of the forest, which reveals itself as full of waterfalls and butterflies, and is much easier to get to.

Brazilians love to eat meat and some restaurants serve nothing but meat, by the plateful. However, there is no shortage of excellent vegetarian restaurants in most Brazilian cities. Many are open only at lunchtime and serve fixed-price buffet meals, including selections of fresh salads, fruity salsas and adaptations of traditional dishes. The cosmopolitan nature of Rio has encouraged a more eclectic choice of ingredients than is found anywhere else in South America.

A view of the Amazon jungle in the rain

On my first day in the rainforest, downriver with one of the guides in a canoe, we misjudged some rapids and knocked the outboard motor out of action. With 20 km (12 miles) of uncut jungle between us and the camp, and piranhas in the water, I felt a very long way from home. Eventually the guide managed to fix the motor with his machete, and we made it back to base thankful to have avoided a twenty-day hack though the forest.

That night the wives of the guides cooked a huge pot of stew for everyone in the camp, a version of the dish cozido (which usually contains pork and sausages), using mounds of fresh vegetables that we had brought with us from Boa Vista.

COZIDO v

SERVES 4–6

300g/10oz 'Buddhist meat' or deep-fried tofu, sliced
350g/12oz (prepared weight) pumpkin, peeled, deseeded and cubed
5 tablespoons olive oil
1 plantain, cut into 1cm/½in slices
125g/4oz okra, sliced lengthwise
1 onion, thinly sliced
2 garlic cloves, crushed
1 heaped teaspoon coriander seeds, crushed
2 small turnips, cubed
225g/8oz hard white cabbage, cubed
300g/10oz marrow, peeled and deseeded, cut into 2.5cm/1in cubes
300g/10oz sweet potatoes, cut into 2.5cm/1in cubes
300ml/½ pint stock
handful of fresh parsley, chopped
salt and pepper

For the marinade
2 garlic cloves, crushed
1 teaspoon coriander seeds, crushed
handful of fresh parsley, chopped
1 onion, thinly sliced
1 dessertspoon balsamic vinegar
3 tablespoons tamari or soy sauce
3 bay leaves
1 tablespoon olive oil

Combine the marinade ingredients and pour them over the sliced Buddhist meat or tofu in a bowl. Allow to stand for 1 hour. Pour off the marinade, retaining the liquid, and set the Buddhist meat or tofu to one side.

Meanwhile, cook the pumpkin in boiling salted water until soft. Drain, retaining the pumpkin water. Mash the pumpkin and set aside.

Heat half the oil in a large pan, add the sliced plantain and fry until browned. Remove from pan. Add the marinated Buddhist meat or tofu and the okra, and fry until both are browned. Remove from pan. Heat the remaining oil and add the onion and garlic. When these begin to soften, add the crushed coriander seeds. Stir and add the turnip, cabbage, marrow and sweet potato. Stir to coat the vegetables in the oil and coriander. Add the stock, 300ml/½ pint of the reserved pumpkin water and the reserved marinade. Simmer until the vegetables are soft.

Stir in the mashed pumpkin, then add the fried Buddhist meat or tofu, the okra and the plantain. Simmer gently for a few minutes to allow the flavours to infuse. Add the parsley and season to taste. Serve with rice.

BLACK BEAN STEW

SERVES 4–6

250g/9oz black turtle beans, soaked
  overnight in cold water
1 large red onion, diced
4 garlic cloves, crushed
3 red chillies, finely chopped
2 tablespoons olive oil
30g/1oz butter
450g/1lb sweet potatoes, cubed
225g/8oz turnips, cubed

2 carrots, cubed
1 red pepper, deseeded and cubed
250g/9oz tomatoes, finely diced
150ml/¼ pint stock
2 large handfuls of coriander,
  chopped, plus more to garnish
handful of parsley, finely chopped
2 bay leaves
salt and pepper

Drain the black beans, place in a saucepan and cover with water. Bring to the boil, then simmer, with the lid on, until the beans are soft.

Meanwhile, fry the onion, garlic and chilli in the olive oil until soft. Remove one-third of the soft black beans and their cooking liquid, and add this to the fried onion. Mash the onion and beans with a potato masher, until the beans start to break down. Return to remaining beans and cooking liquid.

Melt the butter in a large pan, add the sweet potato, turnip, carrot and red pepper, and fry until they start to soften. Add the chopped tomato and fry until the tomato breaks down. Add the black beans and their broth, the stock, coriander, parsley and bay leaves. Simmer until vegetables are soft and the flavours combined. Season with salt and pepper to taste.

MANGO SALSA V

SERVES 4–6

1 large ripe mango, peeled and cubed
2 small carrots, diced
2 celery stalks, diced
1 orange, peeled and cut into cubes

1 green chilli, finely chopped
handful of coriander, chopped
juice of 1 lime
pepper

Combine all the ingredients, season with pepper to taste and chill for about 30 minutes before serving.

This colourful black bean recipe is an adaptation of a traditional Brazilian dish. When it is served with mango salsa, the bright reds and yellows contrast strikingly with the black turtle beans.

Black Bean Stew with Mango Salsa

BOLIVIA

La Paz is the highest capital city in the world, and my arrival there was a dramatic one. By a twist of fate, having nearly missed the flight from Santa Cruz, I had been invited to fly in the last remaining seat — in the cockpit with the pilot. The view of the Andes rising out of the Amazon Basin, as seen through the windscreen of a 737, was an incredible novelty. As the aeroplane passed over the snowy peaks in the half-light of dusk they seemed only a hundred metres below us; beyond them, La Paz came into view, a bowl of lights sunk in the dark expanse of the altiplano. We descended through

Shadowy figures in the La Paz fog

shafts of lightning from an electrical storm to a runway 3,660 metres (12,000 ft) above sea level. The air is cold and thin at this altitude. The effort of carrying my bags up to a third-floor hotel room was exhausting and my sleep full of nightmares.

Bolivia was in the midst of its own nightmare, an economic one. Inflation was running at 45,000 per cent. The exchange rate for US dollars rose several times daily, the banks were closed, and on street corners men in leather jackets exchanged pesos by the carrier-bag from tea-chests full of notes. A cup of coffee cost two million pesos; eating out meant taking along a bag of money to pay the bill. For the first time in my life I was a millionaire. La Paz was a city of millionaires, many of them desperately poor.

SWEETCORN STEW v

Bolivia in general is not great for vegetarians. La Paz is. Near the university I found possibly the best vegetarian restaurant in South America. However, the style of food in the vegetarian cafés was as much Californian as Bolivian. The best local dish I ate was a sweetcorn stew we had in a hillside restaurant on the way back from an exhilarating day out on the highest ski-slope in the world.

This is a very tasty way of eating sweetcorn, which takes on all the flavours of the gravy in which it is boiled.

SERVES 4–6

- 3 carrots, diced
- 3 medium potatoes, peeled and diced
- 4 tablespoons sunflower oil
- 2 onions, finely chopped
- 4 garlic cloves, crushed
- 1 jalapeño chilli, finely chopped
- 2 large ripe plum tomatoes, cubed
- 1 tablespoon sweet paprika
- 1 handful of fresh oregano, chopped
- 1 handful of fresh parsley, chopped
- 3 large handfuls of spinach, finely shredded
- 4 sweetcorn cobs, cut into rounds about 2.5cm/1in thick and parboiled
- 600ml/1 pint stock
- salt and pepper
- handful of coriander leaves, chopped, to garnish

Parboil the carrots and potatoes in salted water until they start to soften.

Heat the oil in saucepan and, when hot, fry the onion, garlic and chilli until soft. Add the tomatoes, paprika, oregano and parsley. Stir well.

Add the parboiled carrots and potatoes with the spinach. Fry, stirring constantly, until the spinach wilts.

Add the sweetcorn and the stock. Cover and simmer until the vegetables are nice and soft. Add salt and pepper to taste, then lightly mash the carrots and potato into the sauce.

Serve garnished with the chopped coriander and accompanied by crusty bread and a leafy green salad.

PERU

The jungles, deserts, mountains and coast of Peru offer an abundance of exciting photographic opportunities, but a dearth of stimulating culinary experiences. Although many of the landscapes are well worth going a little hungry for, when we did find good food it was very welcome.

We entered Peru from Bolivia by ferry across Lake Titicaca in torrential rain. We were travelling through the Andes in midsummer – the wettest time of year. The floating reed islands of the Uros Indians out on the lake were soggy and decaying; the islanders looked bedraggled and unhappy. The only produce in the flooded vegetable market in Puno was rotting coriander. Much of the railway line was under water, but we just managed to catch the last slow train over the altiplano.

Despite the weather, we walked the last day of the Inca Trail up to Machu Picchu, the spectacular 'lost city of the Incas' hidden high in the Urubamba valley. Later, I went back alone to the site at dawn. I climbed the tower of Wayna Picchu and looked down on the deserted city through the swirling clouds from the Temple of the Moon. Machu Picchu stays in my memory as one of the highlights of all my travels.

Dawn in the Andes

POTATO CAKES WITH CUCUMBER RELISH

In Cuzco, better food and accommodation, the colonial splendours of the capital and the dramatic ruins of Inca cities all combined to take our minds off the incessant rain. We ate these fried potato cakes with a vegetable filling and a spicy cucumber relish in the Plaza de Armas, where every evening women set up their stalls.

SERVES 4–6

1kg/2¼lb potatoes,
    peeled and cubed
about 3 tablespoons milk
45g/1½oz butter
salt and pepper
2 onions, finely chopped
2 fresh red chillies, finely chopped
4 garlic cloves, crushed
handful of coriander stalks,
    finely chopped
2 carrots, finely diced

2 red peppers, finely diced
oil for frying

For the cucumber relish
1 large cucumber, grated
2 green chillies, finely chopped
handful of coriander leaves,
    finely chopped
juice of 1 lemon
2 teaspoons honey
salt

Cook the potatoes in boiling salted water until soft. Drain and mash with a little milk and half the butter until smooth. Season to taste.

Gently melt the remaining butter in a frying pan. Add the onions, red chillies and garlic, and fry until these are soft. Add the coriander stalks, carrots and red pepper, and fry until these are soft.

Now make up the potato cakes: take a handful of the mashed potato, press an indentation into its centre and fill with a little of the carrot and pepper mixture. Work the potato around to seal the stuffing and form into a cake with a diameter of about 7.5cm/3in. Repeat with the remaining potato and filling until all are used up.

Fry the potato cakes in very hot oil in a non-stick frying pan, until golden and crunchy on both sides.

Make the cucumber relish by combining all the ingredients with salt to taste.

Serve the potato cakes with the relish, any of the remaining carrot and pepper mixture and a green leaf salad. Alternatively, they are wonderful with poached eggs.

PERUVIAN ANDES POTATOES

This is a version of the traditional Quechua dish known as papa a la huancaina *that has survived the Spanish conquest, although there is an addition of black pepper introduced from India by the invaders.*

Originally it would have been made with Peruvian yellow-fleshed potatoes but is fine with new potatoes. To give the dish its characteristic yellow colour, we have substituted turmeric for the Peruvian herb palillo, as this is more readily available. For similar reasons we suggest a yellow 'Scotch Bonnet' chilli as a substitute for the harder to find yellow aji amarillo *chilli that is popular in Peru, and feta cheese as the type most similar to the Peruvian equivalent. In Peru the dish is usually served with hard-boiled egg, but we prefer it with a fried or poached egg for a lively breakfast.*

'Scotch Bonnet' chillies are very hot and need to be treated with care. Wash your hands thoroughly after chopping and keep them away from eyes and sensitive skin.

SERVES 4–6

- 1kg/2lb new potatoes, peeled and boiled until soft
- 200g/7oz feta cheese
- 250ml/9fl oz milk
- 4 tablespoons olive oil
- 1 yellow 'Scotch Bonnet' chilli, finely chopped
- 4 garlic cloves, finely chopped
- 1kg/2lb onions, thinly sliced
- ½ teaspoon ground black pepper
- ½ teaspoon turmeric
- 150g/5oz sweetcorn kernels
- salt to taste
- 1 egg per person, fried or poached
- about 20 black olives
- handful of coriander leaves, chopped

Slice the boiled potatoes into ½cm/¼in thick slices. In a blender, combine the feta cheese and the milk until smooth. Heat the oil in a large frying pan and gently fry the chilli, garlic and onion until soft and golden brown. Add the black pepper and turmeric, fry for 1 minute, lay the sliced potatoes on top and then add the corn. Pour the milk and cheese into the pan. Gently simmer until the sauce has reduced. Add salt to taste if necessary (remembering how salty feta cheese is).

Serve topped with an egg, black olives and a garnish of coriander leaves.

Peruvian Andes Potatoes

LIMA BEAN AND PUMPKIN STEW

Serves 4—6

450g/1lb potatoes, cubed

450g/1lb pumpkin, peeled,
  deseeded and cubed

salt and pepper

4 tablespoons sunflower oil

2 onions, finely chopped

3 garlic cloves, crushed

1 jalapeño chilli, finely chopped

1 large ripe plum tomato, cubed

handful of fresh thyme, chopped

2 teaspoons ground cumin

175g/6oz cooked lima beans or
  butter beans

85g/3oz fresh or frozen peas

85g/3oz fresh or frozen sweetcorn
  kernels

handful of parsley, finely chopped,
  to garnish

125g/4oz feta cheese, crumbled,
  to serve

Boil the potatoes and pumpkin in a pan of salted water until they begin to soften. Drain and retain the cooking water.

Heat the oil in a saucepan and, when hot, fry the onion, garlic and chilli until soft. Stir in the tomato, thyme and ground cumin. Add the parboiled potato and pumpkin. Cook with a little of the retained water for a couple of minutes.

Add the beans, peas and corn, and cook for a further 10 minutes. Add salt and pepper to taste.

Serve garnished with the chopped parsley and feta cheese on top, accompanied by rice or crusty bread.

In Lima we found relief from the rain that dogged our stay in Peru. The coastal deserts of Peru along the Pacific Ocean are some of the driest places on earth. Lima itself was a tense city with curfews every night.

We were staying with friends, who took us on day-trips into the desert and out for fine meals in the evening. However, we found our most interesting Peruvian meal on a trip to the Cordillera Blanca Mountains. Along the mountain roads women cooked stews on camp-fires. Among the bubbling pots of foul-smelling concoctions we found a woman selling a lima bean and pumpkin stew. It was very good and set us up brilliantly for our trek into the hills.

**Lima Bean and
Pumpkin Stew**

ECUADOR

The best dish we ate in Ecuador was a creamy pumpkin, potato and paprika soup flavoured with thyme and oregano. We were served it while staying on a ranch in the Andean foothills near the small town of Vilcabamba. The ranch was set in idyllic countryside, while Vilcabamba itself seemed like a Wild West town, with saddled horses tied up outside saloons, and drunks fighting in the town square. We saw a more elegant side of Ecuador in Cuenca, with its cathedral and its gleaming barber-shops, well-stocked pharmacies and tidy cafés around the main square.

For us the highlight of Ecuador was the bustling market town of Otavalo, located at the foot of a volcano, and populated by the best-looking, happiest-seeming and most friendly Indians we met in all of South America. The men wore ponchos and wide-brimmed hats, the women attractive hooped skirts and lots of beads. We watched them play a traditional bat-and-ball game in the streets, although both the bat and the ball were so big that hitting the one with the other was almost impossible and most of the game seemed to be spent chasing after missed balls.

PUMPKIN SOUP

Serves 4—6

3 tablespoons olive oil
1 onion, finely chopped
2 garlic cloves, crushed
1 heaped teaspoon sweet paprika
handful of fresh oregano, chopped
450g/1lb peeled and deseeded
    pumpkin, cubed

350g/12oz sweet potato, cubed
600ml/1 pint stock
salt and pepper
150ml/¼ pint double cream
handful of chopped fresh thyme,
    to garnish

Heat the olive oil in a saucepan and, when hot, fry the onion until golden. Stir in the garlic, paprika and oregano, and fry for 1 minute. Add the pumpkin and sweet potato, and fry until they start to soften.

Add the stock with enough water to cover the vegetables. Bring to the boil, cover and simmer until the vegetables are soft. Add salt and pepper to taste.

In a blender or food processor, blend the contents of the pan until smooth. Stir in the cream and serve garnished with chopped thyme.

Along the outside of the Catholic cathedral in Cuenca the walls are full of
carved effigies in tiny alcoves

COSTA RICA

More than a quarter of Costa Rica is protected natural wilderness. The country's active policy of conservation, and the immense biodiversity afforded by its tropical location, have allowed 'eco-tourism' to thrive. Areas of rainforest have been developed for visitors in a range of low-impact facilities, from campsites to the so-called 'five-star rustic' resorts that offer a taste of the wildness of nature — but in comfort. This sounded seductive yet improbable, so we set out to discover just how 'five-star' rustic can be, heading into the deep south where there are several remote resorts.

We decided to try the Tiskita Jungle Lodge, situated in 100 hectares (250 acres) of virgin rainforest on the Pacific coast. Our accommodation consisted of a wooden cabin in the forest, with an outdoor bathroom and a wide platform veranda looking out over the treetops and the ocean. The meals, eaten in the communal open-sided dining-room, were excellent. The place was definitely more rustic than five-star, but quite comfortable and friendly. However, communing with nature does include sharing your bedroom with a lot more biodiversity than you'd ever expect in a hotel room — including, one night, an alarmingly large scorpion.

The daytime paradise easily made up for any nocturnal horrors. Troupes of monkeys and parades of exotic birds and eccentric insects provided hours of entertainment as we sat on our veranda. But the real adventures were the forest walks. The trails were clear enough for us to wander off on our own and admire the giant plants, the towering, liana-draped trees, the minute psychedelic-coloured frogs around the forest pools, and a boa constrictor wrapped around a branch. Everywhere the sounds of the forest were incredible: unseen insects created an unruly racket, monkeys whooped and chattered, and birdsong filled the canopy.

Another attraction of Tiskita was experimental fruit orchard walks, on which we were urged to sample extraordinary offerings from a variety of trees. And there was yet more walking to enjoy along the miles of deserted, black sand, palm-fringed beach, with the welcome relief of the foaming Pacific on hand. The rainforest comes right down to the ocean, and here, looking back up at the vastness of the green forest or gazing out across the endless blue sea, we truly appreciated the blissful remoteness of our position; and, as a pair of toucans glided overhead, the privilege of experiencing nature so unspoilt.

One of the beautiful, untouched beaches of Costa Rica's Pacific coast

CRUNCHY SALAD WITH LIME JUICE v

SERVES 4—6

150g/5oz white cabbage, shredded

85g/3oz cucumber, diced

1 ripe mango, peeled and diced

1 red pepper, deseeded and diced

6 spring onions, thinly sliced

1 avocado pear, peeled,
   stoned and cubed

2 handfuls of watercress

juice of 2 limes

1 garlic clove, crushed

3 tablespoons olive oil

salt and pepper

This fresh-tasting salad, with its sweet-and-sour mixture of fruit and vegetables, is typical of the dishes we sampled on the Pacific coast of Costa Rica.

Combine all the ingredients, season to taste and mix well. Chill for about 30 minutes before serving.

A short flight away on the Caribbean side of Costa Rica we found a very different coast and equally different cuisine. The recipe given here is a delicious mixture of sweet potato, pumpkin and plantains in a rich mustard, coconut and rum sauce.

Left **Crunchy Salad with Lime Juice**
Below **Caribbean Vegetables in a Mustard, Coconut and Rum Sauce**

CARIBBEAN VEGETABLES IN A MUSTARD, COCONUT AND RUM SAUCE v

SERVES 4–6

2 onions, finely diced
4 garlic cloves
5cm/2in piece of root ginger, peeled and roughly chopped
2 teaspoons coriander seeds
½ teaspoon cloves
5cm/2in piece of cinnamon stick
½ teaspoon cayenne pepper
2 teaspoons mustard powder
1 teaspoon ground turmeric
6 tablespoons sunflower oil
450g/1lb sweet potato, cubed
450g/1lb peeled and cubed pumpkin or squash

4 tablespoons dark rum
250ml/9fl oz stock
2 large plantains, peeled and sliced into rounds about 1cm/½in thick
400ml/14fl oz coconut milk
salt and pepper
juice of 1 lime
chopped oregano leaves, to garnish
mango slices, to serve
chives, snipped into longish pieces, to garnish

In a food processor, blend the onions, garlic and ginger to a paste. Using a spice grinder or mortar and pestle, grind the coriander seeds, cloves and cinnamon. Add the cayenne, mustard powder and turmeric.

Heat 4 tablespoons of the oil in a saucepan, add the onion paste and fry for 2 minutes. Add the sweet potato and pumpkin or squash, and fry until they start to soften. Now add the spices and stir. Add the rum, followed by the stock. Cover and bring to the boil. Simmer with the lid on until the vegetables are soft. Add a little water, as necessary.

Meanwhile, fry the plantain in the remaining oil, until brown and crunchy. Add the plantain to the saucepan with the coconut milk, and simmer gently for 5 minutes. Finally add salt to taste and the lime juice.

Serve garnished with chopped oregano leaves, accompanied by the slices of fresh mango sprinkled with chives and some rice.

Caribbean

Caribbean

While the islands of the Caribbean all have their own favourite and unique cuisines, there are many dishes that seem to turn up in only slightly different styles all around the region. Vegetarian dishes are not usually main meals, so we have adapted some of the typical Caribbean recipes we found by substituting meat or fish with vegetables and tofu; others in this chapter, though, are just as we found them. The islands where we found the most interesting food are Jamaica, Anguilla and Nevis.

Nevis is a small island only 6 x 9 miles (9.5 x 14.5 kilometres) and dominated by a volcano that descends from a misty peak through rainforest and tropical palms to a circle of fine beaches. Columbus spotted and named it on his voyage of discovery to the Americas in 1493. Once Nevis was colonized, the fertile soil made fortunes for the owners of its sugar plantations. They built opulent mansions and the island became a popular haunt of high society.

With the abolition of slavery and the decline of the sugar trade, Nevis slipped into international obscurity. Remains of sugar mills are scattered about the island. Fortunately some of the grand plantation houses have been preserved and are now run as inns, providing stylish retreats from which to discover the island's many charms. Most of these are hidden away on the slopes of the volcano in a district known as Gingerland. Some of the recipes in this chapter are based on the meals we enjoyed while staying at these hotels; others are from the simple beach cafés dotted around the island.

Jamaica is a much larger island, with a reputation for being a bit dangerous. Many of the resorts are sold as 'all inclusive', meaning that guests never need to venture beyond the safety of their walls. We stayed in Negril, where danger didn't seem to be a problem, and ate some of the best food of our stay in local cafés and bars. One of these bars was located on top of a high cliff that plunged hundreds of feet down to the sea. Every evening local guys with extremely athletic bodies and long dreadlocks would entertain tourists by diving off the cliffs into the sea.

Anguilla, even smaller than Nevis, is blessed with some of the finest beaches in the Caribbean. There are plenty of upmarket hotels that can afford to import the finest ingredients to cook some excellent Caribbean dishes. Here we found a recipe for the best 'rice and peas' dish we have had anywhere. Beyond the hotels there are few places to eat and little to do; however, people were very friendly, especially when they found out that we were English. Almost everyone we met on the island seemed to have relatives in England and strangely all of them lived in Slough!

Pages 340–341 **Tobago Cayes in the Caribbean**

Right, clockwise from top right **A plantation inn on Nevis; Fig Tree Church on Nevis; Soufrière bay on St Lucia; fishing boats on Nevis; Grand Anse bay, Grenada; Tobago Cayes in the Grenadines**

Cajun spice mix is a popular Creole seasoning, which blackens when cooked in a hot pan. It can be used to season almost anything, but we think it works particularly well with tofu. The spice mix can be made in advance and stored in an airtight jar.

CAJUN BLACKENED TOFU v

SERVES 4

14oz/400g tofu	1 teaspoon yellow mustard seeds
olive oil	1 teaspoon paprika
	1 teaspoon cayenne pepper
For the spice mix	1 teaspoon dried oregano
8 cloves	2 teaspoons dried thyme
1 teaspoon cumin seeds	1 teaspoon salt
1 teaspoon black peppercorns	

Dry roast the cloves, cumin seeds, peppercorns and mustard seeds in a small frying pan until aromatic. Remove from the heat and grind to a powder. Combine with the remaining spice mix ingredients.

Drain the tofu, cut into eight slices and pat dry with kitchen paper. Brush each side with olive oil and then coat with the spice mix. Preheat a griddle pan or thick-based frying pan until really hot, place the tofu in the pan and cook until the spices blacken; then turn and cook other side. Alternatively cook on the barbecue.

Serve with Mango and Ginger Salsa (below) and Pumpkin and Pigeon Pea Salad with Lime and Allspice Dressing (page 346).

MANGO AND GINGER SALSA v

Salsas are often served with Caribbean dishes to liven up a meal. They are easy to make and look great on the table. This is a particularly delicious one that we were served in Anguilla.

SERVES 4

1 large mango, peeled and chopped	1 dessertspoon tarragon,
2in/5cm piece of ginger, peeled	finely chopped
and grated	juice of 1 lime
1 teaspoon brown sugar	

Blend the chopped mango, grated ginger, brown sugar, tarragon and lime juice until smooth but retaining some bite. Store in the fridge until required.

Cajun Blackened Tofu with Mango and Ginger Salsa

PUMPKIN AND PIGEON PEA SALAD WITH LIME AND ALLSPICE DRESSING v

Pigeon peas originated in Africa and are used in many recipes throughout the Caribbean. They are available in Caribbean stores or the ethnic section of good supermarkets; however, if you find them impossible to locate, substitute black eye peas (or kidney beans).

SERVES 4

12oz/350g pumpkin, peeled and cut into cubes

2 tablespoons olive oil

1 large red onion, finely chopped

2 cloves garlic, finely chopped

1 teaspoon ground cumin

14oz/400g tin pigeon peas or black eye peas, drained and rinsed

10oz/300g cooked brown rice

1 red pepper, cut into small cubes

2 celery sticks, cut into small cubes

chopped coriander leaves, to garnish

For the dressing

3 tablespoons lime juice

grated zest of 2 limes

2 tablespoons olive oil

½ teaspoon allspice

5 stems of thyme, finely chopped

salt and ground black pepper to taste

Put the pumpkin in a saucepan of boiling water and simmer until soft, drain and set to one side. Heat 2 tablespoons of the olive oil in a wok. When hot, add the chopped red onion and garlic and sauté until the onion softens; then add the ground cumin, stirring it into the onions. Add the pumpkin and fry until it starts to brown. Remove from the heat, place in a large bowl and add the pigeon peas or black eye peas, cooked brown rice, red pepper and celery.

Make the dressing by whisking together the lime juice and grated zest, the remaining 2 tablespoons of the olive oil, allspice, chopped thyme, salt and freshly ground black pepper. Pour over the salad and combine well.

You can either eat the salad warm or chill it in the fridge for 30 minutes. Serve garnished with chopped coriander leaves.

A fishing boat on Pinney's beach, Nevis

COU-COU

Cou-cou is the Caribbean version of polenta, made from cornmeal and okra. It is used as a side dish to any meal.

SERVES 4

1½ pints/750ml water

1 teaspoon salt

8oz/225g okra, sliced into

½ in/1cm rounds

6oz/175g cornmeal or fine polenta

6fl oz/175ml coconut milk

good dash of Tabasco

½ teaspoon freshly ground

black pepper

2 tablespoons butter, softened

Bring the water and salt to boil in a heavy saucepan, add the okra and boil for 10 minutes with the lid on; then remove the okra with a slotted spoon and keep to one side. Slowly pour in the cornmeal or fine polenta, stirring constantly with a whisk. Whisk in the coconut milk, and then add the okra. Stir constantly until a thick mixture forms. Add the Tabasco and the freshly ground black pepper. Pour the cou-cou into a bowl and spread the butter on top. Serve immediately.

SEASONING-UP BARBECUE MARINADE V

This also makes a good marinade for ingredients to be cooked under the grill or in the oven.

1 large onion, roughly chopped

3 garlic cloves, roughly chopped

½–1 Scotch bonnet chilli,

roughly chopped

1 tablespoon chopped marjoram

1 tablespoon chopped thyme

1 tablespoon chopped chives

1 teaspoon paprika

½ teaspoon ground cloves

½ teaspoon freshly ground

black pepper

3 tablespoons lime juice

3 tablespoons sunflower oil

salt to taste

Place all the ingredients in a food processor and blend until smooth. The marinade can be stored in a jar in the fridge until needed.

To serve, brush the marinade over your favourite barbecue ingredients – we suggest sweet corn cobs, thick-cut slices of sweet potato or tofu. Allow to marinate for 1 hour before cooking on the barbecue or under a hot grill, or baking in the oven. Serve with Papaya and Mango Salsa (page 351).

Horse riding in Jamaica

SPINACH WITH COCONUT MILK, THYME AND CHIVES

Traditionally known as callaloo, this dish is usually made with callaloo leaves, but we find them hard to get, so we use spinach instead.

SERVES 4

1oz/30g butter
1 large onion, diced
2 garlic cloves, chopped
1lb/450g peeled and cubed pumpkin
1 green pepper, cut into cubes
4oz/115g okra, cut into ½ in/1cm slices
1 tablespoon chopped thyme
8floz/250ml vegetable stock
10oz/300g spinach, washed, stems removed and roughly chopped
14fl oz/400ml coconut milk
1 tablespoon chopped chives
salt and freshly ground black pepper to taste

Melt the butter in a large saucepan, add the onion and garlic, and sauté until the onion is soft. Add the pumpkin, green pepper and okra, and fry until the pumpkin starts to soften. Add the thyme and vegetable stock, bring to the boil, cover with a lid and simmer for 10 minutes. Add the spinach, and when it has wilted down, add the coconut milk and chives. Gently simmer for a further 10 minutes, taking care not to boil the coconut milk as it will split. Finally add salt and freshly ground black pepper to taste.

JAMAICAN JERK TOFU

1 onion, roughly chopped

1 Scotch bonnet chilli, chopped

2 garlic cloves, chopped

1in/2.5cm piece of ginger,
    peeled and grated

2 tablespoons honey

2 tablespoons sunflower oil

3 tablespoons soy sauce

2 tablespoons red wine vinegar

2 teaspoons dried thyme

1 teaspoon allspice

1 teaspoon ground cinnamon

1 teaspoon ground cloves

freshly ground black pepper to taste

11b 2oz/500g tofu

Blend all the ingredients except the tofu in a food processor until smooth. Drain the tofu, pat it dry with kitchen paper and cut into 12 pieces. Coat with the jerk sauce and allow to marinate for half an hour. Cook on a barbecue or under a hot grill until brown on both sides. Any remaining sauce can be kept in the fridge, in a jar with a tight-fitting lid, until next time. Serve with Negril Tomato Catch-up (opposite) and Caribbean Rice and Peas (below).

CARIBBEAN RICE AND PEAS

Peas and rice are served all over the Caribbean and everyone has their own special recipe. This recipe, which we found in Jamaica, also works well with black eye peas.

12oz/350g basmati rice

1 large onion, finely chopped

2 garlic cloves, finely chopped

1 tablespoon chopped thyme

1 teaspoon salt

½ teaspoon freshly ground black pepper

1 dessertspoon honey

1 teacup kidney beans, soaked
    overnight and cooked until soft, or
    14oz/400g tin, rinsed

14fl oz/400ml coconut milk

8fl oz/250ml water

chopped coriander leaves, to garnish

Rinse the rice until the water runs clear, and then place in a saucepan with a tight-fitting lid. Add the onion, garlic, thyme, salt, pepper, honey and kidney beans. Add the coconut milk and water, cover with the lid and bring to the boil; then reduce the heat to a minimum and gently cook until the rice is tender, adding more water if necessary. Serve garnished with chopped coriander leaves.

Jerk seasoning is probably the most famous taste to come out of Jamaica. It is a sweet and spicy marinade, and stalls selling it can be found all over the island, grilling meat on barbecues made out of huge oil drums cut in half. The smell is irresistible. We like it as a marinade for tofu and it works both on the barbecue in summer or under the grill.

PAPAYA AND MANGO SALSA v

1 medium mango, peeled and cut into
  small cubes
1 papaya, peeled, deseeded and cut
  into small cubes
1 red pepper, cut into small cubes

1 red chilli, finely chopped
juice of 1 lime
¼ teaspoon grated nutmeg
1 tablespoon chopped marjoram

Combine all the ingredients and chill in the fridge for 1 hour before serving.

NEGRIL TOMATO CATCH-UP

This spicy Caribbean version of tomato ketchup is a good accompaniment to any Caribbean meal. It can be made in advance and kept in a jar in the fridge.

1lb 4oz/565g ripe tomatoes
2 tablespoons sunflower oil
1 medium onion, finely chopped
2 garlic cloves, finely chopped
2 green chillies, finely chopped
½ teaspoon ground ginger
1 teaspoon ground coriander
½ teaspoon ground cinnamon

½ teaspoon ground cloves
½ teaspoon ground nutmeg
1 teaspoon paprika
½ teaspoon ground mace
½ teaspoon salt
¼ teaspoon freshly ground
  black pepper
1 dessertspoon honey

Chop the tomatoes in a blender and set to one side. Heat the oil in a saucepan. When hot, add the onion and garlic and gently fry until the onion is soft but not brown. Add the chopped chillies and the spices, and turn in the oil for 1 minute or so. Add the chopped tomatoes, salt, pepper and honey and bring to the boil; then reduce the heat and gently simmer, uncovered, for 15 minutes until the tomatoes have reduced and the catch-up coats the back of a spoon.

MARINATED BUTTERNUT SQUASH AND SWEET PEPPERS WITH HOT TOMATO SAUCE

In this dish the peppers and butternut squash are marinated and cooked on the barbecue or under the grill and then served with a hot, spicy tomato sauce.

1lb/450g butternut squash, peeled
   and cut into ¾in/2cm chunks
2 large red onions, cut into
   ¾in/2cm chunks
3 red peppers, cut into ¾in/2cm cubes

For the marinade
1 tablespoon chopped thyme
1 tablespoon chopped chives
2 tablespoons fresh lime juice
1 tablespoon soy sauce
3 tablespoons olive oil
1 dessertspoon honey

For the tomato sauce
2 tablespoons sunflower oil
1 large onion, diced
2 garlic cloves, finely chopped
½–1 Scotch bonnet chilli,
   finely chopped
4oz/115g okra pods, chopped in
   ½in/1cm rounds
14oz/400g ripe tomatoes, cut into cubes
3 bay leaves
1 tablespoon chopped thyme
1 tablespoon lime juice
salt and black pepper to taste

Parboil the squash in a saucepan of boiling water until it is just starting to soften but is still firm. Drain and place in a large bowl with the onions, peppers and marinade ingredients. Stir well to coat all the vegetables with the marinade and set to one side for 1 hour.

Meanwhile make the tomato sauce. Heat the sunflower oil in a saucepan. When hot, add the onion, garlic, chilli and okra, and gently fry until soft. Add the tomatoes, bay leaves, thyme and lime juice, and bring to the boil; cover the pan and simmer until the sauce has reduced and the oil returns. Add salt and black pepper to taste.

Skewer the onions, peppers and butternut squash and cook either on the barbecue or under a hot grill until brown on all sides. Any remaining marinade can be added to the tomato sauce and heated through.

Serve the skewers topped with the sauce, with rice on the side.

Marinated Butternut Squash and Sweet Peppers with Hot Tomato Sauce

CARIBBEAN PEPPERPOT v

Pepperpot is one of the Caribbean's most famous dishes. It can be served as a soup or as a meal in a bowl. It is usually made with whatever vegetables are in season.

3 tablespoons sunflower oil
1 large onion, diced
4 garlic cloves, finely chopped
½–1 Scotch bonnet chilli,
    finely chopped
1 large red-skinned sweet potato,
    peeled and cut into chunks
20 okra pods, sliced in
    ½ in / 1 cm rounds
1 tablespoon chopped thyme
1 teaspoon allspice
1 teaspoon ground cloves
1 teaspoon ground cinnamon

½ teaspoon ground nutmeg
½ teaspoon ground mace
½ teaspoon ground black pepper
10oz / 300g kale, washed with stems
    removed and roughly chopped
1 pint / 500ml vegetable stock
6oz / 175g spinach leaves,
    washed, stems removed and
    roughly chopped
1 tablespoon chopped chives
1 tablespoon chopped marjoram
4 spring onions, sliced
salt to taste

Heat the oil in a large saucepan. When hot, add the onion, garlic and chilli, and sauté until the onion is soft. Add the sweet potato and okra, and cook until the okra starts to brown, stirring to prevent the okra from sticking. Stir the thyme and spices into the pan; then add the kale, stock and enough water to cover the vegetables. Bring to the boil, cover the pan and reduce the heat, and simmer until the sweet potato is just soft. Add the spinach, chives, marjoram, spring onions and salt to taste, and cook for a further 5 minutes.

    Ladle into bowls and serve immediately.

Seaside fun in Jamaica

CUBA

There was only one flight a week between London and Havana in the winter of 1994, and that was on a rather old and ill-equipped Russian aeroplane operated by Cubana out of Stansted Airport. The lack of in-flight entertainment was partly compensated for by the freely available Havana Club rum. The biggest shock was a stopover in the frozen north of Canada, where we had to endure sub-zero temperatures as we walked to and from the terminal building dressed for the Caribbean in T-shirts and sandals.

It can be uncomfortable arriving in a strange city at night with no accommodation booked. But, far from being besieged by taxi-drivers competing to whisk us into the unknown for a huge fare, we found the Havana Airport taxi-men playing guitars under a tree in the tropical evening. After a sedate drive down almost empty roads at a fixed fare to the heart of Old Havana, we found a fine room in a hotel rich, like Havana itself, in faded splendour. The elegant Spanish colonial architecture, the brightly coloured 1950s American cars, the post-revolutionary street art, the subtle pastels of the back alleys, and the friendly Cuban people — all made photography a pleasure. Eating was another matter. Seduced into restaurants by stunning interiors and smiling staff, we inevitably found nothing to back up the optimistic words on the menus, while the big hotels seemed content to serve dishes reminiscent of boarding-school meals of the 1960s. We were beginning to despair when rescue came from what seemed a most unlikely source.

At first we had been rather intimidated by the gangs of young men hustling to sell dodgy merchandise in the shadows. But after a couple of days we discovered that they were much less threatening than they appeared, and in fact quite friendly and keen to chat in English. Having turned down their suggestions of various substances to smoke, sniff or sip we found there was something else on offer. A boy who introduced himself as José was our guide to this elusive pleasure. Reluctant at first to follow him down the quiet, narrow streets into the midst of Old Havana's decay, we nonetheless stayed close behind him, drawn by his promise of tasty, home-cooked Cuban dishes for a few dollars.

José introduced us to Rosa, his aunt. Rosa was an old hand at saving foreigners from Havana's dearth of nutritious satisfaction. With her passion for traditional Cuban cooking, she provided some of our most pleasant and enduring memories of Cuba. After her delicious meals we would spend the warm Havana nights sipping Mojito rum cocktails in one of the foodless bars or cafés, followed by live Afro-Cuban dance music at an open-air club, against a background of Atlantic waves crashing on the shore.

Above **One of the many big old American cars to be seen on the streets of Havana**

CUBAN GREEN RICE v

SERVES 4–6

3 tablespoons olive oil
1 large onion, finely chopped
1 green pepper, deseeded and
   finely chopped
large handful of fresh parsley,
   chopped

large handful of fresh coriander
   leaves, chopped
500g/1lb 2oz rice, rinsed
about 700ml/1¼ pints stock
salt and pepper

Heat the oil in the saucepan in which you are going to cook the rice. When hot,
fry the onion and pepper until they start to soften.

   Stir in the chopped parsley and coriander. Add the drained rice and stir to coat
all the grains in oil. Add just enough stock to cover the rice and bring to the boil,
then reduce the heat and cook with the lid on until all the moisture is absorbed.
Adjust the seasoning if necessary.

A pot in a Havana street
forms a casual still-life

HAVANA BEANS

SERVES 4–6

325g/11oz black beans, soaked
  overnight in cold water
6 tablespoons olive oil
2 large red onions, thinly sliced
6 garlic cloves, crushed
2 red peppers, deseeded and
  thinly sliced
2 yellow peppers, deseeded and
  thinly sliced
450g/1lb white cabbage,
  finely shredded
large handful of coriander stalks,
  chopped, and a large handful of
  chopped coriander leaves

large handful of chopped oregano
  leaves, plus more to garnish
Tabasco sauce
5 tablespoons red wine
salt and pepper

For the garnish
slices of plum tomato
chopped fresh oregano
olive oil

Drain the soaked black beans, add enough fresh water to cover generously, bring
to the boil and simmer until soft. Drain the beans, retaining the cooking liquor.

Meanwhile, heat 4 tablespoons of the olive oil in a large pan and, when hot,
fry the red onions and garlic. When they start to soften, add the red and yellow
peppers, followed shortly thereafter by the cabbage. Fry, stirring constantly, until
the vegetables are nice and soft, and caramelized.

Add the coriander stalks, oregano and Tabasco to taste – it should be quite
spicy! Stir well and add the wine. When the wine has reduced by about half, add
the cooked beans and the remaining olive oil, followed by enough of the reserved
bean cooking liquor to make a sauce. Simmer for 5 minutes.

Finally add salt and pepper to taste and the chopped coriander leaves. Stir
until well incorporated.

Serve immediately, garnished with chopped oregano leaves, and accompanied
by Cuban Green Rice (page 357) and plump plum tomato slices drizzled with
olive oil.

Puddings

ORANGE, DATE AND CINNAMON FRUIT SALAD

This simple, delicious fruit salad is popular in Morocco. It is a great way to finish a meal.

5 medium oranges, peeled and
    thinly sliced
12 fresh dates, stoned and
    thinly sliced

handful of flaked almonds
1 tablespoon orange flower water
ground cinnamon to taste
natural yoghurt, to serve

Lay the oranges on a large platter and sprinkle over the dates, flaked almonds, orange flower water and cinnamon to taste. Serve with natural yoghurt.

TROPICAL FRUIT PLATTER WITH CHAT MASALA v

In India fruit is served sprinkled with a spice mix called chat masala, a delicious sweet and savoury combination. You can use any fruit you have in the fruit bowl, but tropical fruit works particularly well. Make the chat masala in advance and store it in an airtight container until required.

tropical fruit, such as pineapple,
    papaya, mango, melon, star fruit or
    chikoo, peeled, deseeded and cut
    into slices
good squeeze of lime juice
2 limes, cut into wedges, to garnish

For the chat masala
2 teaspoons black peppercorns
2 teaspoons cumin seeds
2 teaspoons dried pomegranate seeds
1 teaspoon caraway seeds
2 teaspoons ground mango powder
½ teaspoon ground chilli
1 teaspoon garam masala
salt to taste

Dry roast the pepper, cumin, pomegranate and caraway seeds in a small frying pan until aromatic. Allow to cool a little and then grind to a powder. Combine with the remaining ingredients. Store in an airtight jar.

Arrange the fruit slices on a large platter, squeeze over a good splash of lime juice and garnish with the lime wedges. Just before serving, sprinkle over the chat masala to taste.

Orange, Date and
Cinnamon Fruit Salad

POMEGRANATE GRANITA

Granita is a water ice, thought to have been introduced to Venice when Marco Polo returned from his travels in China. Pomegranate syrup is available in Middle Eastern stores. If you find it impossible to buy, experiment with puréed soft fruit or juice of your choice. Strawberries work well (use approximately 1lb/500g).

5fl oz/150ml pomegranate syrup
6oz/175g castor sugar
1 pint/500ml water

juice of 2 limes
sliced strawberries, to garnish

Blend all the ingredients in a food processor until the castor sugar has dissolved. Pour into a plastic container and place in the freezer.

After 1 hour, remove from the freezer and break up, with a fork, any ice crystals that have formed; this is to prevent the granita from becoming one solid block. Repeat every hour or so, until all the liquid has frozen – it should have the consistency of crushed ice. Store in the freezer until required. We serve it piled into glasses topped with sliced strawberries or, at home, with a slug of vodka.

CHILLI AND LIME ICE CREAM

Chillies work really well in desserts, particularly in this ice cream. The sugar and cream perfectly balance the heat of the chilli.

grated zest of 2 limes
juice of 2 limes
2 red chillies, roughly chopped
7oz/200g castor sugar

3fl oz/100ml water
1 pint/500ml double cream
lime slices or star fruit, to garnish

Blend the lime zest, lime juice, chillies, sugar and water in a food processor until the chilli is finely chopped and the sugar has dissolved. Lightly whip the cream until sloppy, stir in the chilli and lime mix and then pour into a plastic container. Place in the freezer.

After 1 hour, remove from the freezer and break up, with a fork, any ice crystals that have formed. Repeat every hour or so until the cream has completely frozen.

Serve piled into glasses and garnished with lime slices.

PISTACHIO KULFI

Brought to India by the Mughals, kulfi is basically ice cream, but it differs in flavour and texture as it is made with reduced milk. It is traditionally made in cone-shaped receptacles; however, as these are quite hard to buy, we make them in tart trays and pile three on top of each other with sliced fruit in between. Kulfi is usually very sweet but we have cut down the sugar content so that you can taste all the different flavours.

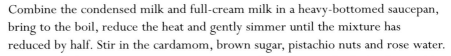

1lb/450g condensed milk
1 pint/500ml full-cream milk
½ teaspoon ground cardamom
3 dessertspoons brown sugar

1oz/30g pistachio nuts, ground
1 dessertspoon rose water
sliced strawberries and physalis, to
   garnish

Combine the condensed milk and full-cream milk in a heavy-bottomed saucepan, bring to the boil, reduce the heat and gently simmer until the mixture has reduced by half. Stir in the cardamom, brown sugar, pistachio nuts and rose water.

Meanwhile prepare your tart trays – you will need two – by lining them with cling film. Pour the kulfi mixture into a jug and carefully pour into the individual segments of the tart trays. Place in the freezer overnight; then remove from the freezer and lift the cling film away from the tray – the kulfi will come away with it. Place the frozen kulfi in a plastic tub and store in the freezer until required.

Serve piled three high, garnished with sliced strawberries and physalis.

Above **Chilli and Lime Ice Cream**
Below **Pistachio Kulfi**

APPLE, DATE AND CINNAMON CAKE v

We had a lot of demand for vegan cakes in the café, so we created this cake, which non-vegans enjoy as well.

4oz/115g dairy-free margarine
4oz/115g brown sugar
1fl oz/30ml sunflower oil
2fl oz/60ml soya milk
7oz/200g self-raising flour
1 teaspoon baking powder
1 heaped dessertspoon
   ground cinnamon

½ teaspoon salt
3 red apples, grated
handful of dates, finely chopped
handful of mixed nuts, chopped
brown sugar
fresh fig slices and soya or whipped
   double cream, to serve

Preheat the oven to 350°F/180°C.

Blend the margarine and brown sugar in a mixer (or with a hand whisk) until creamy. While still mixing, add the oil, followed by the soya milk, and mix until well incorporated. Reduce the speed of the mixer and gradually add the self-raising flour, baking powder, cinnamon and salt. Add the grated apple and chopped dates, and pour into a greased 9in/23cm loose-bottomed cake tin. Sprinkle the chopped nuts and a little brown sugar over the top of the cake, and gently press into the mixture. Place in the oven and bake for 1 hour 15 minutes or until a knife comes out clean.

Allow to cool and serve with fresh fig slices and soya or whipped cream.

Apple, Date and Cinnamon Cake

CARROT CAKE

This is a recipe my mother gave me. It was so popular with one of our customers, who had moved to Scotland, that when her husband was in town he had to take a piece back to her in Scotland. We have also developed a vegan version, which is printed below.

7oz/200g brown sugar

4fl oz/125ml sunflower oil

1 dessertspoon ground cinnamon

½ teaspoon salt

2 medium free-range eggs

6oz/175g self-raising flour

2 medium carrots, grated

handful of sultanas

Preheat the oven to 375°F/190°C.

Blend the sugar, oil, cinnamon, salt and eggs in a mixer, or using a hand whisk, until creamy. Reduce the speed and gradually stir in the flour; when it is well combined add the grated carrot and sultanas. Pour the mixture into a loaf tin, lined with baking paper, and bake in the oven for 1 hour 15 minutes or until a knife inserted comes out clean, as it can sometimes take longer. Allow to cool a little and then remove from the tin.

CARROT CAKE v

7oz/200g brown sugar

6fl oz/175ml sunflower oil

2½fl oz/75ml soya milk

1 dessertspoon ground cinnamon

½ teaspoon salt

8oz/225g self-raising flour

1 teaspoon baking powder

2 medium carrots, grated

handful of sultanas

Make the cake as described above, blending the sugar, oil, soya milk, cinnamon and salt, and then adding the self-raising flour and baking powder, followed by the carrots and sultanas.

MANGO AND PASSION FRUIT CHEESECAKE

7oz/200g digestive or ginger biscuits,
    roughly broken
2oz/60g butter, melted
7oz/200g cream cheese
4 free-range eggs
7oz/200g castor sugar
4 heaped tablespoons natural yoghurt

1 mango, peeled and grated
2 passion fruit, passed through a sieve
    to remove the pips
grated zest of 2 limes
juice of 2 limes
double cream and extra passion fruit,
    to serve

Preheat the oven to 350°F/180°C.

Blend the broken biscuits in a food processor until finely chopped. Add the melted butter and turn out into a greased, loose-bottomed 9in/23cm cake tin. Press into the bottom.

Make the filling by blending the cream cheese, eggs, sugar and yoghurt until smooth and creamy. Stir in the mango, sieved passion fruit, lime zest and juice, and pour into the cake tin. Place in the oven for 1 hour 15 minutes.

The cheesecake is cooked when there is a slight wobble when you shake the cake tin. Turn off the oven and cut around the edge of the cheesecake, but leave the cheesecake in the oven for a further 10 minutes. This should prevent it from cracking.

Serve with whipped double cream and passion fruit scooped over the top.

GUATEMALAN FLAN

In this dish, popular throughout the whole of Latin America, custard is baked over caramel to make a pudding similar to crème caramel, the ultimate comfort food. You will need a flan dish big enough to hold 2 pints/1 litre of milk.

7oz/200g castor sugar
1 tablespoon water
5 free-range eggs
2 pints/1 litre full-fat milk

1 vanilla pod, slit down the middle lengthwise
4in/10cm piece of cinnamon

Preheat the oven to 325°F/170°C.

Place half the sugar and the water in a heavy-bottomed pan, and heat on a medium heat until the sugar melts. Reduce the heat and simmer, stirring regularly, until the sugar becomes like caramel. Pour into your flan dish and spread over the bottom. Set to one side while you make the custard.

Break the eggs into a large bowl and beat with a whisk until creamy. Place the milk, vanilla pod, cinnamon and remaining sugar in a saucepan. Bring to the boil, reduce the heat and gently simmer for a couple of minutes. Remove from the heat and allow to cool a little.

Pull out the vanilla pod and cinnamon stick, and pour the milk into the beaten eggs, whisking constantly. Pour the custard into the flan dish. Place the flan dish into a bain marie, made by filling a baking tray with enough water to come halfway up the side of the flan dish. Carefully place in the oven and bake for about 50 minutes, until the custard has set.

Allow the flan to cool before spooning into dishes and serving.

CHOCOLATE CAKE

In nearly all the countries we have travelled in, the most common dessert is fresh fruit. However, in the café we served a French chocolate cake, which is probably our most requested recipe. Up to now we have always tried to keep it a secret, but this book would not be complete without it.

SERVES 8–10

225g/8oz unsalted butter, plus
    more for the cake pan
200g/7oz plain chocolate,
    broken into pieces
6 large eggs, separated

200g/7oz caster sugar
icing sugar, for dusting
crème fraîche, to serve
strawberries, to serve

Preheat the oven to 190°/375°F/gas 5 and grease a 23cm/9in loose-bottomed cake tin well with butter (the cake mixture can be runny, so it is best to use the type of pan that is tightly secured by a clip).

In a small saucepan set over a larger pan of simmering water, melt the chocolate and the butter. Mix together well and set aside to cool.

Meanwhile, using a whisk – preferably in a food mixer – beat the egg whites until really stiff. While still whisking, slowly add the sugar followed by the egg yolks. The result should be a creamy mixture.

Using a metal spoon, quickly combine the chocolate butter sauce with this cake mixture. Pour and spoon into the prepared cake tin.

Bake for approximately 55 minutes. The cake will puff up in the oven but will sink back down again when removed from the heat, to give it its characteristic appearance.

Dust with lost of icing sugar and serve with crème fraîche and strawberries.

Chocolate Cake

A

achiote 314, 317

advieh 56

ahimaa 286, 289

ajwain 213

amok 238, 241

with spinach and tofu **241**, *241*

Amritsar 134, *140, 144, 169*

Anguilla 342, 345

annatto seeds 317

Antigua 314, *314, 319*

apple, date and cinnamon cake **364**, *364*

apricot: paneer, cashew nut and Hunza apricot masala **213**, *213*

aubergine

baba ganoush 57, **63**

Bangkok stir-fry **251**

beetroot and brinjal black curry **130**

brinjal pickle **118**

Calcutta aubergine **160**, *160*

Cambodian yellow curry **245**, *245*

chu chee red curry **256**

Imam's aubergine **65**, *65*

Mekong stir-fry with puréed aubergine **235**

Melakan devil's mushroom curry **281**

Nalagarh brinjal **200**

in a puréed date sauce **69**

royal baby aubergines **146**

salad **19**

tempeh stuffed aubergines **247**

Thai green curry **254**, *254*

avocado: guacamole 297, **302**, *302*, **319**

B

baba ganoush 57, **63**

baked papaya and banana poe **293**

baked sweet potato with West African tsire **77**

Bali 275, 276, *277*

Balinese gado gado **275**, *275*

banana *111*

baked papaya and banana poe **293**

banana and chilli fritter with passion fruit dip **110**

raita **157**

Bangkok stir-fry **251**

barbeque marinade **348**

Batu Apoi Forest Reserve 258–9, *272*

bean sprouts: tempeh goreng and beansprouts **276**

beancurd and beansprout spicy salad **255**

Bedouin 52–3

beetroot

beetroot and brinjal black curry **130**

deep-red Rajasthani vegetables in a poppy-seed sauce **179**, *179*

pomegranate, beetroot and walnut salad with goat's cheese **21**, *21*

salad **58**

Belize 314, *314*

Bengal 158, *159, 169, 171*

Bengali five spice 164

Bengali panch phoron spice mix **159**

Bengali panch phoron spiced vegetables **159**

berberé paste **80**

biryanis: Hyderabadi kacchi biryani **140–41**

black beans

corn and black bean salsa with toasted pumpkin seeds **318**, *319*

Havana beans **359**

paste 268

refried beans **320**

stew **324**, *324*

black eye peas

Caribbean rice and peas **350**

pumpkin and pigeon pea salad with lime and allspice dressing **346**

black-eyed beans

West African beans and okra **72**

Zanzibar beans in coconut sauce **79**

blimbi 112

Bolivia 326–7, *326*

Borneo 224, 258–9, *258*, 272

Borneo rainforest vegetables **272**, *272*

Brazil 322–3, *322*

bread 52

spicy rice flat bread **119**

breakfast dishes

ful medames **58**, 58, *58*

Guatemalan **319–20**, 320, *320*

huevos rancheros **309**

lablabi **51**

Nepalese breakfast potatoes **221**

Turkish **64**

uttapam **137**, *137*

brinjal pickle **118**

briq à l'oeuf **48**, *48*

Brunei 258–9

'Buddhist meat' and shitake mushrooms **231**

Burma 224, *224, 226, 226*, 228

burus berakutz 206

butterbeans

lima bean and pumpkin stew **332**, *332*

white bean and mint puree with duqqa **41**

butternut squash

carri coco curry **98**, *98*

cinnamon and coconut milk curry **123**

creole pumpkin chutney **113**

Maldivian mango and chickpea curry **103**, *103*

marinated butternut squash and sweet peppers with hot tomato sauce **352**, *352*

C

cabbage

coconut cabbage **151**

deep-red Rajasthani vegetables in a poppy-seed sauce **179**, *179*

Havana beans **359**

red cabbage with harissa and coriander **33**

cachumbers **150**

cajun blackened tofu **345**, *345*

cakes

apple, date and cinnamon cake **364**, *364*

carrot **365**

chocolate **368**, *368*

mango and passion fruit cheesecake **366**

Calcutta 160, *163*

Calcutta aubergine **160**, *160*

callaloo 349

Cambodia 238, *238, 247, 248*

Cambodian yellow curry **245**, *245*

capsicum 120

cashew nut stuffed capsicum in a coconut and curry leaf sauce **120**, *120*

Caribbean Islands 342, *342*

Caribbean pepperpot **355**

Caribbean rice and peas **350**

Caribbean vegetables in a mustard, coconut and rum sauce **339**, *339*

carri coco curry **98**, *98*
carrot
  carrot cake **365**
  Gujarati carrot salad
    182, *184*
  mashed carrot salad **67**
  salad **37**
cashew nuts *298*
  Borneo rainforest
    vegetables **272**, *272*
  cashew nut stuffed
    capsicum in a coconut
    and curry leaf sauce
    120, *120*
  paneer, cashew nut and
    Hunza apricot masala
    213, *213*
cashew tree *298*
cassava and celery in mung
  dal gravy **84**
cauliflower
  aloo gobi **176**
  cauliflower, fennel and
    pea tajine **39**
  cauliflower and pea masala
    169, *169*
  Kashmiri gobi **198**, *198*
  mustard spiced cauliflower
    137
  Placencia coconut
    cauliflower with melted
    cheese **316**
cayenne pepper **301**
celery: cassava and celery in
  mung dal gravy **84**
chamus (apricot juice) **206**
chana batura **153**
chana masala **153**
chana in a thick spicy gravy
  153
channa dhal **143**, *143*
char masala **56**
chat masala **361**
chayote in a cinnamon-spiced
  tomato sauce **308**
cheela **100**, *103*

cheese
  couscous salad with grilled
    red peppers, tomatoes
    and feta cheese **40**
  Mexico **297**
  Placencia coconut
    cauliflower with melted
    cheese **316**
  pomegranate, beetroot and
    walnut sald with goat's
    cheese **21**, *21*
  seasoned feta cheese **57**
  see also halloumi; paneer
chermoula **36**
chickpeas
  chana in a thick spicy gravy
    153
  chickpea, date and pine nut
    pilau **43**, *43*
  falafel **52**, **62**, *62*
  globe artichoke and
    chickpea couscous with
    onions, honey and raisins
    24–5
  hummus **60**
  lablabi **51**
  Maldivian mango and
    chickpea curry **103**, *103*
  pumpkin with chickpeas
    and panch phoran **164**,
    164
chillies **297**, **300–301**, *300*,
  301
  banana and chilli fritter
    with passion fruit dip
    110
  chilli and lime ice cream
    362, *363*
  en Nogada **297–8**, **298**, *298*
  kapi sauce **242**, *242*
  Peruvian Andes potatoes
    330
  piri piri **86**, **86–7**, **87**, **88**
  sambal sauce **267**
  tofu with crispy fried basil
    and chilli sauce **260**, *260*

whole green chillies in
  tamarind and brazil nut
  sauce **139**
China **224**, **230**, *230*, **232**
Chitwan Park, Nepal **218–20**
chocolate
  cake **368**, *368*
  Oaxacan mole **297**, **305**,
    305
chow chow **308**
chu chee red curry **256**
chutneys **156**
  coconut **143**
  coconut mellun chutney
    108
  coconut sambol **127**
  creole pumpkin chutney
    113
  date and tamarind **101**, **156**
  green coconut **156**, *203*
  onion sambol *127*
  papaya **100**
  prune and date **169**
  sultana and onion **33**
  toasted coconut and
    pineapple **124**
  tomato **164**
  tomato chutney for
    pau bhaji **192**
  tomato and cinnamon **34**
cinnamon
  apple, date and cinnamon
    cake **364**, *364*
  chayote in a cinnamon-
    spiced tomato sauce **308**
  and coconut milk curry
    123
  date, fig and cinnamon
    tajine **38**
  orange, date and cinnamon
    fruit salad **361**, *361*
  tomato and cinnamon
    chutney **34**
Cochin coconut masala **154**
coco pods **9**

coconut
  Borneo rainforest
    vegetables **272**, *272*
  Caribbean rice and peas
    350
  Caribbean vegetables in a
    mustard, coconut and
    rum sauce **339**, *339*
  cashew nut stuffed
    capsicum in a coconut
    and curry leaf sauce
    120, *120*
  chutney **143**
  cinnamon and coconut
    milk curry **123**
  Cochin coconut masala **154**
  coconut cabbage **151**
  coconut mellun chutney
    108
  crisp vegetable and
    coconut salad **267**
  fresh coconut with lime
    103
  green coconut chutney
    156, *203*
  Kuching tamarind and
    coconut milk curry **271**
  Malaccan laksa **282**, *282*
  Placencia coconut
    cauliflower with melted
    cheese **316**
  Polynesian salad with
    coconut milk dressing
    293
  rice **124**
  sambol **127**
  spinach with coconut milk,
    thyme and chives **349**
  and sweet potato soup **290**
  Zanzibar beans in
    coconut sauce **79**
Columbo **119**
condiments
  brinjal pickle **118**
  duqqa **40**, **41**

Index

green mango pickle **111**

harissa **32**, 34

see also chutneys

coriander 297

cheela **100**, *103*

red cabbage with harissa and coriander **33**

corn 297

see also sweetcorn

Costa Rica 336, *336*, 339

cou-cou **348**

couscous

couscous salad with grilled red peppers, tomatoes and feta cheese **40**

globe artichoke and chickpea couscous with onions, honey and raisins **24–5**

Ouarzazate couscous **30–31**, 34

cozido **323**

creole pumpkin chutney **113**

crisp vegetable and coconut salad **267**

crunchy salad with lime juice **338**, *339*

crunchy sweet-and-sour salad **236**, *236*

Cuba 356

Cuban green rice **357**

cucumber

and mint raita **157**

potato cakes with cucumber relish **329**

and sesame seed salad **226**

yoghurt with cucumber **67**

cumin 56

curries

amok **241**

beetroot and brinjal black curry **130**

Cambodian yellow curry **245**, *245*

carri coco curry **98**, *98*

chu chee red curry **256**

cinnamon and coconut milk curry **123**

devilled potato curry **108**

Diu sweetcorn curry **184**, *184*

egg curry **163**, *163*

green vegetable mallung **128**, *128*

jungle **252**, *252*

Kandy leek and potato curry **125**

Kenyan curry with okra and peas, topped with a fried egg **91**

Kuching tamarind and coconut milk curry **271**

Maldivian mango and chickpea curry **103**, *103*

Melakan devil's mushroom curry **281**

omelette curry **105**

panch kol 214, **217**

Sri Lankan okra and potato curry **116**

Thai green curry **254**, *254*

see also amok

curry leaves 116

curry powder: Sri Lankan roasted **119**

D

dates

apple, date and cinnamon cake **364**, *364*

aubergine in a puréed date sauce **69**

chickpea, date and pine nut pilau **43**, *43*

date, fig and cinnamon tajine **38**

date and tamarind chutneys **101**, **156**

orange, date and cinnamon fruit salad **361**, *361*

prune and date chutney **169**

devilled potato curry **108**

dhal

channa dhal **143**, *143*

dal fry **197**

dhal Makhani **210**

kichuri **136**

Rajasthani pumpkin dhal **188**

dhokla **194**

Diu sweetcorn curry **184**, *184*

dressings

coconut milk dressing **293**

lime and allspice dressing **346**

orange flower water dressing **22**

rosewater dressing **41**

see also salads

Dubai 12, *18*

duqqa **40**, 41, 56

E

East Africa 78–9, *78*, 82, *84*, *86*

East African piri piri **86**, 88, *88*

East African Wilderness sweet potato patties **88**, *88*

Ecuador 334, *335*

eggs

briq à l'oeuf **48**, *48*

egg curry **163**, *163*

huevos rancheros **309**

Kenyan curry with okra and peas, topped with a fried egg **91**

ojja **45**

omelette curry **105**

Peruvian Andes potatoes **330**

scrambled **320**

Egypt 52, *53*, 55, *55*

Egyptian bean purée **57**

Egyptian lentil soup **56**

Ethiopia 80

Ethiopian vegetable wat 80, *81*

F

falafel 52, **62**, *62*

fava beans

Egyptian bean purée **57**

ful medames **58**, 58, *58*

fennel

cauliflower, fennel and pea tajine **39**

fennel and orange salad with orange flower water dressing **22**, *22*

fenugreek leaves 138

Fez, Morocco 12, 40–41

figs: date, fig and cinnamon tajine **38**

French Polynesia 286, *286*, 289, *290*, *293*

fresh coconut with lime **103**

fresh fruit salsa **312**

fruit lassi **155**, *200*

ful medames **58**, 58, *58*

G

gado gado **275**, *275*

garam masala 56

garma 206

ghee **147**

globe artichoke and chickpea couscous with onions, honey and raisins **24–5**

granita **362**

green mango pickle **111**

green mango salad **242**

green peppercorns 263

green vegetable mallung **128**, *128*

grilled pepper and tomato salad **19**

guacamole 297, **302**, *302*

Guatemalan breakfast **319**

Guatemala 314, *314*, *317*, *319*

breakfast dishes **319–20**, 320, *320*

Guatemalan flan **367**

Gujarat 172, 173, 190–91

Gujarati carrot salad **182**, *184*

Gujarati dhokla **194**, *194*
Gujarati pumpkin with
    tamarind **183**

H
halloumi 88
    marinated halloumi with
        Seychelloise rougaille
        sauce **112**, *112*
halva 57
haneetze daudo 206
haricot beans: sweet peppers
    and haricot beans **289**, *289*
Harira soup **26**
harissa
    Moroccan 31, **32**, 34, 56
    red cabbage with harissa
        and coriander **33**
    Tunisian **45**
Havana 356, *356*, *359*
herb and noodle salad **261**
hing 191
Hong Kong 230, 231
houmous *see* hummus
Huang Shan Mountains
    224, 230, *232*
huevos rancheros **309**
hummus 57, **60**
Hunza valley 206, *206*, *210*,
    213
Hyderabad 134, *169*
Hyderabadi kacchi biryani
    140–41

I
ice cream **362**, **363**
Imam's aubergine **65**, 65
India 134, *134*, *138*, 146,
    169, *381*
    cumin 56
    Eastern 158, *159*
    Northern 196–7, 198
    puddings 361, 363
    Southern 148, *148*, *151*, *153*
    Western *169*, 172–3, *181*,
        182, 184, 190–91

Indian Ocean islands 94, 96
Indonesia 224, 258
    accompaniments 277

J
jaggery *136*
Jains 190–91
Jaisalmer castle 187–8
Jamaica 342, *348*, 350, *355*
Jamaican jerk tofu **350**
jerk seasoning 350
jollof 73
Jordan 52, *61*
Jordanian rocket salad
    58, **63**, *63*
jungle curry **252**, *252*

K
Kandy 125
kapi sauce 242
Kashmir 196, *196*, 200
Kashmiri gobi **198**, *198*
Kenyan curry with okra and
    peas, topped with a fried
    egg **91**
khadi **181**, *181*
Khmer cuisine 238
kichuri **136**, *136*
kidney beans: Caribbean rice
    and peas **350**
korma Shah Jahan **144**
kreoung 241
    Cambodian yellow curry
        245, *245*
    tempeh stuffed aubergines
        247
Kuala Lumpur 260, *267*
Kuching tamarind and
    coconut milk curry **271**
kulfi 363

L
La Paz 326–7
lablabi 51
Lahore 206, *206*, 208, *209*,
    210

Lahore butter saag **209**
laksa 282
    Malaccan laksa **282**, *282*
laksa noodles 282
Laos 224, 234–5, *234*
lassi **155**, *200*
leeks: Kandy leek and potato
    curry **125**
lemon grass rice **227**
lemons: preserved **34**, *34*
lentils
    chickpea, date and pine
        nut pilau **43**, *43*
    dhal Makhani **210**
    Egyptian lentil soup **56**
lima bean and pumpkin stew
    332, *332*
lime
    chilli and lime ice cream
        362, *363*
    crunchy salad with lime
        juice **338**, *339*
    fresh coconut with lime
        103
    lime and allspice dressing
        346

M
mace *281*
Malacca: Strait of 279–81,
    279
Malaccan laksa **282**, *282*
Malay sambal **270**
Malaysia 224, 258, 260, *267*,
    270, *277*, *381*
    accompaniments 277
Maldive Islands 94, *94*, 105,
    109
Maldivian mango and
    chickpea curry **103**, *103*
Mali 72, 74, 77
mallung 128
mango
    green mango pickle **111**
    green mango salad **242**

Maldivian mango and
    chickpea curry **103**, *103*
mango and ginger salsa
    345, *345*
mango and passion fruit
    cheesecake **366**
papaya and mango salsa
    351
salsa 324
marinades
    cocido **323**
    jerk seasong 350
    marinated butternut squash
        and sweet peppers with
        hot tomato sauce
        352, *352*
    marinated halloumi with
        Seychelloise rougaille
        sauce **112**, *112*
    piri piri 86, 88
    Polynesian maa Tahiti
        tempeh **289**
    seasoning-up barbeque
        marinade **348**
    Yucatan recado **300**
markets 12, *224*
    African 77
    see also souks
Marquesas Islands 286, *286*,
    290, *293*
Marrakesh 14, *17*, 24, 26, *26*
    tajine **28**, *28*
mashed carrot salad **67**
mechouia 12
Mekong stir-fry with puréed
    aubergine **235**
Melaka 279, *280*, 281
Melakan devil's mushroom
    curry **281**
methi aloo **138**
Mexican plate with refried
    beans **307**
Mexican West Coast peppers
    313
Mexico 56, 297–8, 300,
    301, *307*, 308–9, 313

Index

mint
　root vegetables in a spicy
　　mint sauce **177**
　tea **15**
　white bean and mint puree
　　with duqqa **41**
mixed vegetable masala **171**
Mkomazi cardamom-mashed
　sweet potato with pepper
　relish **82**, *82*
mooli
　Bengali panch phoron
　　spiced vegetables **159**
　chu chee red curry **256**
　Cochin coconut masala
　　154
　kichuri **136**
　panch kol **217**
　pumpkin with chickpeas
　　and panch phoran
　　164, *164*
Moroccan mixed salad plate
　37
Morocco 14–15, *17*, 19, 30,
　34, 361
　appetizers **19**
　cumin 56
　harissa 31, **32**, 34
　tajines 38
　see also Fez; Marrakesh
Mountain Pine Ridge stew
　314, **317**
Mozambique 87
Mozambique piri piri **87**
mushrooms
　'Buddhist meat' and shitake
　　mushrooms **231**
　Melakan devil's mushroom
　　curry **281**
　stir-fried vegetables with
　　green peppercorns and
　　shitake mushrooms
　　263, *263*
　tempeh and shitake rice
　　paper rolls **264**, *264*

vegetables in a lemon grass
　and herb-scented broth
　266
mustard
　Caribbean vegetables in a
　　mustard, coconut and
　　rum sauce **339**, *339*
　mustard spiced cauliflower
　　137
mustard seeds 214, 221

N
Nalagarh brinjal **200**
narangi pulao *200*, **201**, *201*
Negril tomato catch-up **351**
Nepal 214, *214*, 217,
　218–20, *219*, *220*
Nepalese breakfast potatoes
　221
Nevis (island) *342*, *342*, *346*
Newari cuisine 214
noodles
　herb and noodle salad **261**
　laksa **282**
　pad thai **257**
Nuka Hiva, Marquesas Islands
　286, *286*, *290*, *293*

O
Oaxaca 305, 308, 312
Oaxacan mole **305**, *305*
ojja **45**
okra
　cou-cou **348**
　Kenyan curry with okra
　　and peas, topped with a
　　fried egg **91**
　Sri Lankan okra and potato
　　curry **116**
　West African beans and
　　okra **72**
olives *15*
Oman 68, *69*
omelette curry **105**
onion sambol *127*

orange
　fennel and orange salad
　　with orange flower
　　water dressing **22**, *22*
　orange, date and cinnamon
　　fruit salad **361**, *361*
　rocket and orange salad
　　with rosewater dressing
　　41
Orissan Jagdish saag aloo **170**
Ouarzazate couscous **30–31**,
　34

P
pad thai **257**
Pakistan 206, *206*, *209*
panch kol 214, **217**
panch phoran 58, 164
　Bengali panch phoron
　　spice mix **159**
　Bengali panch phoron
　　spiced vegetables **159**
　pumpkin with chickpeas
　　and panch phoran
　　164, *164*
paneer 144
　korma Shah Jahan **144**
　paneer, cashew nut and
　　Hunza apricot masala
　　213, *213*
　paneer tikka **118**
　saag paneer **174**, *174*
papaya 100
　baked papaya and
　　banana poe **293**
　chutney **100**
　and mango salsa **351**
paprika 301
passion fruit
　banana and chilli fritter
　　with passion fruit dip
　　110
　mango and passion fruit
　　cheesecake **366**
pau bhaji 191, **192**, *192*
　spice mix **191**

pawa 150
peanuts
　Balinese gado gado
　　275, *275*
　potato and peanut pawa
　　150
　tsire **77**
peas
　cauliflower, fennel and
　　pea tajine **39**
　cauliflower and pea masala
　　169, *169*
　Kenyan curry with okra
　　and peas, topped with a
　　fried egg **91**
　peas and spinach with gram
　　flour and curd **147**
　pumpkin and pigeon pea
　　salad with lime and
　　allspice dressing **346**
Penang *277*, *279*
pepper relish **82**, *82*
pepperpot **355**
peppers
　cashew nut stuffed
　　capsicum in a coconut
　　and curry leaf sauce
　　120, *120*
　chillies en Nogada 297–8,
　　298, *298*
　couscous salad with grilled
　　red peppers, tomatoes
　　and feta cheese **40**
　grilled pepper and tomato
　　salad **19**
　harissa **45**, *45*
　Havana beans **359**
　marinated butternut squash
　　and sweet peppers with
　　hot tomato sauce
　　352, *352*
　Mexican West Coast
　　peppers **313**
　Mountain Pine Ridge stew
　　314, **317**

sweet peppers and haricot
beans **289**, *289*
Yucatan recado sauce **301**
see also chillies
Peru **297**, 328–9, *328*, 332
phitti **206**
Phnom Penh, Cambodia
238, 248
Phnom Penh stir fry with holy
basil **248**
pickles
brinjal pickle **118**
green mango pickle **111**
pilau: chickpea, date and pine
nut pilau **43**, *43*
pineapple
savoury pineapple salad
248, *248*
toasted coconut and
pineapple chutney **124**
pinto beans **306**
Mexican West Coast
peppers **313**
refried beans **306**
piri piri **86**, 86–7, **87**, 88
pistachio kulfi **363**, *363*
Placencia coconut cauliflower
with melted cheese 314,
316
plantain
baked papaya and banana
poe **293**
Caribbean vegetables in a
mustard, coconut and
rum sauce **339**, *339*
Oaxacan mole **305**, *305*
Polynesia *see* French Polynesia
Polynesian maa Tahiti tempeh
289, *289*
Polynesian salad with coconut
milk dressing **293**
pomegranate
granita **362**
pomegranate, beetroot and
walnut salad with goat's
cheese **21**, *21*

potato
aloo gobi **176**
briq à l'oeuf **48**, *48*
devilled potato curry **108**
egg curry **163**, *163*
Kandy leek and potato
curry **125**
methi aloo **138**
Mountain Pine Ridge stew
314, **317**
narangi pulao **201**,
201, *201*
Nepalese breakfast potatoes
221
Orissan Jagdish saag aloo
170
Peruvian Andes potatoes
330, *330*
potato bondas **203**, 203,
203
potato cakes with
cucumber relish **329**
potato and peanut pawa
150
Sri Lankan okra and
potato curry **116**
preserved lemons **34**, *34*
prune and date chutney **169**
puddings 361–8
pumpkin
Caribbean vegetables in a
mustard, coconut and
rum sauce **339**, *339*
with chickpeas and panch
phoran **164**, *164*
deep-red Rajasthani
vegetables in a poppy-
seed sauce **179**, *179*
Gujarati pumpkin with
tamarind **183**
Hyderabadi kacchi biryani
140–41
lima bean and pumpkin
stew **332**, *332*

and pigeon pea salad with
lime and allspice
dressing **346**
Rajasthani pumpkin dhal
188
soup **334**
spicy mashed **145**
spinach with coconut milk,
thyme and chives **349**

Q

quatre épices 289

R

radishes
fresh tomato and radish
salsa **310**, *310*
see also mooli
raitas **157**, 157
Rajasthan 134, *134*, 169,
172, *176*, 187–8, *188*, *381*
Rajasthani pumpkin dhal **188**
ras el hanout 14, **17**, 56
red cabbage with harissa and
coriander **33**
refried beans 297, **306**, 306
with flour tortilla **307**
Guatemalan breakfast **320**
Mexican plate with **307**
rice 9
Caribbean rice and peas
350
chickpea, date and pine nut
pilau **43**, *43*
coconut rice **124**
Cuban green rice **357**
kichuri **136**
lemon grass rice **227**
narangi pulao **201**, 201, *201*
rosewater rice **68**
thyme and lemon **109**
West African jollof rice **73**
rice paper wrappers **264**
rocket
Jordanian rocket salad
58, **63**, 63

rocket and grated carrot
salad **58**
rocket and orange salad
with rosewater dressing
41
root vegetables in a spicy
mint sauce **177**
rosewater rice **68**
royal baby aubergines **146**

S

saag paneer **174**, *174*
saffron 55
salads
aubergine **19**
beancurd and beansprout
spicy salad **255**
Cambodian 238
carrot **37**
couscous salad with grilled
red peppers, tomatoes
and feta cheese **40**
crisp vegetable and
coconut **267**
crunchy salad with
lime juice **338**
crunchy sweet-and-sour
236, *236*
cucumber and sesame seed
226
fennel and orange salad
with orange flower
water dressing **22**, *22*
with ful medames **58**
green mango **242**
grilled pepper and tomato
19
Gujarati carrot **182**, *184*
herb and noodle **261**
Jordanian rocket salad
58, **63**, 63
Malaysian fruit and
vegetable **269**
mashed carrot **67**
Moroccan mixed salad
plate **37**

Index

Polynesian salad with
coconut milk dressing
293

pomegranate, beetroot and
walnut sald with goat's
cheese **21**, *21*

pumpkin and pigeon pea
salad with lime and
allspice dressing **346**

rocket and orange salad
with rosewater dressing
41

savoury fruit salad **181**

savoury pineapple **248**, *248*

sweet apple **97**, *98*

sweet potato **22**

tabbouleh *58*, **61**

tomato, cucumber and
green pepper **65**

yoghurt with cucumber **67**

salsas **297**, 309, 310

corn and black bean salsa
with toasted pumpkin
seeds **318**, *319*

fresh fruit **312**

fresh tomato and radish
salsa **310**, *310*

fresh tomato salsa **310**

Guatemalan breakfast **319**

mango **324**

mango and ginger **345**, *345*

papaya and mango **351**

ranchera **309**

sambals **267**, **277**, *277*

sambols 127

samla soup **246**

sauces

kapi sauce **242**, *242*

Negril tomato catch-up
351

sweet and sour dipping
sauce **264**

Yucatan recado sauce **301**

see also salsas; sambals

savoury fruit salad **181**

savoury pineapple salad **248**,
248

scrambled egg **320**

seasoned feta cheese **57**

seasoning-up barbeque
marinade **348**

seitan 231

sesame 57

cucumber and sesame seed
salad **226**

Seychelle Islands 94, *94*,
96–7, *96*, 100, *101*, 108,
111

shitake mushrooms *see*
mushrooms

Siem Reap, Cambodia
238, *242*

Singapore 268, 279, 280

souks 12, *14*, *33*, 40–41, 52,
55, 62

soups

coconut and sweet potato
290

Egyptian lentil **56**

Harira **26**

lablabi **51**

pumpkin **334**

samla **246**

vegetables in a lemon grass
and herb-scented broth
266

South China stir-fry **232**

spices 8–9

achiote 314, 317

berberé paste **80**

cajun 345

chat masala 361

chilli 297, 300–301,
300, *301*

cumin 56

curry leaves 116

duqqa *40*, 41

hing 191

pau bhaji mix **191**

ras el hanout **17**

saffron 55

sesame 57

souks *33*, 55

Sri Lankan roasted curry
powder **119**

traders 169, 191, 279

see also panch phoran

spicy garlic-fried green
vegetables **268**, 268

spicy mashed pumpkin **145**

spicy rice flat bread **119**

spinach

amok with spinach and tofu
241, *241*

chana in a thick spicy gravy
153

with coconut milk, thyme
and chives **349**

Lahore butter saag **209**

Orissan Jagdish saag aloo
170

peas and spinach with gram
flour and curd **147**

saag paneer **174**, *174*

Sri Lanka 94, 108, 114,
118–19, *123*, 125, *126*,
130

Sri Lankan okra and potato
curry **116**

Sri Lankan roasted curry
powder **119**

stir-fry

Bangkok stir-fry **251**

Mekong stir-fry with
puréed aubergine **235**

Phnom Penh stir fry with
holy basil **248**

South China **232**

spicy garlic-fried green
vegetables **268**, 268

in tamarind gravy **228**, *228*

vegetables with green
peppercorns and shitake
mushrooms **263**, *263*

sultana and onion chutney **33**

sweet apple salad **97**, *98*

sweet capsicums 120

sweet date and tamarind
chutney **156**

sweet peppers and haricot
beans **289**, *289*

sweet potato

baked sweet potato with
West African tsire **77**

Caribbean vegetables in a
mustard, coconut and
rum sauce **339**, *339*

carri coco curry **98**, *98*

cassava and celery in
mung dal gravy **84**

in a cayenne, ginger and
groundnut sauce **74**, *74*

coconut and sweet potato
soup **290**

East African Wilderness
sweet potato patties
88, *88*

Mkomazi cardamom-
mashed sweet potato
with pepper relish
82, *82*

Oaxacan mole **305**, *305*

pumpkin soup **334**

salad **22**

Zanzibar beans in coconut
sauce **79**

sweet and sour dipping sauce
264

sweetcorn

corn and black bean salsa
with toasted pumpkin
seeds **318**, *319*

Diu sweetcorn curry
184, *184*

Oaxacan mole **305**, *305*

stew **327**, *327*

T

tabbouleh *58*, **61**

tahina 57

tajines 38

cauliflower, fennel and
pea **39**

date, fig and cinnamon **38**
Marrakesh **28**, *28*
vegetable and chickpea **17**
tamales **297**
tamarind
  date and tamarind chutneys
    101, **156**
  Gujarati pumpkin with
    tamarind **183**
  Kuching tamarind and
    coconut milk curry **271**
  stir-fry in tamarind gravy
    228, *228*
  whole green chillies in
    tamarind and brazil nut
    sauce **139**
tarato **57**
tempeh **88**, **247**
  Borneo rainforest
    vegetables **272**, *272*
  Mexican West Coast
    peppers **313**
  Polynesian maa Tahiti
    tempeh **289**, *289*
  and shitake rice paper rolls
    264, *264*
  tempeh goreng and
    beansprouts **276**
  tempeh stuffed aubergines
    247
Thai green curry **254**, *254*
Thailand **224**, **250–51**, *250*,
  252, *256*, *381*
thyme and lemon rice **109**
toasted coconut and
  pineapple chutney **124**
tofu **88**, **231**, **255**
  amok with spinach and tofu
    241, *241*
  Bangkok stir-fry **251**
  beancurd and beansprout
    spicy salad **255**
  cajun blackened tofu
    345, *345*
  cozido **323**

with crispy fried basil and
  chilli sauce **260**, *260*
herb and noodle salad **261**
Jamaican jerk tofu
  350, *350*
Malaccan laksa **282**, *282*
tomato **37**, **297**
  chayote in a cinnamon-
    spiced tomato sauce
    308
  chutneys **34**, **164**, **192**
  and cinnamon chutney **34**
  couscous salad with grilled
    red peppers, tomatoes
    and feta cheese **40**
  fresh tomato and radish
    salsa **310**, *310*
  fresh tomato salsa **310**
  grilled pepper and tomato
    salad **19**
  marinated butternut squash
    and sweet peppers with
    hot tomato sauce
    352, *352*
  Negril tomato catch-up
    351
  tomato, cucumber and
    green pepper **65**
  tomato and cucumber salad
    58
  Yucatan recado sauce **301**
tortillas **297**
  refried beans with flour
    tortilla **307**
Trincomalee, Sri Lanka **94**,
  108, **118**, **119**
tropical fruit platter with chat
  masala **361**
Tunisia **45**, **51**, *51*
  harissa **45**, 45
  tajines **38**
  Tunis medina **12**, **45**, *48*
Turkey **64**

U
urid dhal **210**
uttapam **137**, 137

V
vanilla **301**
vegan cakes **364**, **365**
vegetable and chickpea tajine
  17
vegetables in a lemon grass
  and herb-scented broth
  266

W
water chestnuts: Melakan
  devil's mushroom curry
  281
West Africa **72**, *73*
West African beans and okra
  72
West African jollof rice **73**
wheat gluten **231**
white bean and mint puree
  with duqqa **41**
whole green chillies in
  tamarind and brazil nut
  sauce **139**
World Food Café **7–8**, **65**,
  74, **98**, **306**, **368**

Y
yoghurt
  with cucumber **67**
  fruit lassi **155**, *200*
  khadi **181**, 181
  Nalagarh brinjal **200**
  narangi pulao **201**, 201,
    201
  raitas **157**
Yucatan recado sauce **301**

Z
Zanzibar **79**, *381*
Zanzibar beans in coconut
  sauce **79**

Captions for index illustrations

Pages 370–371
The Malabar Coast of India was for centuries a major centre of the world spice trade

Page 377, clockwise from top right Harvesting rice at Dhara Dhevi in Chaing Mai; the roof of a Thai house; a reclining Buddha in Phuket; limestone cliffs at Krabi; a water pot; sandals at Pankor Laut spa village

Page 378
Dhows are the ubiquitous sailing craft of the Indian Ocean, and have been since the beginning of the spice trade. Around the island of Zanzibar and along the Swahili coast of East Africa, they are still in everyday use

Pages 382–383 View over Lake Pichola from the lake palace in Udaipur, Rajasthan